MLA Handbook

Ninth edition

The Modern Language Association of America
New York   2021

© 2021 by The Modern Language Association of America

Published by The Modern Language Association of America
85 Broad Street, Suite 500, New York, New York 10004-2434
www.mla.org

Second case binding 2021

To order MLA publications, go to mla.org/books. For wholesale and international orders, see mla.org/Bookstore-Orders.

Library of Congress Cataloging-in-Publication Data

Name: Modern Language Association of America.
Title: MLA handbook / Modern Language Association of America. Other titles:
    MLA handbook for writers of research papers.
Description: Ninth edition. | New York, New York : The Modern Language Association
    of America, 2021. | Includes bibliographical references and index.
Identifiers: LCCN 2020039581 (print) | LCCN 2020039582 (e-book) |
    ISBN 9781603293518 (paperback) | ISBN 9781603295611 (hardcover) |
    ISBN 9781603295628 (spiral bound) | ISBN 9781603293525 (EPUB)
Subjects: LCSH: Report writing—Handbooks, manuals, etc. | Research—Handbooks,
    manuals, etc.
Classification: LCC LB2369 .M52 2021 (print) | LCC LB2369 (ebook) |
    DDC 808.02/7—dc23
LC record available at https://lccn.loc.gov/2020039581
LC e-book record available at https://lccn.loc.gov/2020039582

Contents

Preface

We at the Modern Language Association are proud to bring you this ninth edition of the *MLA Handbook*, a publication that has for more than forty years helped writers produce credible research projects and clear prose.

The MLA, though, is many things besides MLA style. It was founded in 1883 as an organization representing language and literature researchers and teachers. In addition to publishing books that support their teaching, we provide opportunities for members to share their research—in *PMLA*, the premier journal in language and literary studies, for example, and at our annual convention and other events.

Teachers who want ideas about how to teach contemporary Latin American literature, *Wuthering Heights*, digital literacy, or young adult literature can find the help they need in books we publish. Our members assemble resources to collaborate with one another on our online network, *MLA Commons*, and they provide professional development for new scholars and higher education administrators through workshops and seminars we sponsor.

Our members work together to strengthen humanities education and research. They advocate for fair working conditions for college teachers and for better learning environments for students.

The MLA exists to support learning—at every level. MLA resources serve the high school student who seeks guidance on evaluating sources and avoiding plagiarism, the college student who uses our textbooks to learn a language, and the faculty member who wants new ways to teach. Our work goes far beyond MLA style. Check us out at mla.org.

Acknowledgments

We are grateful for the questions, comments, and suggestions received from readers who use MLA style every day. Hearing from you on the *MLA Style Center*, on *Twitter*, by e-mail, at workshop and webinar Q&As, at conferences, and during the various stages of review helped shape this edition in important ways. Thanks are due also to the various reviewers who provided feedback on drafts of this handbook.

The following MLA staff members contributed to the writing, editing, design, and production of this edition of the *MLA Handbook*: Judith H. Altreuter, Zahra Brown, Susan Doose, Angela Gibson, John D. Golbach, Laura Kiernan, Barney Latimer, Sara Pastel, Jennifer A. Rappaport, Kevin Romoser, Michael Simon, Leighton Snyder, Erika Suffern, and Joseph Wallace. The handbook benefited also from the insights of various freelance editors and indexers, including Aileen B. Houston, Erika Millen, Do Mi Stauber, Dana Symons, and Megan J. W. Zid.

Introduction

Building confidence in the information and ideas we share with one another is perhaps more important today than ever before, and for nearly a century it has been the driving principle behind MLA style, a set of standards for writing and documentation used by writers to find and evaluate information, alert their audience to the trustworthiness of their findings through citation, and shape the expression of their ideas in conversation with others. What we call "MLA style" has never been a static method, instead changing over time to meet the needs of writers. Its goals, however, have generally remained the same since the appearance of the first officially published edition (titled the *MLA Style Sheet*) in 1951: establishing uniform standards for documentation and citation, encouraging the widespread adoption of those standards by writers, and instructing students. This edition carries forth those goals, updating and expanding the MLA's long-standing guidance on paper formatting, prose mechanics, quoting and paraphrasing, in-text references, and the list of works cited.

The MLA's method for creating bibliographic entries has, however, changed significantly over time. This edition retains the MLA's unique system of documentation, established in the eighth edition of the handbook in 2016. Entries in the list of works cited are created using a template of core elements—facts common to

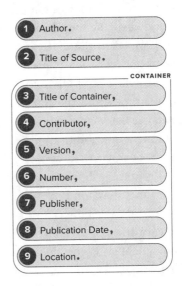

The MLA template of core elements.

most sources, like author, title, and publication date—that allows writers to cite any type of work. Instead of asking writers to document a work by first identifying its publication format (for example, book or journal article) and then applying a formula for citing that format, the MLA's method asks writers to evaluate sources using a comprehensive set of standard criteria and then to create bibliographic entries based on that evaluation. Source evaluation and the development of information literacy are therefore central to the MLA's system of documentation. Given that it is flexible enough to cite any type of source, it is also applicable to different kinds of works in various disciplines and to new and rarely encountered types of sources.

This edition goes much further, however, in explaining the system of documentation and other aspects of MLA style, and it does so in response to feedback from readers like you. We regularly receive questions and suggestions through the online *MLA Style Center*. Although feedback from style users has always shaped editions of the *MLA Handbook*, this edition was created in direct, sustained dialogue with the instructors, librarians, professional writers and editors, and students around the world who use MLA style every day. We heard calls from many of you for a more comprehensive resource with more examples, a reorganized handbook where information could easily be found, and explanations of the documentation system that responded to the many questions you had while using it. We also sought targeted feedback from reviewers about every aspect of this handbook, from which sections to include and how to organize them to the diversity of examples and the clarity of instruction. Above all, we aimed to strike a balance between providing guidelines for those who want them and establishing a method that gives writers discretion to cite sources in ways that work best for their projects. This edition is meant to serve as a reference guide and textbook for anyone using MLA style.

One question instructors and students sometimes ask us is whether materials assembled for use in courses should cite the instructional context or the original publication information, often provided by instructors on syllabi and reproduced as permissions lines in course packs and online learning platforms but not collected by students directly from the source. While this handbook advises writers to cite the version of the work they consult, it acknowledges, too, that students practice documenting sources in the classroom as if they had encountered them in research contexts. If a work is unique to a course—for example, a guest lecture or a photograph taken by an instructor—and cited for an audience other than the class it-self, the classroom context is unquestionably important to include in the citation. Otherwise, instructors may wish to initiate a conversation acknowledging that the instructional environment is meant as training for real-world applications.

New in the Ninth Edition

Writers will find much that is new in this edition. It expands and improves the explanation of how to use MLA style, including the MLA's system of documentation; features new guidelines to answer common questions; restores and updates key sections from previous editions that readers told us they valued; and adds chapters and plentiful visual examples to support writers.

Manuscript Formatting (Chapter 1)

Reintroduced in this edition are the MLA's time-tested guidelines for formatting a research paper, which have been widely adopted by instructors and educational institutions to standardize manuscript formatting. Advice has been added on formatting lists, identifying collaborative projects, and presenting tables and figures and documenting their sources.

Writing Advice (Chapters 2 and 3)

Previous editions of the handbook included a section on the many mechanical decisions that writers face when crafting prose—matters like spelling, punctuation, capitalization of terms in various languages, and the use of italics in prose—and this edition updates and expands those recommendations in chapter 2, which also provides guidance on styling names of persons, organizations, and groups; titles of works; and numbers.

The new guidelines on inclusive language in chapter 3 set forth principles to help writers use language thoughtfully when discussing race and ethnicity, religion, gender, sexual orientation, ability, age, and economic or social status. Included is a discussion of capitalization and styling, pronoun choice, and more.

Principles of Documentation (Chapter 4)

Chapter 4 serves as a brief introduction to the principles of citation. It explains how to recognize and avoid plagiarism, understand the purpose of quoting and paraphrasing (the mechanics of which are detailed later, in chapter 6), and identify the special cases when documentation is not needed.

The List of Works Cited (Chapter 5)

Chapter 5 reorganizes and significantly expands the MLA's guidance on the list of works cited. After a precise introduction to the method of using the template (5.1), the core elements on the template are described in detail. New to this edition, the following three sections appear for each core element:

- What It Is—explains what each element is and the range of situations it applies to
- Where to Find It—provides visual examples of where to locate publication information for each element in a variety of sources
- How to Style It—gives advice on the details of styling elements in works-cited-list entries

By integrating descriptions of the template elements with the mechanics of using them to build an entry, we have made information easier to find in this edition. Key updates for each element are detailed below.

Author. This section offers updated guidance on how to include pseudonyms, stage names, and the like in entries and how to cite works by the same person that are published under different names. This edition also provides expanded, easy-to-follow options for styling the names of authors of government publications, encouraging writers to treat the names of government authors as they find them in the source. (The previous handbook's guidance, to consolidate entries by government, is given as an option for professional scholars, writers, and editors working with complex projects.)

Title of Source. Expanded guidance is given on how to provide a description in place of a title, how to shorten a title, how to list titled and untitled front and back matter like introductions and afterwords, and how to style titles.

Title of Container. This edition elaborates significantly on the explanation of the Title of Container element, providing charts and graphics detailing what kinds of works contain other works and when a website title should appear in the Title of Container element. New advice is given for citing works contained in apps and databases.

Contributor (formerly labeled "Other Contributors"). Guidance on when to use this element is more comprehensive in this edition. Distinguishing between key and other contributors receives special attention. Specific instructions are given for documenting a source that has multiple contributors in the same role.

Version. This edition expands the range of cases showing when the Version element might be used and explains how to use the element when citing an e-book.

Number. Recommendations for using this element remain largely unchanged, although the range of examples is now more expansive.

Publisher. After an extensive demonstration of what constitutes a publisher, this edition offers simplified instructions on determining the publisher of a book and updated recommendations for listing divisions of both nongovernmental organizations and government agencies in the Publisher element. Guidance on abbreviating publishers' names now appears in the section "Publisher: How to Style It" (5.59) instead of in a separate section on abbreviations.

Publication Date. This edition clarifies the variety of date types writers may need to record: not just dates traditionally thought of as publication dates (like those listed in books or on print journal articles) but also the date of composition for unpublished material (like letters), the date of revision for online works, and the date on which the writer attended a live event or performance, as well as the label "forthcoming" for works not yet published. The handbook now recommends that writers lowercase a season that appears in the Publication Date element (e.g., *spring 2019*), just as the seasons would be written in prose.

Location. This edition defines the Location element more systematically and includes a chart for quick reference. Although a rationale for including URLs is provided and examples of works including URLs appear throughout the handbook, the handbook also notes that they should be considered optional. The components of URLs are explained, and pointers are given on how to truncate them, how to break them at the end of a line, when to include the terminal slash, and how to style them in documents treating them as links.

Chapter 5 also includes a series of figures in sections 5.100–5.103 that show sample works-cited-list entries alongside filled-in templates. These figures are newly categorized by the number of containers, if any, the entry uses. The aim is to help writers learn how to use the template and visualize how entries are commonly structured. The following section, "One Work Cited Different Ways" (5.104), illustrates the principle that a work's citation format depends on where and how the work is accessed.

A new section (5.105–5.119) is devoted to explaining supplemental elements (formerly called "optional elements"). Supplemental elements can be added to the core elements on the template. Sometimes they are optional, but in other cases they are necessary—hence the name change. This edition specifies what types of information a writer might provide as supplemental elements and the various places in an entry supplemental elements are likely to appear.

By popular demand, a section has been added on creating an annotated bibliography (5.132).

Citing Sources in the Text (Chapter 6)

Although the MLA's guidelines on in-text citations have not changed in the past few editions, we continue to receive a steady stream of questions about their most basic aspects. Thus, in this edition we adjusted the approach to explaining in-text citations in the first part of chapter 6, first articulating core principles that apply to all in-text citations (namely, they must point to entries in the list of works cited unambiguously and as concisely as possible) and then listing use cases in a more comprehensive, granular way. To help elucidate how in-text citations correspond to entries in the list of works cited, this handbook pairs citations with entries. New guidance appears on how to style titles in parenthetical citations, including how to shorten titles; how to style titles enclosed in quotation marks that start with a title in quotation marks; and how to style titles enclosed in quotation marks that begin with a quotation. An additional section, "When Author and Title Are Not Enough" (6.15), explains what to do when two or more works by an author have the same title or when works listed by title have the same title. Examples showing how to cite numbered notes in parenthetical citations have been added (6.29).

The section on quoting now incorporates information on paraphrasing sources (6.31–6.77). More subheads have been added for easier navigation, and additional explanations and examples have been developed. New to this section are tips for making citations more concise and for differentiating one's own ideas from those of the source; a greater range of examples showing punctuation introducing quotations and the capitalization of quotations; focused discussion of the placement of parenthetical citations; tips for citing multiple works in a single citation; advice on what to do when the material you are quoting contains note numbers or symbols, parenthetical citations, cross-references, or figure numbers; examples of citing dialogue in drama, prose, and poems; and pointers on how to quote the same passage more than once.

Notes (Chapter 7)

This new chapter offers guidance on how writers can use notes in MLA style alongside in-text citations. It includes examples demonstrating when and how to use bibliographic notes and content notes, how to style notes, and where to place notes in the text.

Appendixes

In appendix 1, a list of common abbreviations used in documentation now appears at the end of the handbook for easy reference. Readers asked that the handbook also continue to include the MLA's list of abbreviations for the Bible, Chaucer, and Shakespeare, which can be used in some research projects as an alternative method of referring to works in parenthetical citations (see 6.13). Since works by many other authors and in various literary traditions could benefit from abbreviations, new to this edition is an additional list of sample abbreviations alongside guidance for abbreviating the title of any work.

Instructors and students asked for sample works-cited-list entries for quick glossing and comparison. Thus, appendix 2 collects over two hundred new examples of entries for common and uncommon types of sources, organized by publication format.

Navigating the Handbook

The handbook is designed for easy navigation. Sections are numbered continuously through each chapter. A comprehensive index in the back of the book uses this numbering system for seamless wayfinding between the print and e-book versions. Cross-references appear in shaded capsules at the end of sections, pointing out related information covered elsewhere in the handbook. If a styling matter is the same in prose and in documentation (for example, the capitalization of a surname), it is covered in chapter 2, "Mechanics of Prose," and cross-referenced in the later chapters on documentation. Otherwise, any styling issues unique to the list of works cited appear in the How to Style It sections in chapter 5. The table of contents lists all the section heads throughout the handbook. For quick reference, appendix 2, which shows examples of works-cited-list entries, has its own table of contents.

Learner's Tour through the Handbook

The following sections will be of special value to those new to MLA style and might be read before proceeding to use the rest of the handbook as a reference:

- chapter 4, "Documenting Sources: An Overview"
- 5.1–5.2, an overview of creating and formatting entries and an introduction to the template of core elements
- the What It Is and Where to Find It sections for each element in chapter 5, which explain the range of situations each element applies to and provide visual examples of where to find information in a variety of sources
- 5.100–5.103, which show the three most common types of entries and how to use the template to create works-cited-list entries
- 5.105–5.119, which describe supplemental elements to the template
- 6.1–6.2, which provide an overview of in-text citations
- 7.1–7.2, which explain when to use bibliographic and content notes

Throughout the handbook, advanced tips for specialists, scholars, and those writing long-form works are given. This edition collects those tips together in the index entry "specialist contexts."

Companion Resources

The online *MLA Style Center* (style.mla.org) features a continually growing set of resources that support use of the *MLA Handbook*, including

- sample papers in MLA style
- guidelines for avoiding plagiarism
- a works-cited quick guide providing an overview of how to use the template of core elements
- an interactive version of the template that can be used for practice and instruction
- hundreds of additional example citations, including examples grouped by format
- answers to Ask the MLA questions about writing, citation, and research
- writing tips from the MLA editors

- teaching resources, including lesson plans
- quizzes on various aspects of writing
- a free online course on research using the *MLA International Bibliography*

The MLA also publishes companion guides on research and writing, including

- *The MLA Guide to Digital Literacy*, by Ellen C. Carillo, which provides hands-on, structured activities, prompts, and lesson plans that give students strategies for evaluating the credibility of sources, detecting fake news, understanding bias, crafting a research question, and effectively conducting searches

- *The MLA Guide to Undergraduate Research in Literature*, written by two experienced librarians, Elizabeth Brookbank and H. Faye Christenberry, which introduces resources available through college and university libraries, identifies relevant databases and research guides, explains different types of sources used in researching and writing about a literary text, and offers guidance on organizing research

A number of other resource guides for teachers, students, and writers can be found on mla.org/books.

1. Formatting Your Research Project

The following guidelines have been widely adopted by instructors and educational institutions to standardize manuscript formatting, making it easier for instructors to evaluate papers and theses and for writers to focus on making decisions about their research, ideas, and prose. Although these guidelines follow common conventions, acceptable variations exist. Follow the directions of your instructor, school, or publisher if you are asked to use different formatting guidelines. You should also be responsive to the specific demands of your project, which may have unique needs that require you to use a formatting style not described below.

[1.1] Margins

Leave margins of one inch at the top and bottom and on both sides of the text. See **fig. 1.3** for margins used with a running head.

[1.2] Text Formatting

Always choose an easily readable typeface (Times New Roman is just one example) in which the regular type style contrasts clearly with the italic, and set it to anywhere between 11 and 13 points, unless your instructor specifies a different font size. Generally use the same typeface and type size throughout the paper (however, see 7.3 on the formatting of note numbers, which most word processing programs automatically apply styles to).

Do not justify the lines of text at the right margin, and turn off the automatic hyphenation feature in your word processing program. It is unnecessary to divide words at the ends of lines in a manuscript. (When checking word breaks in a professionally typeset text, consult your dictionary about where words should break.) Double-space the entire research paper, including quotations, notes, and the list of works cited. Indent the first line of a paragraph half an inch from the left margin. Indent block quotations half an inch as well. Leave one space after a period or other concluding punctuation mark, unless your instructor prefers two spaces.

> Block quotations: 6.35, 6.38.

[1.3] Title

One inch from the top of the first page and flush with the left margin, type your name, your instructor's name (or instructors' names, if there is more than one instructor), the course name and number, and the date on separate double-spaced lines. On a new double-spaced line, center the title **(fig. 1.1)**. Do not italicize or underline your title, put it in quotation marks

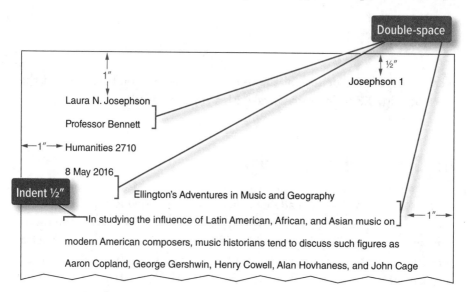

Fig. 1.1. The top of the first page of a research paper.

or boldface, or type it in all capital letters. Follow the rules for capitalization set forth in 2.90 and italicize only the words that you would italicize in the text.

Social Media Coverage of International News Events

Concepts of Justice in *To Kill a Mockingbird*

The Use of the Words *Fair* and *Foul* in Shakespeare's *Macbeth*

Romanticism in England and the *Scapigliatura* in Italy

Do not use a period after your title or after any heading in the paper (e.g., Works Cited). Begin your text on a new double-spaced line after the title, indenting the first line of the paragraph half an inch from the left margin. A research paper does not normally need a title page, but if the paper is a group project, create a title page and list all the authors on it instead of in the header on page 1 of your essay (**fig. 1.2**). If your teacher requires a title page in lieu of or in addition to the header, format the title page according to the instructions you are given.

Sujata Das

José Rodriguez

Stephanie Smith

Professor Green

Humanities 206

21 October 2019

Film Adaptations of Stanisław Lem's *Solaris*

Fig. 1.2. The title page of a paper written by several students.

[1.4] Running Head and Page Numbers

Number all pages consecutively throughout the research paper in the upper right-hand corner, half an inch from the top and flush with the right margin. Type your surname, followed by a space, before the page number (**fig. 1.3**). If a project has several authors and all authors' surnames do not fit in a running head, include only the page number. Do not use the abbreviation "p." before the page number or add a period, a hyphen, or any other mark or symbol. Your word processing program will probably allow you to create a running head of this kind that appears automatically on every page.

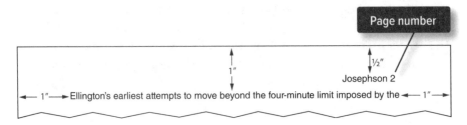

Fig. 1.3. The running head of a research paper.

[1.5] Internal Headings and Subheadings

Headings and subheadings in the body of your research project can help organize and structure your writing, but you should avoid overusing them. Headings should never be used to compensate for poor structure or to explain an underdeveloped idea, and they are generally not needed in short, essay-length works. When headings are called for in your writing project, keep them short and observe the basic guidelines below.

Consistency in the styling of headings and subheadings is key to signaling to readers the structure of a research project. Word processing software often has built-in heading styles. Headings in the body of your research project should be styled in descending order of prominence. After the first level, the other headings are subheadings—that is, they are subordinate. Font styling and size are used to signal prominence. Each level 1 heading should appear in the same style and size, as should each level 2 heading, and so on. In general, a boldface, larger font indicates prominence; a smaller font, italics, or lack of bold can be used to signal subordination. For readability, avoid using all capital letters for headings (in some cases, small capitals may be acceptable).

Heading Level 1

Heading Level 2

Heading Level 3

No internal heading level should have only one instance. For example, if you use a level 1 heading, you should have at least one other level 1 heading. (The exceptions are the paper or chapter title and the headings for notes and the list of works cited.)

In the body of the paper, headings should be flush with the left margin, not indented or centered. For readability, include a line space above and below a heading.

Generally avoid using numbers and letters to designate headings unless you are working in a discipline where using them is conventional.

Capitalize and punctuate headings like the titles of works as explained in 2.90–2.119.

[1.6] Placement of the List of Works Cited

The list of works cited appears at the end of the paper, after any endnotes. Center the heading, Works Cited, an inch from the top of the page (**fig. 1.4**). If the list contains only one entry, make the heading Work Cited. Double-space between the heading and the first entry. Begin each entry flush with the left margin; if an entry runs more than one line, indent the subsequent line or lines half an inch from the left margin. This format is sometimes

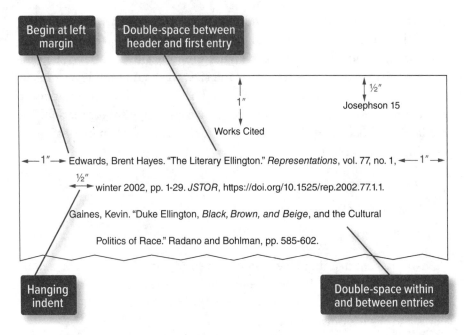

Fig. 1.4. The top of the first page of a works-cited list.

called *hanging indent*, and you can set your word processing program to create it automatically for a group of paragraphs. Hanging indent makes alphabetic lists easier to use. Double-space the entire list.

[1.7] Tables and Illustrations

Place tables and illustrations as close as possible to the parts of the text to which they relate. A table is usually labeled Table, given an arabic numeral, and titled. Type both the label and title flush left on separate lines above the table, and capitalize them as titles (do not use all capital letters). Place the source of the table and any notes in a caption immediately below the table. To avoid confusion between notes to the text and notes to the table, designate notes to the table with lowercase letters rather than with numerals. Double-space throughout; use dividing lines as needed (**fig. 1.5**).

Any other type of illustrative visual material—for example, a photograph, map, line drawing, graph, or chart—should be labeled Figure (usually abbreviated Fig.), assigned an arabic numeral, and given a caption.

A label and caption ordinarily appear directly below the illustration and have the same one-inch margins as the text of the paper. If the caption of a table or illustration provides complete information about the source and the source is not cited in the text, no entry is needed for the source in the

Table 1

Degrees in Modern Foreign Languages and Literature Conferred by Degree-Granting Institutions of Higher Education in the United States[a]

Year	Bachelor's Degrees	Master's Degrees	Doctor's Degrees
1996–97	13,053	2,470	793
1997–98	13,618	2,367	819
1998–99	14,163	2,267	757
1999–2000	14,186	2,228	804
2000–01	14,292	2,244	818
2001–02	14,236	2,284	780
2002–03	14,854	2,256	749
2003–04	15,408	2,307	743
2004–05	16,008	2,517	762
2005–06	16,762	2,637	777

Adapted from: U.S. Department of Education, Institute of Education Sciences, National Center for Education Statistics. *Digest of Education Statistics*, 2007 ed., June 2007, table 297, nces.ed.gov/programs/digest/d07/tables/dt07_297.asp.

a. These figures include degrees conferred in a single language or a combination of modern foreign languages and exclude degrees in linguistics, Latin, classics, ancient and Middle and Near Eastern biblical and Semitic languages, ancient and classical Greek, Sanskrit and classical Indian languages, and sign language and sign language interpretation.

Fig. 1.5. A table in a research paper.

works-cited list. If you provide full bibliographic details in a caption, punctuate the caption like a works-cited-list entry but do not invert the name of the author or artist that appears at the beginning of the caption (**fig. 1.6**). Otherwise, use commas to separate elements in a caption and provide full publication details in the works-cited list (**fig. 1.7**).

Fig. 1.6.
A figure in a research paper, with full bibliographic details in the caption.

Fig. 1. Berthe Morisot. *Reading.* 1873, Cleveland Museum of Art.

Fig. 1.7.
A figure in a research paper, with a caption that points to a works-cited-list entry.

Fig. 1. Edward Topsell, *Manticore,* woodcut, 1658.

Work cited

Topsell, Edward. *Manticore. Curious Woodcuts of Fanciful and Real Beasts,* by Konrad Gesner, Dover, 1971, p. 8. Originally published in *The History of Four-Footed Beats and Serpents* . . . , by Topsell, London, 1658.

Ex. 1. Ludwig van Beethoven, Symphony No. 3 in E-flat, Opus 55 (*Eroica*), first movement, opening.

Fig. 1.8. A musical example in a research paper.

Musical illustrations are labeled *Example* (usually abbreviated *Ex.*), assigned an arabic numeral, and given a caption. A label and caption ordinarily appear directly below the example and have the same one-inch margins as the text of the paper (**fig. 1.8**).

Punctuation of works-cited-list entries: 5.120.

[1.8] Lists

Lists can help you organize information and present it economically. The goal of any list is to help readers easily understand information. Overusing lists, however, can have the opposite effect, making prose difficult to follow. Lists can be incorporated into your prose or set vertically. They can be numbered when enumeration is essential to your point.

[1.9] Integrated into Your Prose

It is preferable to integrate lists into your prose, rather than to set them vertically, whenever the information can be readily understood in this format. A colon is often used to introduce an integrated list unless the list is grammatically essential to the introductory wording—for example, when the list is the object of the verb that introduces it, as in the second example below (where the list is the object of the verb *include*). Punctuate items in an unnumbered, integrated list just as you would words in a sentence.

> Chimamanda Ngozi Adichie has written four books of fiction: *Purple Hibiscus, Half of a Yellow Sun, The Thing around Your Neck,* and *Americanah.*

> Chimamanda Ngozi Adichie's books of fiction include *Purple Hibiscus, Half of a Yellow Sun,* and *The Thing around Your Neck.*

Numerals in lists in your prose should be enclosed in parentheses.

> The workshop will walk students through five key stages in the research process: (1) selecting a topic, (2) searching for sources, (3) evaluating sources, (4) reading and taking notes from relevant sources, and (5) refining the topic.

> Serial commas with lists: 2.12. Semicolons with lists: 2.26. Colons to introduce lists: 2.27.

[1.10] Set Vertically

Vertical lists are best used when the information presented is lengthy, has many component parts, or benefits from being set apart from the main prose. Below are examples of vertical lists—which may be unnumbered, numbered, or bulleted—and how to introduce, punctuate, and capitalize them. Word processing programs automatically define styles for lists so that they are indented and thus clearly distinguished from the text and so that each item in the list forms a unit.

[1.11] Lists introduced with a complete sentence

A list may be introduced with a complete sentence followed by a colon, as in the examples below. The items in the list can be composed of complete sentences or fragments but should be consistent in using one or the other.

If the list items are complete sentences, the first letter of the first word of each item should be capitalized, and the item should be followed by closing punctuation, such as a period or question mark.

> Students were asked to address one of the following questions in their group presentation:
>
> > What signs of the ancien régime continue to influence the social mores of characters in the novel?
> >
> > How is realism evinced in the novel, and when does the novel retreat from realism?
> >
> > How are workers depicted in the novel's urban scenes?
> >
> > How do the moments of magical realism in the novel relate to the subplot of the dictator's coup?

In bulleted lists, elements begin with a lowercase letter (unless the first word is normally capitalized, such as a proper noun), and no punctuation follows list elements unless they are composed of a full sentence.

> The *MLA Style Center* (style.mla.org), a free companion to the *MLA Handbook*, is the only official website devoted to MLA style and provides a number of useful features:
>
> - the opportunity to submit questions about MLA style
> - sample research papers
> - teaching resources
> - tools for creating works-cited-list entries

If the list items are not complete sentences and the list is not bulleted, then, whether the list is numbered or not, begin each item with a lowercase letter and punctuate the fragments like parts of a sentence. Use semicolons between the list items and write *and* or *or* before the final item. A period should conclude the list.

The specific contexts influencing the author's work fall into four main areas:

1. ideas about free will and the change and mutability that attend human decision-making, derived from Boethius;

2. teachings about the importance of translating the Bible into English;

3. humanism's founding precepts and, especially, the writings of Petrarch; and

4. the political insurrection that took place as a result of heavy taxation to continue funding of the Hundred Years' War.

[1.12] Lists that continue the sentence introducing them

A list may also start with a sentence continued in the list, as shown in the examples below. No colon should appear before such lists. In most cases, list items continuing the sentence introducing them will not be complete sentences, and each item can therefore begin with a lowercase letter.

In formal contexts, you may punctuate the fragments in numbered and unnumbered lists like parts of a sentence. Use semicolons between the list items and write *and* or *or* before the final item. A period should conclude the list.

The campus health clinic is expanding its advocacy efforts by

launching a twenty-four-hour care hotline;

developing strategic partnerships with community health care providers; and

running a website that provides reliable, up-to-date health information, mental health resources, nutritional advice, and more.

In bulleted lists, elements begin with a lowercase letter (unless the first word is normally capitalized, such as a proper noun), and no punctuation follows list elements unless they are composed of a full sentence.

A free companion to the *MLA Handbook* and the only official website devoted to MLA style, *The MLA Style Center* (style.mla.org) provides

- the opportunity to submit questions about MLA style
- sample research papers
- teaching resources
- tools for creating works-cited-list entries

[1.13] Paper and Printing

If you print your paper, use only white, 8½-by-11-inch paper. Use a high-quality printer. Some instructors prefer papers printed on a single side because such papers are easier to read, but others allow printing on both sides to conserve paper.

[1.14] Proofreading and Spellcheckers

Proofread and correct your research paper carefully before submitting it. Spellcheckers and usage checkers can be helpful but should be used with caution. They do not find all errors, such as words spelled correctly but misused, and they sometimes label correct material as erroneous, such as many proper nouns as well as terms from languages other than English.

[1.15] Binding a Printed Paper

Pages of a printed research paper may get misplaced or lost if they are left unattached or merely folded down at a corner, so be sure to use a staple or paper clip. Although a plastic folder or a binder may seem an attractive finishing touch, most instructors find that such devices make it harder to read and comment on students' work.

[1.16] **Electronic Submission**

If you are asked to submit your paper electronically, follow your teacher's guidelines for formatting, mode of submission (e.g., by e-mail or on a website), and so forth.

2. Mechanics of Prose

Presenting information in a standardized, consistent manner will make your writing clear and effective. This chapter focuses on the mechanics of prose—that is, the many technical questions that writers must contend with, like those of spelling, punctuation, capitalization, and the styling of numbers.

[2.1] Spelling

Spelling should be consistent in a paper. Some words can acceptably be spelled more than one way. So if you write *acknowledgment* in one place, use that spelling throughout instead of the variant spelling *acknowledgement*. (Quoted text, however, must follow the spelling shown in the source: see 6.32.)

[2.2] Dictionaries

To ensure consistency, use a single dictionary, such as *Merriam-Webster* (merriam-webster.com); if an entry has variant spellings, generally adopt the spelling listed first.

[2.3] Plurals

The plurals of nouns are generally formed by appending *-s* (*kids*, *laws*, *stars*, *Fridays*, *Obamas*) or, for words ending in *-ch*, *-s*, *-sh*, *-x*, and *-z*, appending *-es* (*sketches*, *masses*, *Dickenses*, *brushes*, *taxes*, *Kleenexes*, *spritzes*).

Consult a dictionary for guidance about nonstandard plurals. These include some words ending in *-f* (the plural of *serif* is *serifs*, but the plural of *thief* is *thieves*), *-fe* (the plural of *gaffe* is *gaffes*, but the plural of *wife* is *wives*), *-o* (the plural of *mosquito* can be *mosquitoes* or *mosquitos*), and *-y* (the plural of *guy* is *guys*, but the plural of *allegory* is *allegories*). There are also irregular plurals (the plural of *child* is *children*), compound plurals (*fathers-in-law*, *poets laureate*, *nurse practitioners*), and terms that retain the plural forms of their original language (*foci*, *phenomena*). Some words even have different forms of the plural with different meanings (e.g., the plural of *mouse* is *mice* when referring to rodents but *mouses* when referring to the computer component). When the dictionary provides more than one plural form (as for *mosquito*), generally use the first term listed.

If the term has not been naturalized into English—that is, if it is labeled "foreign term," "French phrase," or the like in a dictionary—add an *s* (e.g., *mise en abyme* becomes *mise en abymes*). Terms such as these should appear in italics in your prose.

Some words, like *data* and *politics*, can be construed as singular or plural. The dictionary usually tells you when this is the case.

> Possessive plurals: 2.50–2.51. Foreign words in an English-language text: 2.63. Plurals of numbers: 2.134.

[2.4] Punctuation

The primary job of punctuation is to make your writing clear and readable. Punctuation clarifies sentence structure by separating some words and grouping others. The guidelines set forth here cover common punctuation issues.

[2.5] Commas

The comma is an essential tool for effective communication. Commas can be necessary, incorrect, or optional.

[2.6] When a comma is necessary

[2.7] *Before a coordinating conjunction joining independent clauses*

Use a comma before a coordinating conjunction (*and, but, for, nor, or, so, yet*) joining independent clauses in a sentence.

> Congress passed the bill, and the president signed it into law.

> Synonyms have a basic similarity of meaning, but they cannot always be used interchangeably.

> The poem is sentimental, yet the poet takes a pragmatic view of death.

But the comma may be omitted when the coordinating conjunction joins short independent clauses: see 2.25.

[2.8] *Between coordinate adjectives*

Use a comma between coordinate adjectives—that is, adjectives that separately modify the same term.

> Critics praise the novel's unaffected, unadorned style.
> *The adjectives* unaffected *and* unadorned *each modify* style.

But when the adjectives do not modify the same term—that is, when they are not coordinate—do not use a comma.

> A famous photograph shows Marianne Moore in a black tricornered hat.
> *The adjective* black *modifies* tricornered hat.

Adjectives that denote size, color, age, material, temperature, shape, and quantity are usually not coordinate.

> a big white dog

> a large brown rectangular briefcase

> seven cold metal stools

A noun can be modified by a combination of coordinate and noncoordinate adjectives.

> The author crafted an unremitting, forceful narrative persona.
>
> *The adjectives* unremitting *and* forceful *both modify* narrative persona.

[2.9] *To set off parenthetical comments*

Use commas to set off a parenthetical comment, or an aside, if the comment is brief and closely related to the rest of the sentence.

> The Ming dynasty, for example, lasted nearly three hundred years.
>
> His testimony is not, I submit, an accurate account.

[2.10] *After long introductory phrases and clauses*

Use a comma after a long introductory phrase or clause (see 2.23 for commas with a short introductory phrase or clause).

Phrase

After years of intensive research for her dissertation, Amy Vuong received her PhD.

Clause

Although theorists of comedy tend to agree that there is no universal sense of humor, they note that what most forms of comedy have in common is a sense of incongruity.

[2.11] *With contrasting phrases*

Use commas to set off alternative or contrasting phrases.

> Julio, not his mother, sets the plot in motion.

But do not use commas if the phrase expresses a relation between two terms.

> Several cooperative but autonomous republics were formed.
>
> *The conjunction* but *expresses the relation between* cooperative *and* autonomous.

[2.12] *In series*

Use commas to separate words, phrases, and clauses in a series. The final comma in a series is known as the serial (or Oxford) comma.

Words

Ta-Nehisi Coates has written books, comics, and works of journalism.

Phrases

Anne Frank's diary has been translated into many languages, adapted for the screen, and turned into a play.

Clauses

In the Great Depression, millions of people lost their jobs, businesses failed, and charitable institutions closed their doors.

But use semicolons when items in a series have internal commas: see 2.26.

[2.13] *With dates and locations*

Use a comma in a date presented in month-day-year style. If such a date comes in the middle of a sentence, include a comma after the year.

Roberto Bolaño was born on April 28, 1953, and died on July 15, 2003.

But commas are omitted for dates presented in day-month-year style.

Roberto Bolaño was born on 28 April 1953 and died on 15 July 2003.

Commas are also omitted between a month and a year and between a season and a year.

The events of July 1789 are as familiar to the French as those of July 1776 are to Americans.

I passed my oral exams in spring 2007.

Use a comma to set off the components of a place-name (e.g., a city from a state, a province from a country, a campus from its main institution, and so on).

> The book tour started in Auckland, New Zealand, and ended in Limuru, Kenya, the author's hometown.

> The University of Toronto, Mississauga, is located about twenty miles west of Toronto, Ontario.

[2.14] *With nonrestrictive modifiers*

Modifiers are parts of a sentence, whether a word or group of words, that qualify other parts of the sentence. Use commas to set off a modifier that could be dropped without changing the main sense of the sentence. Such a modifier is termed *nonrestrictive* because it does not restrict, or limit, what is being modified. For example, in the sentence *The teacher, who answers every question patiently, asked if the students had any more questions*, the clause *who answers every question patiently* merely provides additional detail and can be omitted without changing the main point of the sentence. Thus, commas surround the clause.

Dropping a *restrictive* modifier, in contrast, would change the main sense of the sentence. For example, in the sentence *The child to the left raised her hand*, the phrase *to the left* modifies *child* and tells you which specific child is meant. A *restrictive* phrase affects the meaning of a sentence—here, the meaning of *child* is restricted to the child *to the left*. Do not use commas around restrictive modifiers.

Words in apposition—that is, two nouns that refer to the same thing (like *Olga Tokarczuk* and *the Polish writer* in the examples below) can be restrictive or nonrestrictive.

Nonrestrictive

Olga Tokarczuk, the Polish writer, won the 2018 Nobel Prize in Literature.
> *Dropping the phrase* the Polish writer *does not change the meaning of the sentence.*

Restrictive

The Polish writer Olga Tokarczuk won the 2018 Nobel Prize in Literature.
> *Without* Olga Tokarczuk *it is unclear which Polish writer is meant.*

Practices vary on the use of *that* and *which* to introduce restrictive and non-restrictive clauses. Usage in what is called American English has *which*, preceded by a comma, introduce only nonrestrictive clauses and has *that*, not preceded by a comma, introduce restrictive clauses. An alternative practice, where *that* and *which* are both used to introduce restrictive clauses, and no comma precedes *that* or *which*, is observed by British English usage. The examples below reflect American English usage.

Nonrestrictive

Novels, which can be published in hardcover, paperback, or e-book formats, are seeing their best sales in years.

> *The clause* which can be published in hardcover, paperback, or e-book formats *can be dropped without changing the meaning of the sentence.*

Restrictive

Novels that are bound in hardcover are seeing their best sales in years.

> *The clause* that are bound in hardcover *cannot be dropped; only those novels are seeing increased sales.*

Who, whom, and *whose* are used to introduce both types of clauses.

Nonrestrictive

Kamau Brathwaite, who wrote *Born to Slow Horses,* won a PEN award in 2018.

Restrictive

The poet who wrote *Born to Slow Horses* won a PEN award in 2018.

Nonrestrictive

Edith Wharton, whose works illuminate the complexities of class and power in New York City during the Gilded Age, was the first woman awarded a Pulitzer Prize for fiction.

Restrictive

The first woman to win a Pulitzer Prize for fiction was a novelist whose works illuminate the complexities of class and power in New York City during the Gilded Age.

Whether a comma appears before an adverbial phrase or clause affects the meaning.

Nonrestrictive

The novel takes place in China, where many languages are spoken.
> *The clause* where many languages are spoken *can be dropped.*

Restrictive

The novel takes place in a country where many languages are spoken.
> *The clause* where many languages are spoken *cannot be dropped.*

[2.15] When a comma is incorrect

Do not use commas between the following sentence elements.

[2.16] *Subject and verb*

What makes Sartre's theory of commitment relevant to our discussion **[no comma]** is its insistence that choice in today's world can be only political.

Sometimes, however, a pair of commas will surround a phrase or clause that comes between a subject and verb.

Many of the characters who dominate the early chapters and then disappear, often leaving behind no trace other than a farewell letter, are portraits of the author's friends.

[2.17] *Verb and object*

The agent reported **[no comma]** that the vehicle had been traced to an underground garage.

[2.18] *Parts of a compound subject*

A dozen wooden chairs **[no comma]** and a window that admits a shaft of light complete the stage setting.

[2.19] *Parts of a compound object*

Ptolemy devised a system of astronomy accepted until the sixteenth century **[no comma]** and a scientific approach to the study of geography.

[2.20] *Two verbs that share a subject*

He composed several popular symphonies **[no comma]** but won the most fame for his witticisms.

[2.21] *Two subordinate elements that are parallel*

From his darkness, Lear has gained insight into himself as a fallible man and negligent king **[no comma]** and into the evil of Goneril and Regan.

The current economic climate has given rise to a technology sector that demands workers receive training in basic coding skills **[no comma]** but that is unwilling to pay for it.

[2.22] When a comma is optional

In the following examples, the commas are not required, but it is not wrong to include them.

[2.23] *With short introductory phrases and clauses*

If you use commas after short introductory phrases and clauses, do so consistently throughout your work.

With comma

By 2010, smartphone use was widespread.

In the fall, students attend convocation.

Without comma

By 2010 smartphone use was widespread.

In the fall students attend convocation.

[2.24] *Around specific words*

Commas are optional around words and phrases like *perhaps, therefore, indeed*, and *of course* that come in the middle of a sentence when the sentence does not conjoin two independent clauses.

> This assumes, of course, that we finish the test on time.

> The instructor saw our confusion and is therefore going to explain the principle again.

> We could, perhaps, approach the problem from another angle.

> Rather than speculate further, we could indeed consult a reference work.

But when the word or phrase joins two independent clauses, a comma is needed.

> This assumes that we finish the test on time; of course, we may not.

[2.25] *Before some coordinating conjunctions*

When a coordinating conjunction joins short independent clauses, the comma is optional.

With comma

Wallace sings, and Armstrong plays cornet.

Without comma

Wallace sings and Armstrong plays cornet.

[2.26] Semicolons

Semicolons mark a stronger separation than commas. They are commonly used in a sentence to link two or more independent clauses not joined by a conjunction.

> Don't touch the stove; it's hot.

In some cases, when a sharp break is intended, a dash can be used instead.

Don't touch the stove—it's hot.

Semicolons should always be used between items in a series when the items contain commas.

Present at the symposium were Henri-Guillaume Durand, the art critic; Sam Brown, the *Daily Tribune* reporter; and Maria Rosa, the conceptual artist.

Semicolons are also used in constructions where the verb is elided with a comma.

Some writers favor semicolons; others, dashes; yet others, commas.

[2.27] Colons

Like semicolons, colons connect two independent clauses, but they have other uses as well. Colons are used to introduce an elaboration of what was just said, the formal expression of a rule or principle, or a list.

Lowercase what follows a colon unless it is a word normally capitalized or when the colon introduces a series composed of more than one sentence, a rule or principle, or a question.

Elaboration

The plot is founded on deception: the protagonist has a secret identity.

The moderator then posed a question to the panelists: In what ways has the New Queer Cinema amplified the visibility of queerness in film?

Rule or principle

Many books would be briefer if their authors followed the logical principle known as Occam's razor: Explanations should not be multiplied unnecessarily.

List

The musicology syllabus includes three genres: jazz, blues, and hip-hop.

Do not use a colon before a list if the list is grammatically essential to the introductory wording—for example, when the list is the object of the verb that introduces it. In the first example below, the list is the object of the verb *are*, so the colon is incorrect. To revise, recast the sentence so that what precedes the colon is a full sentence, or omit the colon.

Incorrect

The three assigned topics for your essay on *Infinite Jest* are: tennis, lenses, and mathematics.

Correct

These are the three assigned topics for your essay on *Infinite Jest*: tennis, lenses, and mathematics.

The three assigned topics for your essay on *Infinite Jest* are tennis, lenses, and mathematics.

> Formatting lists integrated into your prose: 1.9.
> Colons to introduce quotations: 6.35, 6.49.

[2.28] Dashes and Parentheses

Dashes and parentheses indicate an interruption in thought. They are used to provide additional information, clarify a word or statement, or set apart other kinds of commentary from the main text. Whether to mark an interruption in thought in a sentence with commas, dashes, or parentheses is often a matter of choice. Because both dashes and parentheses break the continuity of a sentence more sharply than commas do, overusing them often distracts readers and makes prose less readable. Another caution: using one unpaired dash or more than two paired dashes in a sentence might make readers unsure of what is being set off and what is not.

Dashes can be rendered as two hyphens in manuscripts or as the em-dash symbol—that is, a dash the length of the letter *m*—which is conventional in professionally typeset publications like this one. No space comes before or after the dash. When two hyphens are used to indicate the dash, no space appears between them. Various examples of using dashes and parentheses are given below.

[2.29] To enclose an interruption

Use dashes or parentheses to enclose a sentence element that interrupts the train of thought.

> The play's "hero" (the townspeople see him as heroic, but he is the focus of the author's satire) introduces himself as a veteran of the war.

[2.30] To prevent misreading

Use dashes or parentheses to set off a parenthetical element that contains a comma and that might be misread if set off with commas.

> The qualities of Corinne's character—honor, patience, and kindness—are lacking in her fellow countrywoman, the play's antagonist.

[2.31] To introduce an elaboration or an example

Use a single dash before a phrase like *for example, that is*, or *namely* when the phrase introduces an elaboration of what was just said.

> She argues against limiting her speech to the court to only one style—for example, a formal register.

> The figure may by its insistence become performative—that is, may produce the appearance of newness.

> The play's lead had one thing on her mind—namely, making up for lost time.

[2.32] To introduce a list

A dash may also be used instead of a colon to introduce a list.

> The course covers three epics from different literary traditions—the *Odyssey*, the *Tale of the Heike*, and *Omeros*.

[2.33] Hyphens

Hyphens indicate the relation between words by joining two or more words. They also join prefixes to words. In prose, hyphens are primarily used to prevent misreading. One of the most common uses of hyphens is to form compound adjectives.

Compound words—that is, words that are formed from more than one word—may be written as separate words (*hard drive*), with hyphens (*hard-boiled*), and as single words (*hardheaded*). The dictionary indicates the styling of many compounds. When used as a noun, a compound word not in the dictionary should generally be written as separate words (*knitting needle*).

[2.34] When to hyphenate compound adjectives before a noun

[2.35] *Adverbs*

A compound adjective that begins with an adverb such as *better, best, ill, lower, little,* or *well* is hyphenated when it comes before a noun.

> ill-prepared student
>
> well-earned applause

The same type of compound is unhyphenated when it appears after the noun it modifies.

> The flowers were well arranged.

[2.36] *Number-noun combinations*

A compound adjective formed from a number, including an ordinal number, and a noun is hyphenated.

> fifteen-day trips
>
> thirteenth-century architecture

When an adjective appears before a compound adjective like *thirteenth-century*, attach it with a hyphen.

> early-thirteenth-century architecture

The same type of compound is unhyphenated when it appears after the noun it modifies.

The trips took place over a period of fifteen days.

The book surveys architecture of the early thirteenth century.

[2.37] *Prepositional phrases*

A compound adjective formed from a prepositional phrase is hyphenated.

on-campus activities

The same type of compound is unhyphenated when it appears after the noun it modifies.

The activity is on campus.

[2.38] *Clarity*

Sometimes a hyphen is necessary in a compound adjective in order to prevent misreading.

three-layer cakes

The hyphen indicates that the term refers to cakes with three layers, not to three cakes with layers.

Swiss-cheese maker

The hyphen makes it clear that the term refers to a maker of Swiss cheese, not to a cheese maker who is Swiss.

ocean-blue bird

The hyphen indicates that the bird is a certain shade of blue, not a blue bird from the ocean.

[2.39] When not to hyphenate compound adjectives before a noun

[2.40] *Adverbs*

Do not hyphenate an adjective that includes an adverb ending in *-ly*.

thoughtfully presented thesis

No hyphen is needed in a compound adjective that begins with *too, very*, or *much*.

> much beloved teacher

[2.41] *Comparatives and superlatives*

Likewise, no hyphen is needed in a compound adjective that includes a comparative or superlative description formed with *less, least, more, or most*.

> less expensive option
>
> most likely outcome

[2.42] *Familiar compound terms*

When the adjective is formed from familiar unhyphenated compound terms, such as compound terms that are listed in the dictionary, do not use a hyphen.

> civil rights legislation
>
> high school reunion

When you are writing for a specialized field, no hyphen is needed in a compound adjective formed from unhyphenated compound terms that are familiar in that field (often called *terms of art*).

> second language acquisition
>
> tort reform law

[2.43] *Foreign language terms*

When the adjective is formed from a phrase derived from a language other than English or when the adjective is a foreign language term, a hyphen is not needed.

> ad hoc solution
>
> *mise en abyme* figure

Foreign words in an English-language text: 2.63.

[2.44] *Proper nouns*

No hyphen is used in a compound adjective formed from unhyphenated proper nouns.

> Asian American students
>
> Pulitzer Prize ceremony

[2.45] Hyphens before suppressed words

When words are suppressed from a compound phrase—whether hyphenated or not—add a space after the hyphen unless a punctuation mark follows.

> five- and ten-dollar bills
>
> pre- and postwar literature
>
> first-, second-, and third-semester students

[2.46] Hyphens with prefixes

The dictionary can help you determine when to include a hyphen after a prefix (e.g., *pre-*, *semi-*). The dictionary shows that many words formed with a prefix do not use a hyphen. Here are some examples:

antiwar	overpay	semiretired
coworker	postwar	subculture
multinational	prescheduled	unambiguous
nonjudgmental	reinvigorate	underrepresented

The dictionary often shows when words formed with a prefix require a hyphen. Here are some examples:

> anti-academic
>
> non-biblical
>
> co-occuring

Use hyphens after prefixes when the dictionary shows the term with a hyphen, when vowels are doubled (*anti-itch*), when the prefix precedes a capitalized word (*post-Victorian*), and when the hyphen helps distinguish different meanings of a word (*re-cover*, meaning "cover again," distinct from *recover*, meaning "get back" or "recuperate").

[2.47] Hyphens in fractions

Use a hyphen in simple fractions, no matter their part of speech.

He watched only one-third of the movie.

The glass is three-quarters full.

Use of numerals or words to express numbers: 2.127.

[2.48] Hyphens versus en dashes

If a lowercase compound that would not be hyphenated under the above guidelines forms a single adjective with another word or a prefix, hyphenate the entire adjective.

civil rights legislation → post-civil-rights legislation

cultural studies approach → cultural-studies-based approach

But when a compound is formed from a prefix and a proper noun composed of more than one word, use an en dash (a dash the length of the letter *n*) in place of a hyphen. The en dash indicates that the prefix is meant to connect to the entire capitalized term that follows and not only to the first word of the capitalized term.

World War II era → post–World War II era

In research papers and other manuscripts, hyphens can also be used to indicate number ranges. Professionally typeset publications like this one, however, use en dashes in number ranges (see 2.139).

[2.49] Apostrophes

Apostrophes are used to form some plurals and to indicate possession. They are also used to form contractions (*can't, wouldn't*), generally to be avoided in scholarly writing and other contexts where a formal tone is called for.

[2.50] Singular and plural nouns

To form the possessive of a singular noun, add an apostrophe and an *s*.

a poem's meter

To form the possessive of a plural noun ending in -*s*, add only an apostrophe.

firefighters' trucks

To form the possessive of a noun that ends in -*s* in both the singular and plural form, add an apostrophe.

ethics' contribution to philosophy

To form the possessive of an irregular plural noun not ending in -*s*, add an apostrophe and an *s*.

women's studies

[2.51] Proper nouns

To form the possessive of any singular proper noun, add an apostrophe and an *s*.

Du Bois's essays

Rome's ancient monuments

To form the possessive of a plural proper noun, add only an apostrophe.

the Democrats' legislation

the Dickenses' economic woes

[2.52] Nouns expressing shared possession

To form the possessive of nouns in a series, add a single apostrophe and an *s* if the ownership is shared. But if the ownership is separate, place an apostrophe and an *s* after each noun.

> Palmer and Colton's book on European history is on the syllabus.
>
> Mom's and Dad's cars are both at the shop.

[2.53] Letters

Use an apostrophe to form the plurals of letters used as letters.

> The word *accommodation* has two *c*'s and two *m*'s.
>
> She ended her message by typing three *Z*'s.

Also use an apostrophe to form the plurals of letter grades.

> She got three A's this semester.

> Letters referred to as letters: 2.62.

[2.54] Plural abbreviations and numbers

Do not use an apostrophe to form the plural of an abbreviation or a number.

> PhDs
>
> 1960s
>
> fours
>
> TVs

[2.55] Quotation Marks

Quotation marks are used to quote from a source and to style the titles of some works. They have two other main uses in your prose.

[2.56] To flag provisional meaning

Quotation marks can be placed around a word or phrase to indicate skepticism, disapproval, or purposeful misuse. These quotation marks, often called *scare quotes*, should be used sparingly and with caution because their intended purpose is not always clear.

> A silver dome concealed the robot's "brain."

> Many "experts" offer advice on training babies to sleep on a schedule.

Quotation marks are not needed after *so-called*.

> Many so-called experts offer advice on training babies to sleep on a schedule.

[2.57] To mark translations of words or phrases

Use quotation marks to indicate when you have translated a foreign word or phrase. Place the translation in double quotation marks with parentheses or in single quotation marks without parentheses.

> The first idiomatic Spanish expression I learned was *irse todo en humo* ("to go up in smoke").

> The first idiomatic Spanish expression I learned was *irse todo en humo* 'to go up in smoke.'

> Styling titles in prose: 2.106. Translating titles in prose: 2.125. Quoting: 4.9–4.11. Translating titles in the works-cited list: 5.30. Integrating quotations into prose: 6.32–6.42. Translations of quotations (bilingual quotations): 6.75.

[2.58] Slashes

The slash, or diagonal, is rarely necessary in formal prose, except between two nouns paired as opposites.

> Examining fundamental binaries like good/evil, East/West, and aged/young deeply affects one's understanding of history and culture.

Use a hyphen rather than a slash when such a compound precedes and modifies a noun.

nature-nurture conflict

> Slashes for copublishers: 5.61. Slashes for line breaks in poetry: 6.37.

[2.59] Periods, Question Marks, and Exclamation Points

A sentence can end with a period, a question mark, or an exclamation point. Periods end declarative sentences. Question marks follow interrogative sentences. Except in direct quotations, avoid exclamation points in formal prose.

> Marking the end of a quotation: 6.51–6.53.

[2.60] Italics in Prose

Italics are used in prose to indicate when words and letters are referred to as words and letters and to distinguish words in languages other than English. The use of italics for emphasis ("Felski does *not* claim . . .") is a device that rapidly becomes ineffective and should be used sparingly.

[2.61] Words and Phrases Referred to as Words

Italicize words and phrases that are referred to as words.

The word *albatross* probably derives from the Spanish and Portuguese word *alcatraz*.

When scholars refer to *open access*, they could be referring to various models of publication.

[2.62] Letters Referred to as Letters

Italicize letters referred to as letters.

> Shaw spelled *Shakespeare* without the final *e*.

[2.63] Foreign Words in an English-Language Text

In general, italicize foreign words used in an English-language text.

> The Renaissance courtier was expected to display *sprezzatura*, or nonchalance, in the face of adversity.

The numerous exceptions to this rule include quotations entirely in another language ("Julius Caesar said, 'Veni, vidi, vici'"); non-English-language titles of works like poems, short stories, and articles published within larger works, which are placed in quotation marks and not italicized ("Unidad," the title of a poem by Pablo Neruda); proper nouns (the Kremlin), except when italicized through another convention (e.g., the names of ships and aircraft, such as the *Amistad*); and foreign words that have been naturalized into English through frequent use. A dictionary can help you decide whether a foreign expression requires italics (in *Merriam-Webster*, for example, such words will be accompanied by a label like "French phrase").

[2.64] Capitalization of Terms

[2.65] English

For English-language terms, capitalize the following:

- the first letter of the first word of a sentence
- the subject pronoun *I*
- the names and initials of persons (except for some particles)
- the names of months of the year and days of the week

- titles that immediately precede personal names (*Senator McCain*) but not a person's title used alone (*the senator, a professor of English*)
- proper nouns (*Canada*)
- most adjectives derived from proper nouns (*Canadian wildlife*)
- musical notes (*middle C*)
- academic grades (*I got a B in algebra*)

In general, lowercase generic forms of proper nouns.

the United States Army, the army

President Kennedy, the president

the Brooklyn Bridge, the bridge

the Housatonic River, the river

[2.66] French

French capitalization is the same as English capitalization except that the following terms are not capitalized in French unless they begin sentences or, sometimes, lines of verse:

- the subject pronoun *je* ("I")
- the names of months of the year and days of the week
- the names of languages and nationalities
- adjectives derived from proper nouns
- titles preceding personal names
- the words meaning *street*, *square*, *lake*, *mountain*, and so on in most place-names

Examples

Un homme m'a parlé anglais près de la place de la Concorde.

Hier j'ai vu le docteur Maurois qui conduisait une voiture Ford.

Le capitaine Boutillier m'a dit qu'il partait pour Rouen le premier jeudi d'avril avec quelques amis normands.

[2.67] German

In German capitalize all nouns—including adjectives, infinitives, pronouns, prepositions, and other parts of speech when they are used as nouns—as well as the pronoun *Sie* ("you") and its possessive, *Ihr* ("your"), and their inflected forms. The following terms are generally not capitalized unless they begin sentences or, usually, lines of verse:

- the subject pronoun *ich* ("I")

- the names of languages and of days of the week used as adjectives, adverbs, or complements of prepositions

- adjectives and adverbs formed from proper nouns, except when the proper nouns are names of persons and the adjectives and adverbs refer to the persons' works or deeds

Examples

Meine Eltern glauben, ich verbringe den Sommer in ihrem Haus.

Er schreibt, nur um dem Auf und Ab der Buch-Nachfrage zu entsprechen.

Fahren Sie mit Ihrer Frau zurück?

Ein französischer Schriftsteller, den ich gut kenne, arbeitet sonntags immer an seinem neuen Buch über die platonische Liebe.

Der Staat ist eine der bekanntesten Platonischen Schriften.

[2.68] Italian

In prose and verse, Italian capitalization is the same as English capitalization except that centuries and other large divisions of time are capitalized in Italian (*il Seicento*) and the following terms are not capitalized unless they begin sentences or, usually, lines of verse:

- the subject pronoun *io* ("I")
- the names of months of the year and days of the week
- the names of languages and nationalities

- nouns, adjectives, and adverbs derived from proper nouns
- titles preceding personal names
- words meaning *street*, *square*, and so on in most place-names

Examples

Un italiano parlava francese con uno svizzero in piazza di Spagna.

Il dottor Bruno ritornerà dall'Italia giovedì otto agosto e io partirò il nove.

[2.69] Spanish

In prose and verse, Spanish capitalization is the same as English capitalization except that the following terms are not capitalized in Spanish unless they begin sentences or, sometimes, lines of verse:

- the subject pronoun *yo* ("I")
- the names of months of the year and days of the week
- the names of languages and nationalities
- nouns and adjectives derived from proper nouns
- titles preceding personal names
- the words meaning *street*, *square*, and so on in most place-names

Examples

El francés hablaba inglés en la plaza Colón.

Ayer yo vi al doctor García en un coche Ford.

Me dijo don Jorge que iba a salir para Sevilla el primer martes de abril con unos amigos neoyorquinos.

[2.70] Latin

Although practice varies, Latin most commonly follows the English-language rules for capitalization, except that *ego* ("I") is not capitalized.

Examples

Semper ego auditor tantum? Numquamne reponam / Vexatus totiens rauci Theseide Cordi?

Quidquid id est, timeo Danaos et dona ferentes.

Nil desperandum.

Quo usque tandem abutere, Catilina, patientia nostra?

> Capitalization of personal names in languages other than English: 2.75–2.80. Capitalization of titles in languages other than English: 2.91–2.98.

[2.71] Names of Persons in Your Prose

[2.72] First Uses of Personal Names

In general, most persons' names should be stated in full when they first appear in your prose and surnames alone given thereafter. Common sense sometimes dictates exceptions to this rule. Very famous persons, such as Cervantes and Shakespeare, may be referred to by their surnames only. Some full names are very long and, by convention, rarely used—Hegel, for example, is rarely called Georg Wilhelm Friedrich Hegel. Dante Alighieri is conventionally referred to by his given name only. Considerations like clarity, consistency, the relative prominence of names in disciplines, and the desire to avoid the appearance of discrimination may argue for the inclusion or exclusion of first names in certain contexts.

When you state someone's name fully, write the name as it appears in your source or in a reference work, including any suffixes, accent marks, and initials.

Henry Louis Gates, Jr.

Ramón del Valle-Inclán

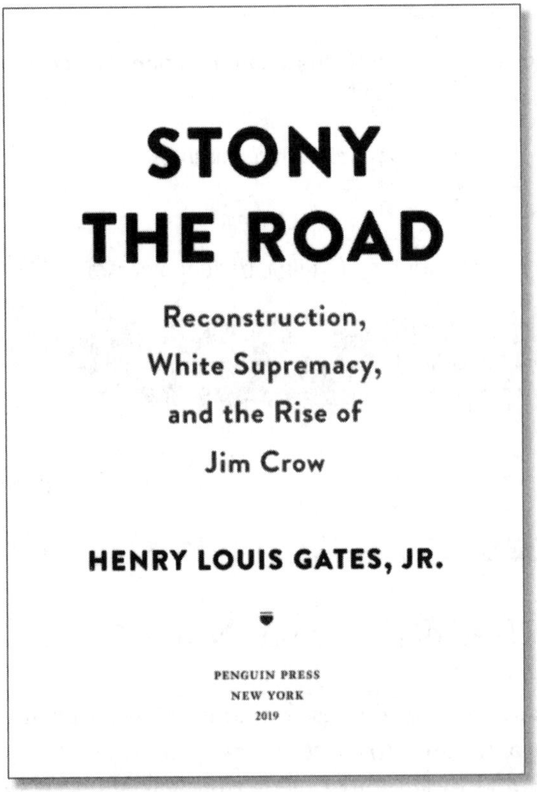
STONY
THE ROAD

Reconstruction,
White Supremacy,
and the Rise of
Jim Crow

HENRY LOUIS GATES, JR.

PENGUIN PRESS
NEW YORK
2019

Fig. 2.1. The title page of a book. The author's name includes the suffix *Jr.*

Do not change the name Henry Louis Gates, Jr., to Henry Louis Gates, for example (**fig. 2.1**), or drop the hyphen or omit the accents in the name Ramón del Valle-Inclán. In subsequent uses, you may refer to a person by the surname only—*Gates* and *del Valle-Inclán* (unless, of course, you refer to two or more persons with the same surname).

> In *Stony the Road,* Henry Louis Gates, Jr., studies visual culture during the period after Reconstruction to tell a story about the origins of structural racism in the United States.

Names in languages other than English: 2.75–2.80.
Premodern names: 2.81. Suffixes: 2.84.

[2.73] Surnames Used Alone

[2.74] English

In general, surnames in English-language contexts retain particles (sometimes capitalized, sometimes lowercased). When surnames are composed of more than one element, they are typically shortened to the last element.

Full name	Surname used alone
James Fenimore Cooper	Cooper
Daniel Defoe	Defoe
Walter de la Mare	de la Mare
Don DeLillo	DeLillo
Thomas De Quincey	De Quincey
W. E. B. Du Bois	Du Bois
Zora Neale Hurston	Hurston
Ursula K. Le Guin	Le Guin
Cormac McCarthy	McCarthy
Edna St. Vincent Millay	Millay
N. Scott Momaday	Momaday
Flannery O'Connor	O'Connor
Harriet Beecher Stowe	Stowe
John Edgar Wideman	Wideman

Exceptions to this practice exist. For guidance consult a dictionary or a reputable publication in which the name appears. If you are working directly with a person you are writing about, ask for their preferred form of reference.

Full name	Surname used alone
David Lloyd George	Lloyd George

For hyphenated surnames, retain both parts of the name.

Full name	Surname used alone
Arthur Quiller-Couch	Quiller-Couch

The element of the name used alone in subsequent references forms the basis for alphabetization in your works-cited list.

> Alphabetizing entries in the works-cited list: 5.123–5.130.

[2.75] French

The French *de* following a given name or a title such as *Mme* or *duc* is usually not treated as part of the surname.

Full name	Surname used alone
Étienne de La Boétie	La Boétie
Guy de Maupassant	Maupassant
Louis-Charles d'Orléans, duc de Nemours	Nemours

When the surname has only one syllable, however, *de* is usually retained.

Full name	Surname used alone
Charles de Gaulle	de Gaulle

The preposition also remains, in the form *d'*, when it is partially elided with a surname beginning with a vowel.

Full name	Surname used alone
Pierre d'Arcy	d'Arcy

The forms *du* and *des*—combinations of *de* with *le* and *les*—are always used with surnames and are capitalized.

Full name	Surname used alone
Bonaventure Des Périers	Des Périers
Charles Du Bos	Du Bos

[2.76] German

The German *von* is generally not treated as part of the surname.

Full name	Surname used alone
Annette von Droste-Hülshoff	Droste-Hülshoff
Heinrich von Kleist	Kleist

Some exceptions exist, especially in English-language contexts.

Full name	Surname used alone
Wernher Von Braun	Von Braun
Maria Von Trapp	Von Trapp

[2.77] Italian

The Italian *da, de, del, della, di,* and *d'* are usually capitalized and treated as part of the surname.

Full name	Surname used alone
Gabriele D'Annunzio	D'Annunzio
Lorenzo Da Ponte	Da Ponte
Oreste Del Buono	Del Buono
Andrea Della Robbia	Della Robbia
Vittorio De Sica	De Sica
Angelo Di Costanzo	Di Costanzo

The names of members of historic families are usually referred to in abbreviated form by surname without the particle, and the particle is lowercased in the full name.

Full name	Surname used alone
Lorenzo de' Medici	Medici

[2.78] Spanish

The Spanish *de* is usually not treated as part of the surname.

Full name	Surname used alone
Salvador de Madariaga	Madariaga
Lope de Rueda	Rueda
Juan de Timoneda	Timoneda

The Spanish *del*, however, which is formed from the fusion of the preposition *de* and the definite article *el*, is capitalized and treated as part of the surname.

Full name	Surname used alone
Ángel Del Río	Del Río

A Spanish surname may include both the paternal name and the maternal name, with or without the conjunction *y*. The surname of a married woman usually includes her paternal surname and her husband's paternal surname, connected by *de*. Consult a biographical dictionary for guidance in distinguishing surnames and given names.

Full name	Surname used alone
Juan Carreño de Miranda	Carreño de Miranda
Gabriel García Márquez	García Márquez
Pero López de Ayala	López de Ayala
Ana María Matute	Matute
José Ortega y Gasset	Ortega y Gasset
María de Zayas y Sotomayor	Zayas y Sotomayor

Authors commonly known by the maternal portions of their surnames, such as Galdós and Lorca, should nonetheless be referred to by their full surnames when shortening.

Full name	Surname used alone
Federico García Lorca	García Lorca
Benito Pérez Galdós	Pérez Galdós

[2.79] Latin

Use the forms of Roman names most common in English.

Full name	Common name
Marcus Tullius Cicero	Cicero
Quintus Horatius Flaccus	Horace
Gaius Julius Caesar	Julius Caesar
Titus Livius	Livy
Publius Ovidius Naso	Ovid
Publius Vergilius Maro	Virgil

Some medieval and Renaissance figures are best known by their adopted or assigned Latin names.

Latin name	Name in original language
Albertus Magnus	Albert von Bollstädt
Copernicus	Mikołaj Kopernik

[2.80] Asian languages

In Chinese, Japanese, Korean, and many other Asian languages, surnames usually precede given names.

Name in source	Surname used alone
Gao Xingjian	Gao
Ariyoshi Sawako	Ariyoshi
Yi Mun-yol	Yi

Note that some names follow the Western name order, where the surname comes last.

Full name	Surname used alone
Haruki Murakami	Murakami

Consult a reference work, the author's or publisher's website, or writing by knowledgeable scholars for guidance on the order of names.

[2.81] Premodern names

Many people who lived during the Middle Ages or the Renaissance are referred to primarily by their given name, since often the surname is derived from a place-name. After referring to them by their full names at first mention, use their given names for subsequent references.

Full name	Given name used alone
Christine de Pizan	Christine
Geoffrey of Monmouth	Geoffrey
Leonardo da Vinci	Leonardo

But other people from this time period, usually those whose surnames are family names and not place-names, are referred to by their surnames after their full names are used at first mention.

Full name	Surname used alone
Giovanni Boccaccio	Boccaccio
Geoffrey Chaucer	Chaucer
Jean Froissart	Froissart

Consult a reference work or other scholarly publication for guidance on how to treat particular premodern names.

[2.82] Transliterated Names

In an English-language context, names of persons, places, and organizations in languages that do not use the Latin alphabet are romanized—that is, spelled in the Latin alphabet as they are pronounced (e.g., Ahmad al-Rahuni, al-Andalus). Various systems of romanization have been devised. If you are uncertain how to romanize terms in a particular language, consult the United States Library of Congress ALA-LC Romanization Tables (www .loc.gov/catdir/cpso/roman.html).

[2.83] Titles with Personal Names

Generally omit a title associated with a personal name when the name is mentioned in the text discussion, even when an author's name in a source you consulted is given with a title—such as *Mrs., Dr., Professor, Captain, Senator, Reverend, Saint,* or *Sir* (**fig. 2.2**).

> Augustine (not Saint Augustine)
>
> Samuel Johnson (not Dr. Johnson)
>
> Philip Sidney (not Sir Philip Sidney)

The appropriate way to refer to persons with titles of nobility can vary. For example, the full name and title of Henry Howard, earl of Surrey, should be given at first mention, and thereafter *Surrey* alone may be used. In contrast, for Benjamin Disraeli, first earl of Beaconsfield, it is sufficient to give *Benjamin Disraeli* initially and *Disraeli* subsequently. Consult a reference work or follow the example of your source in treating titles of nobility.

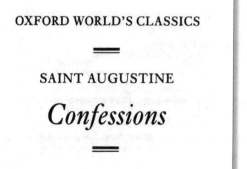

Fig. 2.2.
Part of the title page of a book. The author's name is preceded by the title *Saint*. *Saint* is omitted when the author is discussed in prose.

[2.84] Suffixes with Personal Names

When you cite a person's name in full in the main text of your written work, use a suffix that is an essential part of the name—like those that indicate generation such as *Jr.* in English, *fils* in French, or a roman numeral. Do not place a comma before numbered suffixes.

> John D. Rockefeller IV

Place a comma before suffixes like *Jr.* and *Sr.*

> Henry Louis Gates, Jr.

In your prose, add a comma after suffixes like *Jr.* and *Sr.* if words follow; the suffix is parenthetical.

> On 20 January 2021, Joseph Robinette Biden, Jr., became the forty-sixth president of the United States.

To indicate possession with a name ending in a suffix, reword to avoid forming a possessive.

Incorrect

Martin Luther King, Jr.'s, legacy endures.

Martin Luther King, Jr.,'s legacy endures.

Correct

Martin Luther King, Jr., has an enduring legacy.

[2.85] Given Names and Personal Initials

Capitalize given names of persons and the initials that stand for them. A period and a space follow each initial unless the name is entirely reduced to initials.

Chimamanda Ngozi Adichie	George R. R. Martin
Octavia E. Butler	V. S. Naipaul
JFK	J. R. R. Tolkien

When a given name is hyphenated, retain the hyphen when using initials alone.

Jean-Paul Sartre   J.-P. Sartre

[2.86] Names of Fictional Characters

Refer to fictional characters in your text in the same way that the work of fiction does. You need not always use their full names, and you may retain titles as appropriate.

Dr. Jekyll

Harry Potter (or Harry)

Madame Defarge

[2.87] Names of Organizations and Groups

Capitalize the names of all types of groups and organizations—companies, institutions, learned societies, and so on—according to the rules for styling titles of English-language works. Do not capitalize initial articles with names of groups and organizations.

To conduct the study, the Pew Research Center enlisted a team of statisticians.

Our teacher gave a speech before the Fondo de Cultura Económica.

Bulmer spent twelve hours a day at the Bibliothèque Nationale.

The institution houses the largest archive of the Grateful Dead's live performances.

Will you attend the Conférence Internationale Émile Zola et le Naturalisme à travers le Monde?

A conference sponsored by the Zentralverband der Deutschen Geographen will take place in the fall.

Retain internal capitals in the names of organizations and corporations.

> YouTube

Abbreviating the name of an organization is acceptable in some contexts, in particular if you repeat the name frequently in your prose. Always spell out the name in full and identify how you are going to abbreviate it at the first mention. Avoid abbreviating the name of an organization if you use the name only a few times.

> The University of North Texas (UNT) is a research university recognized for its scholarship in many fields. The division of research at UNT collaborates with the office of the provost on innovative research projects and grants.

[2.88] Names of Literary Periods and Cultural Movements

Capitalize the name of a literary period, cultural movement, or school of thought only when it could be confused with a generic term. By convention, the words *school* and *movement* in such names are not capitalized. Also capitalize any proper nouns in such names.

> Frankfurt school   New Criticism
>
> Harlem Renaissance   New German Cinema
>
> modernism   Romanticism

Consult a dictionary or a reputable, authoritative source for how to capitalize foreign language terms for such periods and movements when you use them in English-language prose.

> Négritude movement
>
> Risorgimento
>
> Sturm und Drang

Literary genres and forms are generally not capitalized.

ghazel

magical realism

terza rima

[2.89] Titles of Works in Your Prose

Whenever you use the title of a source in your writing, take the title from an authoritative location in the work—for example, from the title page of a book and not from the cover. Copy the title without reproducing any unusual typography, such as capitalization or lowercasing of all letters (**fig. 2.3**).

Fig. 2.3. Part of the title page of a book. Standardize capitalization when you copy a title in your text or works-cited list: *Kiss of the Spider Woman*.

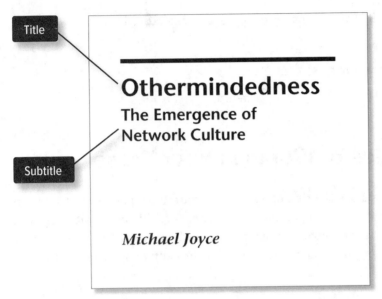

Fig. 2.4. Part of the title page of a book. The type design makes clear the distinction between the title and subtitle. Add a colon between a title and a subtitle when you copy them in your text or works-cited list: *Othermindedness: The Emergence of Network Culture.*

Standardize capitalization of the title and add a colon between the title and the subtitle (**fig. 2.4**).

[2.90] Capitalizing Titles in English

When you copy an English-language title or subtitle or write the title of your own research project, use title-style capitalization: capitalize the first word, the last word, and all principal words, including those that follow hyphens in compound terms. Therefore, capitalize the following parts of speech:

- nouns (*The Flowers of Europe*)
- pronouns (*Save Our Children; Some Like It Hot*)

- verbs (*America Watches Television*; *What Is Literature?*)
- adjectives (*The Ugly Duckling*)
- adverbs (*Only Slightly Corrupt*; *Go Down, Moses*)
- subordinating conjunctions (e.g., *after, although, as, as if, as soon as, because, before, if, that, unless, until, when, where, while*, as in *Life As I Find It*)

Do not capitalize the following parts of speech when they fall in the middle of a title:

- prepositions (e.g., *against, as, between, in, of, to, according to*; as in *The Artist as Critic*)
- coordinating conjunctions (*and, but, for, nor, or, so, yet*; as in *Romeo and Juliet*)
- the *to* in infinitives (*How to Play Chess*)
- articles (*a, an, the*; as in *Under the Bamboo Tree*)

But capitalize an article at the start of a subtitle.

"Building Libraries in Exile: The English Convents and Their Book Collections in the Seventeenth Century"

Do not capitalize the word following a hyphenated prefix if the dictionary shows the prefix and word combined without a hyphen.

Theodore Dwight Weld and the American Anti-slavery Society

When an untitled poem is known by its first line or when a short untitled message can be identified by its full text, the line or full text is used in place of the title, transcribed exactly as it appears in the source (**figs. 2.5, 2.6**).

Gertrude Stein's poem "The house was just twinkling in the moon light" is a love letter to Alice B. Toklas.

The tweet "Avoiding plagiarism: it's easy with the MLA's free online guidelines," by MLA Style (@mlastyle), garnered considerable attention.

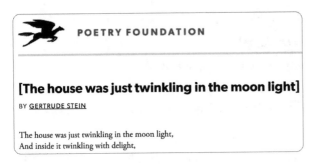

Fig. 2.5.
A poem known by its first line published on a website.

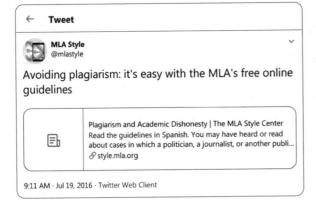

Fig. 2.6.
A tweet. In your prose the full text of a short tweet can serve as its title.

[2.91] Capitalizing Titles in Languages Other Than English

In a title or a subtitle in languages other than English that use the Latin alphabet, capitalize only the first word and all words normally capitalized in prose.

[2.92] French

La chambre claire: Note sur la photographie

Les liaisons dangereuses

La guerre de Troie n'aura pas lieu

"Saisir, décrire, déchiffrer: Les mises en texte du social sous la monarchie de Juillet"

> Capitalizing French terms: 2.66.
> Capitalizing French names: 2.75.

[2.93] German

Lethe: Kunst und Kritik des Vergessens

Ein treuer Diener seines Herrn

"Ein Versuch der Restitution"

Zeitschrift für vergleichende Sprachforschung

> Capitalizing German terms: 2.67.
> Capitalizing German names: 2.76.

[2.94] Italian

L'arte tipografica in Urbino

Bibliografia della critica pirandelliana

Collezione di classici italiani

"Le 'cose vane' nelle lettere di Machiavelli"

Luigi Pulci e la Chimera: Studi sull'allegoria nel Morgante

Studi petrarcheschi

> Capitalizing Italian terms: 2.68.
> Capitalizing Italian names: 2.77.

[2.95] Spanish

Breve historia del ensayo hispanoamericano

Cortejo a lo prohibido: Lectoras y escritoras en la España moderna

La gloria de don Ramiro

Historia verdadera de la conquista de la Nueva España

Revista de filología española

"De técnicas narrativas e influencias cervantinas en *Niebla* de Unamuno"

> Capitalizing Spanish terms: 2.69.
> Capitalizing Spanish names: 2.78.

[2.96] Latin

In the title or subtitle of a classical or medieval work in Latin, capitalize only the first word and all words normally capitalized in prose.

De senectute

Pro Marcello

Titles of postmedieval works in Latin are often capitalized like English-language titles.

Tractatus de Intellectus Emendatione

> Capitalizing Latin terms: 2.70.
> Capitalizing Latin names: 2.79.

[2.97] Other languages in the Latin alphabet

When you copy a title or a subtitle in nearly any language using the Latin alphabet not discussed above, it is appropriate to capitalize only the first word and all words normally capitalized in prose in that language.

[2.98] Languages in non-Latin alphabets

If you are discussing a work in a language not written in the Latin alphabet (e.g., Arabic, Chinese, Greek, Hebrew, Japanese, Russian), give its title consistently, either in the original writing system or in transliteration. Unless you are writing for a specialist audience that has familiarity with the language, include English translations parenthetically whether you give the title in the original script or in transliteration. In a transliterated title or subtitle, capitalize the first word and any words that would be capitalized in English prose—that is, capitalize it like a sentence.

Original script

عَلِيّ و أَمُهُ الرُّوسِيّة (*Ali and His Russian Mother*)

Transliteration

'Alī wa-ummuhu al-Rūsīyah (*Ali and His Russian Mother*)

If you are uncertain how to transliterate terms in a particular language, consult the ALA-LC Romanization Tables (www.loc.gov/catdir/cpso/roman .html).

> Capitalizing foreign language terms in titles: 2.118.
> Capitalizing foreign language titles within titles: 2.119.

[2.99] Punctuation of Titles

Punctuate titles according to the following guidelines.

[2.100] Serial comma

Use the serial comma if it is indicated on the title page (**fig. 2.7**).

After the Wreck, I Picked Myself Up, Spread My Wings, and Flew Away

After the **WRECK**,
I Picked Myself **UP**,
Spread My **WINGS**,
and **FLEW AWAY**

Joyce Carol Oates

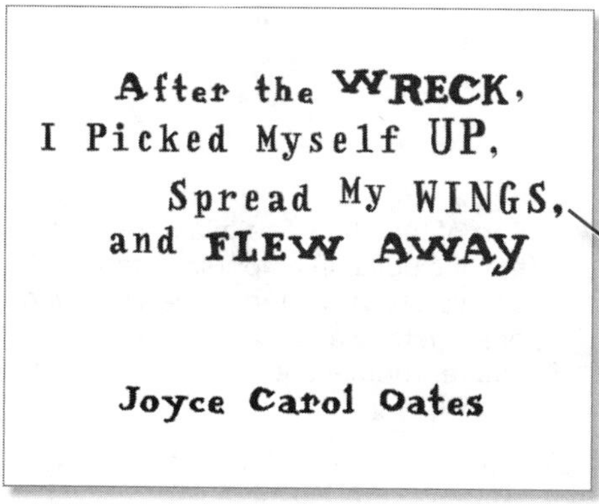

Fig. 2.7.
Part of the title page of a book. The serial comma is retained in your prose.

Serial comma

But when the comma is not indicated, do not add it (**fig. 2.8**).

The Lion, the Witch and the Wardrobe

When the design of the title page does not make it clear whether the comma should be included, consult another authoritative location on the work (for example, the copyright page).

Convert an ampersand in titles to the word *and* and add a serial comma (**fig. 2.9**).

The Extraordinary Secrets of April, May, and June

Serial commas: 2.12.

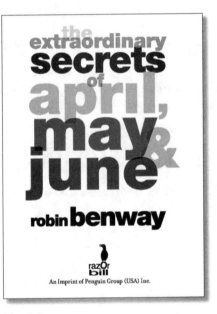

Fig. 2.8.
Part of the title page of a book. The title does not include a comma before the *and*; do not add a serial comma when you reproduce the title in your prose.

Fig. 2.9.
Part of the title page of a book. The title includes an ampersand that should be converted to the word *and*, preceded by a serial comma, when you reproduce the title in your prose.

[2.101] Subtitles

Use a colon followed by a space to separate a title from a subtitle even if your source shows no punctuation between the title and the subtitle (see **fig. 2.4**).

Othermindedness: The Emergence of Network Culture

When a title is followed by two subtitles, use a colon before each subtitle (**fig. 2.10**).

English Literature: Its History and Its Significance for the Life of the English-Speaking World: A Text-book for Schools

When a question mark, exclamation point, or dash separates a title and a subtitle on the title page, do not add a colon (**fig. 2.11**).

Whose Music? A Sociology of Musical Languages

However, when a title contains another title ending in a question mark or exclamation point, add a colon.

Moby-Dick *and* Absalom, Absalom!*: Two American Masterpieces*

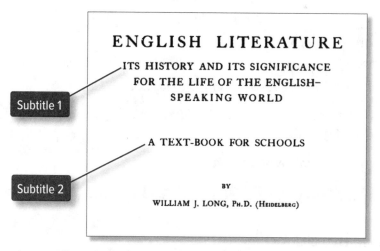

Fig. 2.10. Part of the title page of a book. The title is followed by two subtitles, both of which should be preceded by a colon in your prose.

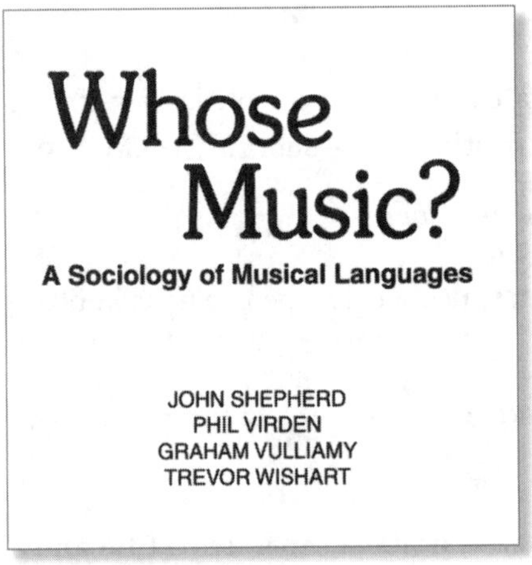

Whose Music?
A Sociology of Musical Languages

JOHN SHEPHERD
PHIL VIRDEN
GRAHAM VULLIAMY
TREVOR WISHART

The East End.
The Story of a Neighborhood

Fig. 2.11.
Part of the title page of a book. A
question mark separates the title
from the subtitle. Do not add a colon
before the subtitle in your prose.

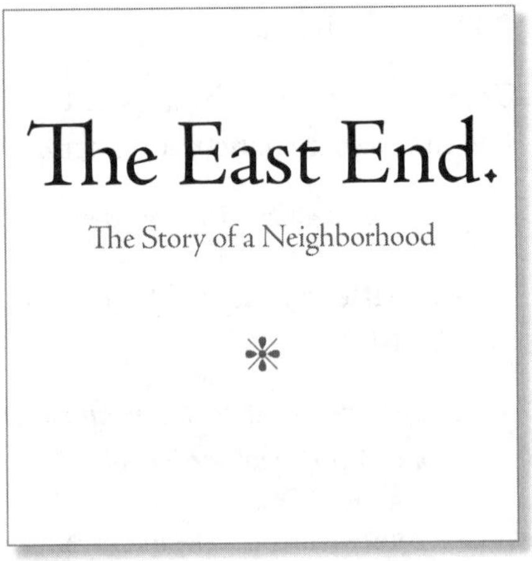

Fig. 2.12.
Part of the title page of a book. A
period separates the title from the
subtitle. Replace the period with a
colon in your prose.

If the title ends with a quotation mark, insert the colon between the quotation mark and the subtitle. In the first example below, the title consists of a quotation from Shakespeare. In the second example, the title of a book contains the title of a short story.

> *"To Be or Not to Be": A Study of Decision-Making in Shakespeare's Tragedies*
>
> *Ken Liu's "Paper Menagerie": Family, Fantasy, and Mourning*

When a period separates a title and a subtitle on the title page, change the period to a colon (**fig. 2.12**).

> *The East End: The Story of a Neighborhood*

Titles within titles: 2.111. Quotations within titles: 2.115.

[2.102] Alternative titles

For an alternative title (also called a *double title*) in English beginning with *or*, use a semicolon after the first title and follow *or* with a comma,

FRANKENSTEIN

OR

THE MODERN PROMETHEUS

BY

MRS. SHELLEY

Fig. 2.13. A double title on the title page of a book. Use a semicolon after the first title and follow *or* with a comma.

GETTING CALLIOPE THROUGH GRADUATE SCHOOL? CAN CHOMSKY HELP? OR, THE ROLE OF LINGUISTICS IN GRADUATE EDUCATION IN FOREIGN LANGUAGES

LINGUISTICS and its place in our foreign language graduate programs has become a concern of some moment in many of our departments. One might approach the topic by posing the most basic question: What value is there for literature students in studying linguistics?

Suzanne Fleischman

Fig. 2.14. A double title on the first page of a journal article. The first part of the title ends with a question mark, so do not add a semicolon.

capitalizing the first word after *or* and all words normally capitalized (**fig. 2.13**). Note that *or* is lowercased.

> *Frankenstein; or, The Modern Prometheus*

But if an English-language title before an alternative title ends with a question mark or exclamation point, the semicolon is not needed (**fig. 2.14**).

> "Getting Calliope through Graduate School? Can Chomsky Help? or, The Role of Linguistics in Graduate Education in Foreign Languages"

[2.103] Dates appended to titles

Add a comma before a date appended to the end of the title of a single-volume work unless the date is part of the title's syntax (**fig. 2.15**).

Melodrama Unveiled: American Theater and Culture, 1800–1850

Split in a Predominant Party: The Indian National Congress in 1969

David Grimsted

Melodrama Unveiled

AMERICAN THEATER AND CULTURE
1800–1850

Fig. 2.15.
Part of the title page of a book. Use a comma before a date range given at the end of the title.

[2.104] Multivolume works

Individual volumes that form part of a multivolume work sometimes lack a unique title. In some cases, the scope of the volume (usually, the period or portion of work covered) is given on the title page, cover, or elsewhere (**fig. 2.16**). Generally do not include this information as part of the title. If you do include this information as part of the title, use a comma before numbered ranges (including those preceded by a label) and a colon before descriptive designations.

Herrumbrosas lanzas, libros 8–12

The Life of Graham Greene, 1904–1939

The Longman Anthology of British Literature: The Twentieth Century

The Poems and Letters of Andrew Marvell: Letters

Citing multivolume works: 5.51, 5.117, 6.27.

Fig. 2.16. Part of a title page of a volume that forms part of a multivolume work, showing the scope of the volume. Generally do not include this information as part of the title in your prose.

[2.105] Punctuation around Titles

If a period is required after a title that ends with a quotation mark, place the period before the quotation mark.

> The study appears in *New Perspectives on "The Eve of St. Agnes."*

> Last night I read Elizabeth Bishop's poem "In the Waiting Room."

For titles ending with a question mark or exclamation point that are incorporated into your prose, include a comma after the title when it is an item in a series or when a nonrestrictive clause is introduced after the title.

> The essay analyzes *Who's Afraid of Virginia Woolf?*, *Oklahoma!*, and *Design for Living*.

> The film version of *What Ever Happened to Baby Jane?*, which united two of Hollywood's greatest stars, was released in 1962.

If the title appears inside quotation marks, the comma should appear inside the quotation marks.

> In D. H. Lawrence's poem "The English Are So Nice!," its title an example of irony, the narrator constantly qualifies the praise lavished on the poem's subject.

When possible, reword the sentence to avoid the need for multiple punctuation marks.

Acceptable

The film version of *What Ever Happened to Baby Jane?*, released in 1962, united two of Hollywood's greatest stars.

Preferred

Released in 1962, the film version of *What Ever Happened to Baby Jane?* united two of Hollywood's greatest stars.

[2.106] Styling Titles

In your prose, most titles should be italicized or enclosed in quotation marks. In general, italicize the titles of long-form works, which are often but not always self-contained and independent of other works (e.g., novels, movies), and the titles of works that contain other works (e.g., anthologies, television and streaming series). Use quotation marks for the titles of short-form works (e.g., poems, short stories, songs) and works contained in other works (e.g., an essay in an edited collection, an episode of a television or streaming series).

These guidelines are followed in the list of works cited as well.

> Styling titles in the works-cited list: 5.25–5.30.

[2.107] Italicized titles

Book

Kiss of the Spider Woman (novel)

Persepolis (graphic narrative)

The Pleasures of Reading in an Age of Distraction (monograph)

Agent of Change: Print Culture Studies after Elizabeth L. Eisenstein (collection of essays)

The Waste Land (poem published as a book)

The Woman I Kept to Myself (collection of poems published as a book)

Play

Hamlet

Newspaper

The New York Times

Journal

PMLA

Magazine

Harvard Business Review

Premodern epic

Iliad

Dissertation

Thinking beyond Modernism: Peripheral Realism and the Ethics of Truth-Telling

Film

Return of the Jedi

Television or streaming series

The Simpsons

Website

CNN (news website)

Facebook (social media platform)

Fondo de Cultura Económica (organization's website)

Merriam-Webster (online dictionary)

MLA International Bibliography (database)

National Endowment for the Humanities (government agency's website)

Nike (corporate website)

Twitter (social media platform)

Wikipedia (online encyclopedia)

The William Blake Archive (scholarly website)

YouTube (video-sharing website)

But when corporations and organizations are discussed as companies and groups, not as websites, do not italicize their names in your prose.

> The National Endowment for the Humanities supports digital scholarship through a grants program.

App

> *Bible Gateway*
>
> *Instagram*
>
> *Spotify*
>
> *TikTok*
>
> *WhatsApp*

Video game

> *Minecraft*

But do not italicize the names of board games, card games, and the like.

Radio program

> *All Things Considered*

Podcast

> *The Adventure Zone*

Music album

> *When We All Fall Asleep, Where Do We Go?*

Long musical composition identified by name

> *The Ring Cycle*
>
> *Symphonie fantastique*

Visual art

> *Infinity Mirrors* (exhibit)
>
> *Migrant Mother* (photograph)
>
> *Studies for the Libyan Sibyl* (drawing)
>
> *We Come in Peace* (sculpture)

By convention, the names of earthworks, ancient artworks, and buildings are not italicized: see 2.110.

Performing arts

The Formation World Tour (titled concert series)

Avenue Q (musical)

The Nutcracker (dance performance)

Court case

Marbury v. Madison

Ships, aircraft, and spacecraft

USS *Titanic*

Enola Gay

Challenger

When an abbreviation such as USS or HMS precedes the name of a ship, the abbreviation is not italicized.

[2.108] Italicized titles of works contained in a larger work

When a work that is normally italicized (such as a novel, play, or serialized graphic narrative) appears in a larger work (*Ten Plays*, *Internet Shakespeare Editions*, and *Eightball* in the examples below), both titles appear in italics.

Euripides's play *The Trojan Women* appears in the collection *Ten Plays*, translated by Paul Roche.

Did you use the edition of Shakespeare's *Hamlet* found on the *Internet Shakespeare Editions* website?

The graphic narrative *David Boring* was serialized in three issues of Daniel Clowes's comic book *Eightball*.

[2.109] **Titles in quotation marks**

Journal article

"Why Milton Is Not an Iconoclast"

Magazine article

"When Michelangelo Went to Constantinople"

Encyclopedia article

"Etruscan"

Essay in a collection

"The Fiction of Langston Hughes"

Short story

"The Lottery"

Poem

"Afterimages"

Chapter in a book

"The American Economy before the Civil War"

Page on a website

"The *Princess Bride* You Don't Know"

Episode of a television or streaming series

"Women's Work"

Song

"Somewhere over the Rainbow"

Video of a song

"Hold Up"

Lecture

"The Future of the Public Mission of Universities"

[2.110] Titles with no formatting

With some exceptions, which are noted below, titles in the following categories are capitalized like titles but are not italicized or enclosed in quotation marks.

Scripture

Bible	Old Testament
Genesis	Talmud
Gospels	Upanishads
Koran *or* Quran *or* Qur'an	

Titles of individual published editions of scriptural writings, however, are italicized and treated like any other published work.

The Interlinear Bible

The Talmud of the Land of Israel: A Preliminary Translation and Explanation

The Upanishads: A Selection for the Modern Reader

Laws, acts, and other political documents

Bill of Rights	Magna Carta
Declaration of Independence	Treaty of Trianon
Improving Broadband Access for Veterans Act of 2016	

Musical compositions identified by form, number, and key

Beethoven's Symphony No. 7 in A, Opus 92

Vivaldi's Concerto for Two Trumpets and Strings in C, RV539

Columns and titled categories in periodicals and on websites

Ask the MLA (titled category of posts on a website or blog)

The Ethicist (newspaper column)

Titled print publication series

Approaches to Teaching World Literature

A Song of Ice and Fire

Informally titled series

Informally titled series of all kinds are usually referred to by the title of the foundational work or the main character featured in the series. When the title of the series includes the main character's name, italics or roman typeface is acceptable as long as styling is applied consistently.

Star Wars movies

Harry Potter novels

Harry Potter novels

But titles of shows that air on television and stream online (often called *series*) are italicized.

The Umbrella Academy

Conferences, courses, workshops, and events

International Symposium on Cultural Diplomacy 2015

MLA Annual Convention

Introduction to Anthropology

Geographic Information Analysis Workshop

Edinburgh International Festival

Terms designating divisions of a work

Terms designating the divisions of a work are not capitalized, italicized, or put in quotation marks when used in your prose (*The author says in her preface* . . . ; *In canto 32 Ariosto writes* . . .).

act 4	introduction
appendix	list of works cited
bibliography	preface
canto 32	scene 7
chapter 2	stanza 20
index	

Earthworks, ancient artworks, and buildings

Arch of Titus	Great Wall of China
Empire State Building	Stonehenge
Fallingwater	Taj Mahal
Great Serpent Mound	Venus de Milo

[2.111] Titles within Titles

When a title appears within a title, the internal title should be clearly distinguished from the surrounding title. How you mark that distinction depends on the way the surrounding title is styled in accordance with guidelines given earlier in this handbook: in quotation marks, in italics, or, at the beginning of your paper, unstyled.

[2.112] Surrounding title in quotation marks

When the surrounding title is in quotation marks and the internal title is italicized (**fig. 2.17**), retain the italics of the internal title.

"The Flawed Greatness of *Huckleberry Finn*" (article about a novel)

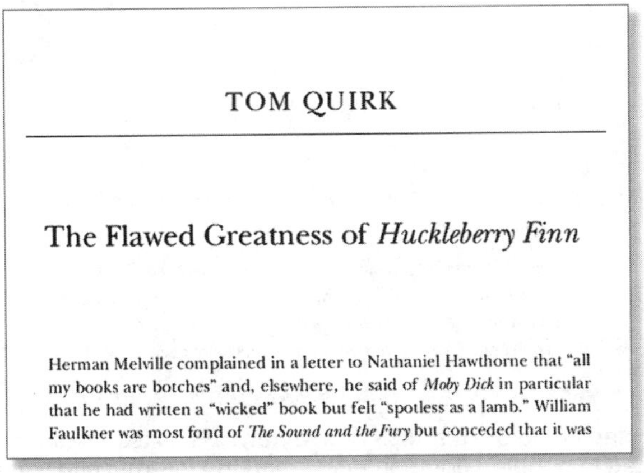

TOM QUIRK

The Flawed Greatness of *Huckleberry Finn*

Herman Melville complained in a letter to Nathaniel Hawthorne that "all my books are botches" and, elsewhere, he said of *Moby Dick* in particular that he had written a "wicked" book but felt "spotless as a lamb." William Faulkner was most fond of *The Sound and the Fury* but conceded that it was

Fig. 2.17. The first page of a journal article about a novel. The article title is placed in quotation marks in your prose and includes an italicized title that remains in italics.

When the surrounding title is in quotation marks and the internal title is in quotation marks (**figs. 2.18, 2.19**), use single quotation marks around the internal title, even when double quotation marks appear in the original or the internal title is one that would normally be italicized.

"'The Yellow Wallpaper' and Women's Discourse" (article about a short story)

"The Age of 'The Age of Innocence'" (article about a novel)

> ## "The Yellow Wallpaper" and Women's Discourse
>
> Paula Treichler's essay "Escaping the Sentence: Diagnosis and Discourse in 'The Yellow Wallpaper'" offers one of the first close and thorough readings of a short story which has long been of interest to feminists but which is also read and employed by psychologists, historians, sociologists, and literary

Fig. 2.18. The first page of an article about a short story. In your prose the surrounding title is placed in double quotation marks and the internal title is placed in single quotation marks.

Fig. 2.19. The beginning of an article from a news website. The surrounding title is placed in double quotation marks and the internal title is placed in single quotation marks in your prose. Follow the source's styling of the novel's title and do not correct to italics.

[2.113] Surrounding title in italics

When the surrounding title is in italics and the internal title is in quotation marks (**fig. 2.20**), retain quotation marks around the internal title.

"Silent Souls" and Other Stories (book with a short story in its title)

When the surrounding title is in italics and the internal title is in italics (**fig. 2.21**), convert the italicized internal title to roman typeface (i.e., no italics).

Approaches to Teaching Murasaki Shikibu's The Tale of Genji (book about a novel)

CATERINA ALBERT

"Silent Souls" and Other Stories

Translated by Kathleen McNerney

Fig. 2.20.
Part of the title page of a book with a short story in its title. In your prose retain quotation marks around the internal title.

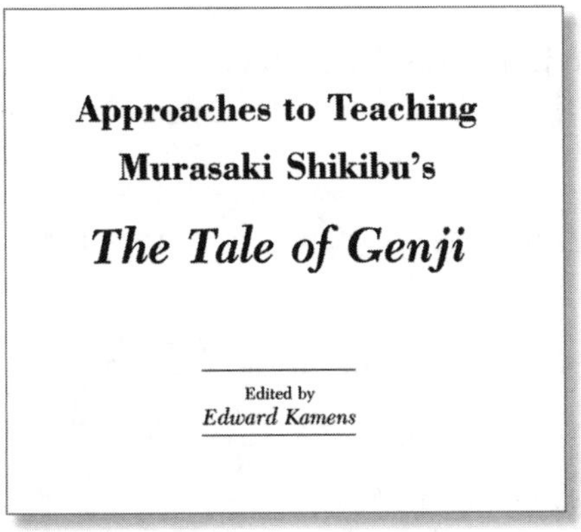

Approaches to Teaching Murasaki Shikibu's

The Tale of Genji

Edited by
Edward Kamens

Fig. 2.21.
Part of the title page of a book. In your prose the surrounding title is italicized and the internal title is in roman typeface (i.e., no italics).

Alfred Hitchcock's Psycho: A Casebook

Robert Kolker,
Editor

Fig. 2.22.
Part of the title page of a book. The entire title appears in roman typeface. Italicize the title of the book but leave the title of the film in roman in your prose.

If an internal title is in the same style as the surrounding title (**fig. 2.22**), apply appropriate styling to the internal title, whether the surrounding title is in quotation marks or italics.

> *Alfred Hitchcock's* Psycho*: A Casebook* (book about a film; the roman typeface indicates the internal title)

[2.114] Surrounding title with no formatting

When a surrounding title is neither in italics nor in quotation marks, italicize a title normally styled in italics according to the rules for styling titles.

> *Romeo and Juliet* and Renaissance Politics (title for a paper you are writing about a play)

> Language and Childbirth in *The Awakening* (title for a paper you are writing about a novel)

When a surrounding title is neither in italics nor in quotation marks, use quotation marks around a title normally enclosed in quotation marks according to the rules for styling titles.

> Lines after Reading "Sailing to Byzantium" (title for a paper you are writing about a poem)

> The Uncanny Theology of "A Good Man Is Hard to Find" (title for a paper you are writing about a short story)

Formatting the title of a research paper: 1.3.
Punctuating titles within titles: 2.101.

[2.115] Quotations within Titles

In English-language titles, capitalize quotations just as you would a title. A title that consists solely of a quotation should also be capitalized as a title. For titles styled in quotation marks, convert the double quotation marks surrounding the quotation to single quotation marks.

> "'Mind's Internal Heaven': Wordsworth's Fair Region"

> *"Full of Fire and Greedy Hardiment": Youth and Coming of Age in* The Faerie Queene

> "'The Figure in the Carpet'"

An exception occurs when the first line of an untitled poem is used as its title, in which case do not standardize the capitalization. Follow your source. If you are creating a title and your source is the poem itself, capitalize it as it appears in the poem.

> "Wordsworth's Vision in the Lyric 'Most sweet it is with unuplifted eyes'"

[2.116] Foreign Language Terms and Titles within Titles

[2.117] Styling

If an English-language title contains a foreign language term or phrase, style the term however it is styled in the source (**figs. 2.23–2.25**).

> *The Death of Procris: "Amor" and the Hunt in Ovid's* Metamorphoses

> *How to Hygge: The Nordic Secrets to a Happy Life*

> *From Romanticism to* Modernismo *in Latin America*

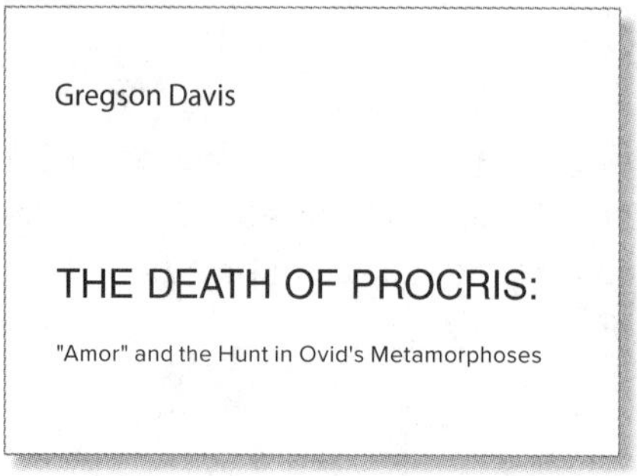

Gregson Davis

THE DEATH OF PROCRIS:

"Amor" and the Hunt in Ovid's Metamorphoses

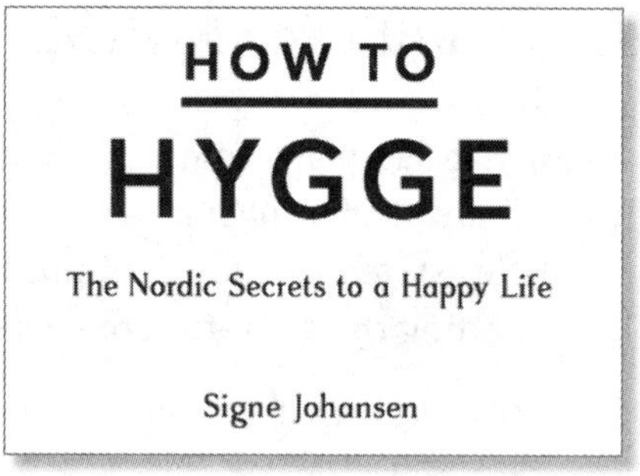

HOW TO

HYGGE

The Nordic Secrets to a Happy Life

Signe Johansen

Fig. 2.23.
The title page of a book. The Latin term *amor* appears in quotation marks in the source, and the quotation marks should be retained.

Fig. 2.24.
The title page of a book. The Norwegian term *hygge* is styled the same way as the English-language words in the title.

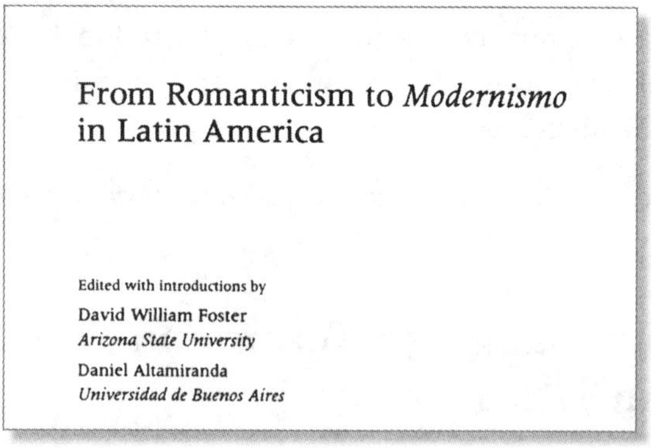

From Romanticism to *Modernismo* in Latin America

Edited with introductions by
David William Foster
Arizona State University
Daniel Altamiranda
Universidad de Buenos Aires

Fig. 2.25. The title page of a book. The Spanish word *modernismo* is italicized in the title. When the rest of the title is placed in italics, the word is styled in roman typeface to indicate it would normally appear in italics.

[2.118] Capitalization

In English-language titles, capitalize foreign words, phrases, and quotations (other than titles of works) according to the rules for capitalizing titles in English.

> "'La Dolce Sinfonia di Paradiso': Can Mere Mortals Compose It?"

> "Omnia Vincit Amor: Incongruity and the Limitations of Structure in Ovid's Elegiac Poetry"

> *The Rhetoric of the* Mise en Abyme *Figure*

[2.119] Titles within titles

Foreign language titles appearing in a title are capitalized according to the system appropriate to the foreign language.

"Cine, teatro y poesía en *The Crying of Lot 49*"

"*Les fleurs du mal*: Documents and Marginalia"

"A geometria necessaria: *Die Leiden des jungen Werthers*"

> Capitalizing titles in languages
> other than English: 2.91.

[2.120] Shortened Titles in Your Prose

When you refer to a title in your discussion, you should generally state the title in full at first reference. Thereafter, if you refer to a title often in your discussion, you can truncate the title (e.g., "Nightingale" for "Ode to a Nightingale").

[2.121] Subtitles

If a title consists of a title and subtitle, you may generally omit the subtitle in your prose (though it should appear in your works-cited-list entry).

In prose

One of the essays in *Women and Deafness* contends that in the first half of the twentieth century local Deaf organizations gave women space to participate as political leaders (Robinson).

Work cited

Robinson, Octavian. "The Extended Family: Deaf Women in Organizations." *Women and Deafness: Double Visions*, edited by Brenda Jo Brueggemann and Susan Burch, Gallaudet UP, 2006, pp. 40–56.

A subtitle should be included at the first reference to a title, however, if the title alone provides insufficient information about the work.

In prose

Krista Thompson's *Shine: The Visual Economy of Light in African Diasporic Aesthetic Practice* includes a chapter that examines the role of light in Jamaican dance halls.

Work cited

Thompson, Krista A. *Shine: The Visual Economy of Light in African Diasporic Aesthetic Practice*. Duke UP, 2015.

[2.122] Conventional forms of titles

Some titles may be known by their short forms. For example, the full title of Shakespeare's *The Tragedy of Hamlet, Prince of Denmark* can be shortened in your prose to *Hamlet*.

[2.123] Very long titles

Some works, particularly older ones, have very long titles.

Philocophus; or, The Deafe and Dumbe Mans Friend, Exhibiting the Philosophical Verity of That Subtile Art, Which May Enable One with an Observant Eie to Have What Any Man Speaks by the Moving of His Lips

To shorten such a title in your prose, include the beginning of the title up to at least the first noun.

Philocophus

Note that when a work has an alternative title, it may be beneficial to include it—again, up to the first noun.

Philocophus; or, The Deafe and Dumbe Mans Friend

[2.124] Punctuating shortened titles

If you need to shorten a title within quotation marks that begins with a quotation or an internal title in quotation marks, use the quotation or the title within the title as the short form and retain the single quotation marks within double quotation marks.

Full title

"'The Yellow Wallpaper' and Women's Discourse"

Shortened title

"'The Yellow Wallpaper'"

Full title

"'These Problematic Shores': Robert Louis Stevenson in the South Seas"

Shortened title

"'These Problematic Shores'"

[2.125] Translating Titles in Languages Other Than English

If you quote or substantively discuss both an original-language work and a published translation of it (or are translating the text yourself), at first reference provide both a translation of the title and the original title and place one of them in parentheses. Style both the original title and the translation in either italics or quotation marks, according to the type of work. Capitalize the translated title according to the rules for English-language titles.

The first line in Albert Camus's *L'étranger* (*The Stranger*)—"Aujourd'hui, maman est morte"—has been controversially translated as "Mother died today."

Franz Kafka explores the pressures and contours of human decision-making in "The Judgment" ("Das Urteil").

In subsequent references, you can use either version of the title, but do so consistently.

If you are working only with a published translation of a work written in a language other than English or are making a passing reference to the work, there is usually no need to provide the original-language title.

Franz Kafka explores the pressures and contours of human decision-making in "The Judgment."

In rare cases, when a work is better known by its title in the original language, the title does not need to be translated.

Petrarch's *Canzoniere* uses similar language to describe both frustration over unrequited love and the honor of bestowing that love.

> Capitalizing titles: 2.90–2.98.

[2.126] Numbers

[2.127] Use of Numerals or Words

In discussions where few numbers appear, spell out those numbers that can be written in a word or two.

one	one hundred	two thousand	three million
two-thirds	thirty-six	ninety-nine	twenty-one

Use numerals when more than two words are needed (for an exception, see 2.131). Numbers not spelled out are most commonly represented by arabic numerals (*1, 2, 3*).

2½	101	137	1,275

Numerals can be used with abbreviations and symbols in the ways shown below.

> Hyphens in fractions: 2.47. Decimal fractions: 2.130.
> Numerals for page numbers: 5.91.

[2.128] Number-heavy contexts

In discussions where numbers appear frequently, such as reports of experimental data, use numerals for all numbers that precede units of measurement and to express ratios.

30 inches	5 kilograms

In such contexts, express related numbers in the same style. Thus, use numerals for numbers usually spelled out if they appear alongside numbers that must be expressed as numerals.

> only 5 of 250 delegates
>
> exactly 3 ships and 129 trucks

[2.129] Street addresses

Use ordinal numbers for numbered streets and do not format the suffix (e.g., -nd, -rd, -th, -st) in superscript.

> 4401 13th Avenue

[2.130] Decimal fractions

Use numerals to express fractions presented as decimals.

> 8.3

[2.131] Percentages and amounts of money

In discussions involving infrequent use of numbers, spell out a percentage or an amount of money if you can do so in three words or fewer.

> one percent   thirty-five dollars
>
> forty-five percent   two thousand dollars
>
> one hundred percent   ten million dollars
>
>   sixty-eight cents

Use numerals with symbols when more than three words would be required.

> $5.35 $970   48.5%

In discussions involving frequent use of numbers, use numerals with symbols (e.g., $, %). Do not combine spelled forms of numbers with symbols.

[2.132] Items in numbered series

In general, use numerals for items in numbered series.

chapter 9   room 601   page 143   phase 3

But some formulations are conventionally spelled out and appear in the dictionary (e.g., *looking out for number one*).

[2.133] Large numbers

Large numbers may be expressed in a combination of numerals and words.

4.5 million inhabitants

[2.134] Plural forms

To form the plural of a spelled-out number, treat the word like an ordinary noun.

threes   sixes   forties

Add an *s* to numerals to form the plural.

1990s   747s

[2.135] At the start of a sentence

Spell out a number that appears at the beginning of a sentence. It is often better to reword the sentence so that the number does not appear at the beginning.

Incorrect

1960 was the beginning of a transformative decade in the United States.

Acceptable

Nineteen sixty was the beginning of a transformative decade in the United States.

Preferred

A transformative decade began in 1960 in the United States.

Spell out a number that appears at the beginning of a sentence even when it is paired with a related numeral that is not spelled out. However, it is often better to reword the sentence so that the number does not appear at the beginning.

Incorrect

250 out of 638 delegates favored the rule change.

Acceptable

Two hundred and fifty out of 638 delegates favored the rule change.

Preferred

The rule change was favored by 250 out of 638 delegates.

[2.136] In titles

In English-language titles, spell out numbers that would be spelled out in text, but follow the source for numbers in foreign language titles (**figs. 2.26, 2.27**).

Moby Dick *and the Whaling Industry of the Nineteenth Century*

Paris, capitale du XIXe siècle

Retain a numeral that precedes an abbreviation in a title.

The Ekopolitan Project: Migrant Histories and Family Genealogies from 19th and 20th c. Lagos

Moby Dick **and the Whaling Industry of the 19th Century**

Graham Faiella

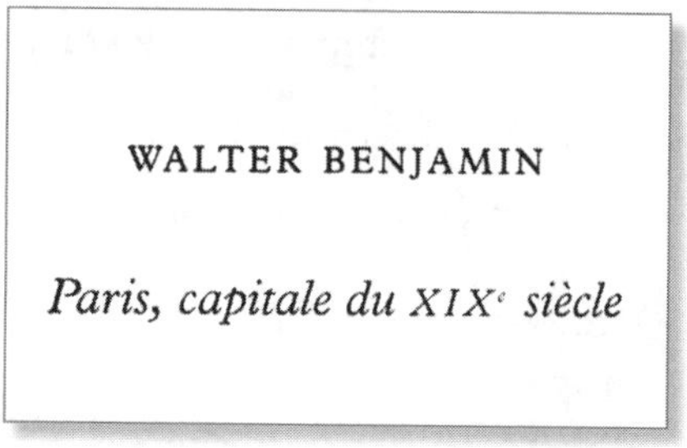

WALTER BENJAMIN

Paris, capitale du XIX⁴ siècle

Fig. 2.26.
Part of the title page of a book. Numerals are used for the century in the title. When reproducing the title in your prose, spell out the numerals.

Fig. 2.27.
Part of the title page of a book with a foreign language title. Numerals are used for the century and are retained in your prose.

[2.137] Commas in Numbers

Commas are usually placed between the third and fourth digits from the right, between the sixth and seventh, and so on, without a space.

1,000   20,000   7,654,321

Commas are not used in page and line numbers, in street addresses, or in four-digit years.

[2.138] Dates and Times

In the body of your writing, do not abbreviate dates. Be consistent in your use of either the day-month-year style or the month-day-year style and use numerals to express numbers.

5 January 2020

January 5, 2020

In works-cited-list entries, use only the day-month-year style. When using the month-day-year style in prose, a comma must be placed after the year unless another punctuation mark follows it.

On December 10, 1920, Clarice Lispector was born.

Clarice Lispector was born on December 10, 1920.

Do not use a comma between month and year or between season and year.

National Poetry Month was started in April 1996 by the Poetry Foundation.

The seminar on modernist poetry was last offered in spring 2019.

Decades can be written out or expressed in numerals. Use one style consistently in your prose.

the eighties   the 1980s

Spell out centuries in lowercase letters.

the twentieth century

Eras are abbreviated in prose and elsewhere: for example, as AD (*anno Domini*, or "in the year of the Lord") and BC ("before Christ"), BCE ("before the common era") and CE ("common era"), and AH (*anno Hegirae*, or "in the year of Hegira"). The abbreviations BC, BCE, and CE follow the year, but AD and AH precede it.

19 BC   AD 565   AH 950

Numerals are used for most times of the day. Generally use the twelve-hour-clock system in prose.

2:00 p.m.

When the time zone needs to be specified, use an abbreviation or spell it out.

4:30 EST   9:45 Pacific Standard Time

Exceptions include time expressed in quarter and half hours and in hours followed by *o'clock*.

five o'clock   half past ten   a quarter to twelve

Date style in works-cited-list entries: 5.77.
Time style in works-cited-list entries: 5.80.

[2.139] Number Ranges

In a range of numerals, give the second number in full for numbers up to ninety-nine.

2–3   21–48

10–12   89–99

For larger numbers, give only the last two digits of the second numeral, unless more are necessary for clarity.

96–101   395–401   1,003–05

103–04   923–1,003   1,608–774

For roman numerals, ranges should be given in full.

ii–iii   x–xii   xxi–xlviii

For alphanumeric numbers, ranges should be given in full.

A110–A112

In a range of years beginning 1000 CE or later, omit the first two digits of the second year if they are the same as the first two digits of the first year. Otherwise, write both years in full.

2000–03   1898–1901   1945–89

In a range of years beginning from 1 through 999 CE, follow the rules for number ranges in general. Do not abbreviate ranges of years that begin before 1 CE.

748–742 BCE   143 BCE–149 CE   800–14

Add a space after the hyphen when you are indicating ongoing, incomplete ranges.

> In an interview with Brian Lamb on C-SPAN, Robert Caro indicated that he was working on the fifth and likely final volume of *The Years of Lyndon Johnson* (1982–).

Styling the Number element in the works-cited list: 5.53.

3. Principles of Inclusive Language

Inclusive language aims to be respectful to others by treating language describing individual and group identity with sensitivity and by avoiding bias that could make some people feel excluded. Writers who strive for inclusivity in language recognize that their audience includes people who come from many different, and sometimes multiple (i.e., intersectional), backgrounds and experiences.

The following principles are intended to help writers choose inclusive language with regard to race and ethnicity, religion, gender, sexual orientation, ability, age, and economic or social status. These guidelines are necessarily generalized; writers should exercise judgment in choosing inclusive language and consider the particular context and audience they are writing for.

[3.1] Make references to identity relevant

Consider whether terms that specify a subject's ethnicity, religion, gender, sexual orientation, disability, age, or economic or social status are meaningful to the context, because including such information (e.g., *African American congresswoman, female conductor, transgender actor*) may imply that this characteristic places the subject outside the norm.

Many gender-specific terms can be reworded for gender neutrality: for example, *human-made* can be used in place of *man-made*. Avoid using *man* to mean *human beings, humankind, humanity,* or *people*.

Gender-specific terms that refer to persons of known gender may be appropriate—for example, an individual might identify as Latino or

Latina—but a nonspecific term, such as *Latinx*, is a more inclusive way to describe a person of unknown gender or a population of mixed genders. Avoid using gender-specific terms (e.g., *poetess, policeman*) to refer to people.

[3.2] Be precise

Broad terms applied to diverse populations may require more specificity. For example, terms such as *the Muslim community* and *Native American language* incorrectly conflate diverse populations and traditions; be specific and, if possible, use the subject's preferred term: for example, *Sunni Muslims in India* and *Chinookan languages*.

To avoid perpetuating stereotypes, refrain from making generalizations about group identities. Try recasting a statement such as *Jews believe . . .* to *A Jewish belief is . . .* or specify the Jewish community you are referring to. Avoid generalizations, too, that assume readers share your understanding of what concepts or texts are referred to by religious terms (e.g., *God, scripture*).

[3.3] Choose terms of identity that respect your subject

When you use people-first language (e.g., *a person with diabetes, a person on probation, a person with autism*) the subject is not defined first of all by a single aspect of their experience. When you use identity-first language (e.g., *a queer person, an autistic person*), the identity is the focus. Identity-first language is preferred by some individuals or groups opting to claim or choose the identity. Both people-first language and identity-first language are generally considered valid approaches, but your choices should always reflect the expressed preferences of individuals or groups when those preferences are known.

[3.4] Be thoughtful about capitalization and styling

The dictionary includes many terms that denote identity, generally capitalizing them only if they derive from proper nouns (e.g., *Egyptian, Mormon*, but *bisexual, retiree*). When the dictionary gives both capitalized and lowercased forms as options, choose one and be consistent. When the dictionary notes that one form is the more commonly used one, as *Merriam-Webster* does for *Black*, generally use the more common form. But when you are working directly with an author or discussing a person or community whose preferences are known, follow that preference. For example, some writers use *Deaf* to refer to the Deaf community and Deaf culture but *deaf* to refer to hearing loss, and individuals who strongly identify as culturally Deaf may prefer *Deaf*.

Avoid language or punctuation that undermines a subject's identity: do not place quotation marks around or italicize words used to define a person's or group's identity or to indicate a transgender person's chosen name or pronoun, even when those terms are neologisms—that is, terms that do not yet appear in the dictionary.

[3.5] Minimize pronouns that exclude

Writers wishing to use inclusive pronouns sometimes use both feminine and masculine pronouns, use only feminine pronouns, or alternate between feminine and masculine pronouns.

> When a student studies abroad, his or her communication skills in the target language are likely to improve dramatically, especially if he or she avoids speaking English with other students.

A revision that recasts the subject as plural or that eliminates the pronoun is often the best solution for expressing an idea or action in which sex or gender is not relevant or for avoiding the assumption that all individuals identify as male or female.

> When students study abroad, their communication skills in the target language are likely to improve dramatically, especially if they avoid speaking English with other students.

> Studying abroad can help students dramatically improve their communication skills in the target language, especially if speaking English with other students is avoided.

Writers who wish to use a non-gender-specific pronoun to refer to themselves may prefer *they* and *their* (or a neologism like *hir*). Likewise, writers should follow the personal pronoun of individuals they write about, if individuals' pronouns are known. *They* may be used in a singular sense as a person's chosen pronoun.

> Jules is writing their research paper on Jane Austen's *Persuasion*.

In addition to this use of *they* to refer to specific individuals, *they* has gained acceptance as a generic, third-person singular pronoun used to refer to hypothetical or anonymous people.

> Each taxpayer must file their tax return by 15 April.

Singular *they* can be used to refer to a specific person whose gender is unknown or not relevant to the context.

> I am impressed by the résumé of T. C. Blake, a candidate for the web developer job, and will schedule an interview with them.

In formal writing, the use of singular *they* has been considered a less desirable option than revising to plural constructions or rephrasing without pronouns. But it has emerged as a tool for making language more inclusive because it helps writers avoid making or enabling assumptions about gender.

Be wary of making assumptions about your audience, and do not assume that your audience shares your own identity, background, geographic location, culture, or beliefs. Language such as *in our society intergenerational households are no longer common* and *we value free-market economics above all* assumes a common culture or set of shared beliefs. For this reason, consider avoiding the first-person plural (*we* and *our*) in your writing. If you do use *we* and *our*, ask yourself whether your language makes it clear who is included and whether any readers are excluded.

[3.6] Avoid negatively judging others' experiences

When writing about a person who has a disability or health condition or who has experienced trauma, avoid descriptions like *suffers from, afflicted with, prisoner of,* or *victim of.* Although appropriate in some contexts, such language can evoke emotions or imagery that may not be accurate.

For example, a person who uses a wheelchair should not be described as *wheelchair-bound* or *confined to a wheelchair*, because such statements make assumptions about the person's experiences.

[3.7] Use a dictionary to check for offensive terms

If you are uncertain about using a term, first look in a recent dictionary. A good, up-to-date dictionary will note when a term is considered offensive or questionable. (Keep in mind that language is constantly changing; the connotations of words and phrases shift over time.) Offensive terms that feature in a work you are discussing should never be repeated as your own words and, when quoted from a source, may merit a note to indicate that the term is offensive. You can also add a dash after the first letter of a term to avoid reproducing it fully. A respectful alternative may be available for use in the discussion (e.g., if you quote from historical documents referring to a "Gypsy," you can use *Rom* in your prose).

4. Documenting Sources: An Overview

Academic writing is a conversation that draws on research about a topic or question. Scholars write for their peers, communicating the results of their research through books, journal articles, and other forms of publication. All scholars—whether in the natural sciences, the social sciences, or the humanities—incorporate, confirm, modify, correct, or refute the work done by previous scholars. In this response, they quote, paraphrase, and cite sources by using a system of documentation like the one described in this handbook.

A system of documentation directs readers to the source of a quotation, paraphrased idea, fact, or other borrowed material. References are formatted in a standard way so that they can be quickly understood by all, just like a common language. Think, for example, about mathematical symbols: the plus sign tells you to add numbers, and the minus sign tells you to subtract them. In the same way, the various elements in a documentation system tell you how to understand and use information (e.g., how to find the source or evaluate claims). A documentation system thus gives writers a comprehensible, verifiable means of referring to one another's work. A documentation system also allows writers to seek out relevant publications in the course of research so that they can learn from and build on the work of others. By giving credit to the precursors whose ideas they work with, scholars allow future researchers interested in the history of a conversation to trace the line of inquiry back to its beginning.

Learning a documentation style prepares writers to recognize the conventions their professional field expects its members to adhere to in their writing. Legal documents must refer to other legal documents in the way

that has been established by the legal profession. Reports on scientific research must refer to earlier research in the way that the particular scientific
field expects. Practicing a consistent documentation style—and learning
how to read a writer's citations—helps establish trust between researchers
and their audience and is a key component of academic integrity.

In the MLA's system, references in the text point to entries in a list of
works cited. Writers use a template of core elements—elements that most
sources have, such as author, title, and publication date—to cite any type of
work. This template allows writers to assess all works according to standard
criteria and provides a comprehensive method for evaluating sources and
creating bibliographic entries based on that evaluation.

The guidelines set forth in this handbook also ensure that academic
writers can clearly distinguish their ideas from the ideas of others, which is
yet another key component of academic integrity.

[4.1] Why Plagiarism Is a Serious Matter

Occasionally an author or public speaker is accused of plagiarism. No doubt
you have had classroom conversations about plagiarism and academic dis-
honesty. Your school may have an honor code that addresses academic dis-
honesty; your school almost certainly has disciplinary procedures meant
to address plagiarism. But you may not be sure what exactly this offense is
and how to avoid committing it.

Plagiarism is presenting another person's ideas, words, or entire work as
your own. Plagiarism may sometimes have legal repercussions (e.g., when it
involves copyright infringement) but is always unethical.

Plagiarism can take a number of forms. Copying a published or unpublished text of any length, whether deliberately or accidentally, is plagiarism
if you do not give credit to the source. Paraphrasing someone's ideas or arguments or copying someone's unique wording without giving proper credit
is plagiarism. Turning in a paper or thesis written by someone else, even if
you paid for it, is plagiarism.

It is even possible to plagiarize yourself. In published work, if you reuse
ideas or phrases that you used in prior work and do not cite your prior work,
you have plagiarized. Many schools' academic honesty policies prohibit the

reuse of one's prior work in papers, theses, and dissertations, even with self-citation. (Sometimes, however, revising and building on your earlier work is useful and productive for intellectual growth; if you want to reuse portions of your previously written work in an educational context, ask your instructor.)

When writers and public speakers are exposed as plagiarists in professional contexts, they may lose their jobs and are certain to suffer public embarrassment, diminished prestige, and loss of credibility. One instance of plagiarism can cast a shadow across an entire career because plagiarism reflects poorly on a person's judgment, integrity, and honesty and calls into question everything about that person's work. The consequences of plagiarism are not just personal, however. The damage done is also social. Ultimately, plagiarism is serious because it erodes public trust in information.

[4.2] Avoiding Plagiarism

[4.3] Careful Research

Many instances of unintentional plagiarism can be traced back to sloppily taken notes during the research process. So be scrupulous in your research and note-taking. When you write, your notes will help you identify all borrowed material. Make sure that you clearly identify when you are copying words from a source (and transcribe them exactly or retain digital images of the passages), when you are summarizing or paraphrasing a source, and when you are jotting down an original thought of your own. Remember to record page numbers for quotations and paraphrased passages in your notes. Note-taking apps can help you collect information about your sources and organize your own ideas.

Steer a middle course between recording too much information and too little. Details, like specific phrases and passages, will help you present evidence in your paper. But also remember to describe in your notes how a writer used those details to arrive at a particular conclusion. Notes that merely list quotations without giving any sense of why they are important, how they relate to the sources they derive from and to one another, and what they collectively mean will be of little help to you once you start writing.

As you do research, collect all the sources you use in one place, which will allow you to double-check that your work acknowledges them. Care needs to be taken even when using a digital reference manager for note-taking or creating documentation, since the data used by the software can be incorrect and must be checked against your source. Thus, manual input is often required. Citation tools are a good starting point, but their output must be verified and edited.

For more on conducting research and on the methods and tools that can help you, see the *MLA Guide to Undergraduate Research in Literature*, the *MLA Guide to Digital Literacy*, and the free tutorials on using the *MLA International Bibliography*, available at www.mla.org/bibtutorials (see also the free online course at style.mla.org/bibcourse/).

[4.4] Giving Credit

Once you have carefully tracked your research, avoiding plagiarism is relatively straightforward: when the work of others informs your ideas, give credit by summarizing or paraphrasing that work or by accurately quoting it—and always cite your source.

Detailed explanations of how to create works-cited-list entries and in-text citations and how to incorporate quotations and paraphrased passages into your work appear in chapters 5 and 6.

[4.5] Paraphrasing

Paraphrasing allows you to maintain your voice while demonstrating that you understand the source because you can restate its points in your own words and with your own sentence structure.

[4.6] *When to paraphrase*

Paraphrase from a source when you want to condense or summarize long passages, arguments, or ideas; make your writing more concise; stay in control of your ideas and argument and maintain your voice; or signal your knowledge of key lines of conversation and concepts from your sources.

[4.7] *How to paraphrase*

A paraphrase should convey the important information in a passage in your own words and sentence structure.

Imagine that you read the following passage about the well-known concept of American exceptionalism (from Walter A. McDougall's *Promised Land, Crusader State: The American Encounter with the World since 1776*).

Passage in source

American Exceptionalism as our founders conceived it was defined by what America *was*, at home. Foreign policy existed to defend, not define, what America was.

Maintaining the sentence structure and plugging in synonyms in your paraphrase is insufficient, because doing so hews too closely to the original.

Paraphrase (unacceptable)

American exceptionalism as the founding fathers envisioned the concept was given meaning by America as a homeland. Programs focused on other countries were there to protect America, not delineate it.

If you write the following sentence, however, you have successfully paraphrased the passage by changing the wording and sentence structure.

Paraphrase (acceptable)

As conceived, American exceptionalism was based on the country's domestic identity, which foreign policy did not shape but merely guarded.

Note that some terms cannot be paraphrased because they represent core concepts, definitions, or principles: it would not make sense, for example, to find a different way to state *American exceptionalism* just as it would not make sense to find a synonym for *capitalism, democracy, freedom*, or any other widely used term.

[4.8] *How to paraphrase and give credit*

To properly give credit to your source in MLA style, you also need to include an in-text citation directing your reader to a works-cited-list entry and, if you are citing a paginated book, the location in the work where the idea is set forth.

In your prose

As Walter A. McDougall argues, for the founding fathers American exceptionalism was based on the country's domestic identity, which foreign policy did not shape but merely guarded (37).

Work cited

McDougall, Walter A. *Promised Land, Crusader State: The American Encounter with the World since 1776*. Houghton Mifflin, 1997.

[4.9] Quoting

Quoting can be effective when someone else's words are the focus of analysis or perfectly express an idea. Quotations are most effective in research-based writing when used selectively. Quote only words, phrases, lines, and passages that are particularly apt, and keep all quotations as brief as possible. Always explain the relevance of the quotation to your point. Your project should be about your own ideas, and quotations should help you explain or illustrate those ideas and how you arrived at them.

[4.10] *When to quote*

Quote from a source when the exact wording is important to your claim, the phrasing is particularly compelling, or you want to focus on the language in the source. Quoting should not be used as a substitute for paraphrasing ideas you do not fully understand. Quoting and paraphrasing can be combined in one sentence, as shown in the example below.

[4.11] *How to quote and give credit*

Quotations should be transcribed accurately from the source and integrated into your prose grammatically and in a way that distinguishes others' ideas from your own.

Imagine, for example, that you read the following passage, which coins a term that you wish to discuss in your paper (from Michael Agar's book *Language Shock: Understanding the Culture of Conversation*).

Passage in source

Everyone uses the word *language* and everybody these days talks about *culture*. . . . "Languaculture" is a reminder, I hope, of the *necessary* connection between its two parts. . . .

If you want to quote from this source in your writing, you must use quotation marks around the borrowed words and give credit to the source. You do this by including an in-text citation that directs the reader to an entry for the work in the list of works cited and to the page number where the quoted material appears in the source.

In your prose (incorrect)

At the intersection of language and culture lies a concept that has been called "languaculture."

In your prose (correct)

At the intersection of language and culture lies a concept that Michael Agar calls "languaculture" (60).

Work cited

Agar, Michael. *Language Shock: Understanding the Culture of Conversation.* HarperCollins Publishers, 2016.

[4.12] When Documentation Is Not Needed

Documentation is required for any work that you quote from or paraphrase; that you refer to substantively, whether the reference is to a specific place in the source (a page, a chapter) or to the source as a whole; or that you acknowledge as the source of facts you provide or ideas you formulate. But documentation is not required for every type of borrowed material.

[4.13] **Common Knowledge**

Information and ideas that are common knowledge among your readers need not be documented. Common knowledge includes information widely available in reference works, such as basic biographical facts about prominent persons and the dates and circumstances of major historical events. When the facts are in dispute, however, or when your reader may want more information about your topic, it is good practice to document the source of the material you borrow.

[4.14] **Passing Mentions**

Documentation is also not required when you mention a work or author in passing. For example, if you state that your favorite graphic narrative is *Fun Home*, you have not quoted from or paraphrased the book, referred to any aspect of it specifically, or used it to advance an idea. You have simply stated that the book exists and given an opinion about it. This is a passing mention. It does not require a source citation.

[4.15] **Allusions**

When you are making an allusion for rhetorical effect—that is, making an indirect or partial reference to a well-known passage that serves as a cultural touchstone—you usually do not need to cite a source.

> The Force was definitely with our team's goalie when she deflected the ball.

> Junior year of high school may not have been the best of times, but it wasn't the worst either.

> The female protagonist's "to be or not to be" moment came when she contemplated the difficulty of the journey ahead.

[4.16] Epigraphs

An epigraph is a short quotation at the beginning of a work that establishes its theme or mood, and they should be used sparingly. Primarily ornamental, epigraphs are not discussed subsequently in the text. Do not place an epigraph in quotation marks. On a line below the epigraph, generally provide only the author and the title of the work the epigraph comes from; no further documentation is needed, and the work is not included in the works-cited list.

> All these beauties will already be familiar to the visitor, who has seen them also in other cities.
>
> —Italo Calvino, *Invisible Cities*

A quotation that you discuss in the essay should not also be treated as an epigraph. Provide documentation for such a quotation as for any other work you cite. See 6.32–6.42 for details on integrating quotations into prose.

The rest of this handbook will show you how to cite sources using the MLA's system of documentation.

5. The List of Works Cited

Each source cited in the text or notes of your project should appear in a list at the end of the paper, after any endnotes. Title the list Works Cited. (If you want to document works you merely consulted but did not cite, give the list a different title, such as Works Cited and Consulted.)

[5.1] Creating and Formatting Entries: An Overview

Entries in the works-cited list are created using the MLA template of core elements—facts common to most sources, like author, title, and publication date (**fig. 5.1**).

To use the template, record the publication information given by the version of the work you consult by first evaluating the work you are citing to see which elements apply to the source. Then, list each element relevant to your source in the order given on the template. Omit any element that does not apply except Title of Source. If no title is given, use your own description of the work as the title. Conclude each element with the punctuation mark shown in the template—but always end your entry with a period.

1 Author.

2 Title of Source.

CONTAINER

3 Title of Container,

4 Contributor,

5 Version,

6 Number,

7 Publisher,

8 Publication Date,

9 Location.

Fig. 5.1.
The MLA template of core elements.

Fig. 5.2.
The MLA template of core
elements with two containers.

Because a work containing another work can itself be contained in a work—such as an article published in a journal and contained in a database—you can repeat the process by filling out the template again from Title of Container to Location, listing all elements that apply to the container (**fig. 5.2**).

Works-cited-list entries in MLA style are based on the template of core elements, but you can add supplemental elements to the template if you want or need to give your reader additional information about the source.

In the works-cited-list entry, generally follow the same guidelines as for prose for the following:

- capitalization of words, names, and titles
- styling of titles (e.g., in italics or quotation marks)
- treatment of names of persons (including how to identify the element of the name to alphabetize)
- number ranges

Capitalization of terms: 2.64–2.70. Personal names: 2.71–2.86. Capitalization of titles: 2.90–2.98. Styling titles: 2.106–2.110. Number ranges: 2.139. Containers: 5.31–5.37. Supplemental elements: 5.105.

[5.2] The MLA Core Elements

Each core element is named with a shorthand label that covers a range of situations.

The element name is not always literal. For example, Publication Date can include an actual date of publication, a date of composition for unpublished material, the date a performance was attended, and other dates relevant to the work you are citing.

The rest of this section defines each element and explains when to use it, provides guidance on finding publication information and other relevant details about each element, and explains styling decisions unique to the list of works cited.

[5.3] Author: What It Is

In the Author element, list the primary creator of the work you are citing. In the example below, Toni Morrison wrote the novel *Song of Solomon* and is therefore its author.

> Morrison, Toni. *Song of Solomon*. Vintage, 2004.

The author of a work can be a writer, artist, or any other type of creator. The author can be an individual, a group of persons, an organization, or a government. Some examples of authors are the author of a play, such as Euripides; the author of an essay, such as Benjamin Franklin; a painter, such as Berthe Morisot; a music group, such as the Beatles; and an intergovernmental body, such as the United Nations. Include pseudonyms, stage names, online usernames, and the like in the Author element, especially if the person is well known by that form of the name (e.g., Stendhal, Mark Twain, and Lady Gaga).

Sometimes a label must be used to describe the role of the person or persons listed in the Author element. This most often occurs when the person is not the primary creator, such as for editors of collections of essays written by various authors, since editors shape the content of the volume.

In the example below, Ignacio M. Sánchez Prado is the editor of the book, not the writer of all the essays, so his name is followed by the label *editor*.

> Sánchez Prado, Ignacio M., editor. *Mexican Literature in Theory.* Bloomsbury Academic, 2018.

When a work is published without an author's name, do not list the author as *Anonymous*. Instead, skip the Author element and begin the entry with the work's title.

> *Lazarillo de Tormes.* Medina del Campo, 1554.

Variant forms of names, pseudonyms, and name changes: 5.12–5.15. When contributors to a work should not be listed in the Author element: 5.41. Labels describing the contributor's role: 5.44.

[5.4] Author: Where to Find It

The author's name is usually prominently displayed in a work. In a book, the author's name is often near the title (**fig. 5.3**). **Figures 5.4–5.9** show the location of the name of the author or other type of creator in other kinds of sources.

THE SYMPATHIZER

VIET THANH NGUYEN

Mexican Literature in Theory

Edited by
Ignacio M. Sánchez Prado

Fig. 5.3.
Part of the title page of a book. The author's name, Viet Thanh Nguyen, is near the title.

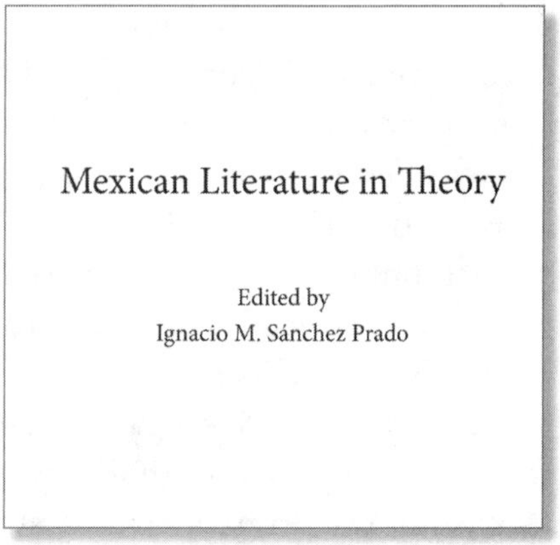

Fig. 5.4.
Part of the title page of an edited book. The title page shows the editor's name.

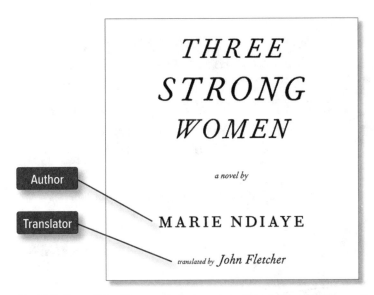

Fig. 5.5. Part of the title page of a translated book. The title page shows the author's name and the translator's name.

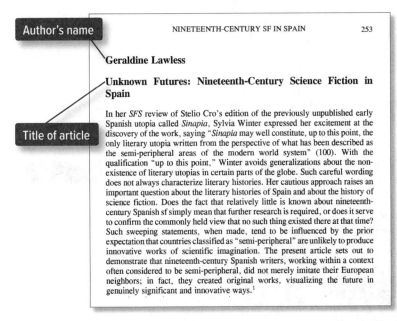

Fig. 5.6. The first page of an essay in a scholarly journal prominently displays the author's name near the title.

Fig. 5.7. An online news site displays the author's name near the article title.

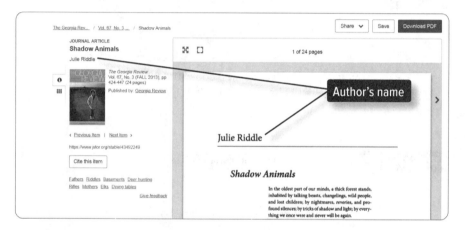

Fig. 5.8. A journal article in an online archive showing the name of the article's author.

Fig. 5.9. A digitized image of a painting published on a website. The text on the site provides the name of the artist.

[5.5] Author: How to Style It

[5.6] One author

When an entry begins with the name of an author who has a family name or other surname, begin the entry with the surname so that the entry can be alphabetized under this name. Follow the surname with a comma and the rest of the name as presented by the work. End the Author element with a period (unless a period that is part of the author's name already appears at the end).

> Baron, Naomi S. "Redefining Reading: The Impact of Digital Communication Media." *PMLA*, vol. 128, no. 1, Jan. 2013, pp. 193–200.
>
> Jacobs, Alan. *The Pleasures of Reading in an Age of Distraction*. Oxford UP, 2011.
>
> Kincaid, Jamaica. "In History." *Callaloo*, vol. 24, no. 2, spring 2001, pp. 620–26.

Surnames used alone: 2.73. Names in languages other than English: 2.75–2.80. Premodern names: 2.81. Names not reversed: 5.9. Languages that order surname first: 5.10. Lack of surname: 5.11. Alphabetizing entries in the works-cited list: 5.123–5.130.

[5.7] Two authors

When a source has two authors, include them in the order in which they are presented in the work (**fig. 5.10**). Reverse the first of the names as described above, follow it with a comma and the word *and*, and give the second name in the normal order. To include a label

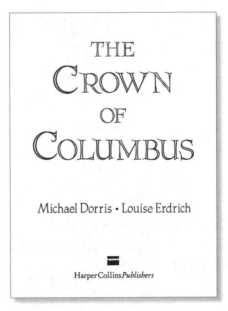

THE
CROWN
OF
COLUMBUS

Michael Dorris • Louise Erdrich

HarperCollins*Publishers*

Fig. 5.10.
The title page of a book showing the names of two authors. In the works-cited list, reverse only the first author's name.

such as *editors* or *translators*, add a comma after the second author's name and then add the label.

> Dorris, Michael, and Louise Erdrich. *The Crown of Columbus.* HarperCollins Publishers, 1999.
> Gilbert, Sandra M., and Susan Gubar, editors. *The Female Imagination and the Modernist Aesthetic.* Gordon and Breach Science Publishers, 1986.

The comma is needed in addition to *and* so that the reader can easily distinguish the two names.

[5.8] Three or more authors

When a source has three or more authors (**fig. 5.11**), reverse the first of the names as described above and follow it with a comma and the abbreviation *et al.* ("and others"). Italicize *et al.* only if it is referred to as a term, as the

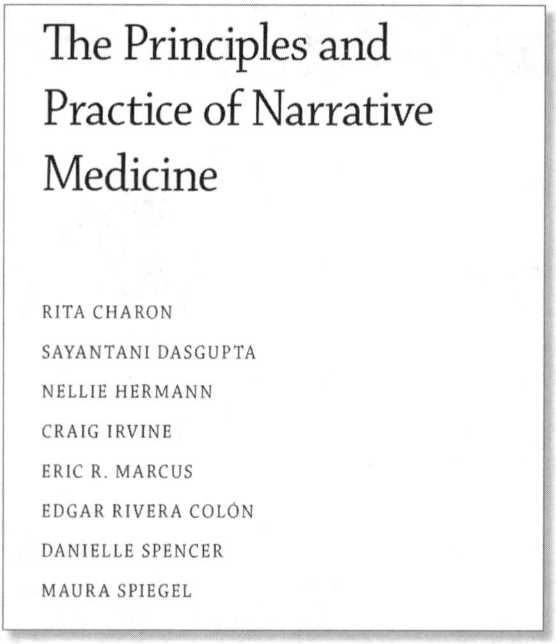

The Principles and Practice of Narrative Medicine

RITA CHARON

SAYANTANI DASGUPTA

NELLIE HERMANN

CRAIG IRVINE

ERIC R. MARCUS

EDGAR RIVERA COLÓN

DANIELLE SPENCER

MAURA SPIEGEL

Fig. 5.11. Part of the title page of a book. The names of eight authors are shown. Only the first, followed by the abbreviation *et al.*, appears in the works-cited-list entry.

example in this sentence shows. In parenthetical citations and works-cited-list entries, the abbreviation should be set roman (i.e., not italicized).

> Charon, Rita, et al. *The Principles and Practice of Narrative Medicine*. Oxford UP, 2017.

[5.9] Names not reversed

[5.10] *Languages that order surname first*

In some languages, such as Chinese, Japanese, and Korean, the surname may be listed before the given name on the title page (**fig. 5.12**). Do not reverse the name in the works-cited list. When a name is not reversed, no comma is needed.

> Shen Fu. *Six Records of a Life Adrift*. Translated by Graham Sanders, Hackett Publishing, 2011.

SHEN FU

Six Records of a Life Adrift

Translated, with Introduction and Notes, by
Graham Sanders

Fig. 5.12. Part of the title page of a book. The surname of the author is given first.

But some names from languages where the surname is normally listed first do not follow this order. Consult relevant parts of the work (like the introduction), a reference work, the author's or publisher's website, or writing by knowledgeable scholars for guidance on the order of the names. If the surname is given last, begin the entry with the surname followed by a comma and the rest of the name.

> Oe, Kenzaburo. *A Quiet Life*. Translated by Kunioki Yanagishita and William Wetherall, Grove Press, 1990.

> Names in Asian languages: 2.80.

[5.11] *Lack of surname*

Do not reverse the following: the name of an author who lacks a surname, some names of nobility and premodern names, pseudonyms (including stage names and online usernames) that do not take the form of a name traditionally reversed, and names of groups and organizations.

> Elizabeth I. *Collected Works*. Edited by Leah S. Marcus et al., U of Chicago P, 2000.
> Film Crit Hulk. "What We Talk about When We Talk about Female Filmmaking." *Film Crit Hulk! Hulk Blog!*, 16 Mar. 2018, filmcrithulk .blog/2018/03/16/what-we-talk-about-when-we-talk-about-female -filmmaking/.
> Geoffrey of Monmouth. *History of the Kings of Britain*. Translated by Michael A. Faletra, Broadview, 2008.
> Lady Gaga. *The Fame*. Interscope Records, 2008.
> United Nations. *Consequences of Rapid Population Growth in Developing Countries*. Taylor and Francis, 1991.

But reverse a pseudonym, screen name, stage name, and the like that takes the form of a name traditionally reversed.

> Tribble, Ivan. "Bloggers Need Not Apply." *The Chronicle of Higher Education*, 8 July 2005, chronicle.com/article/Bloggers-Need-Not-Apply/45022.

[5.12] Variant forms of a personal name

You should generally cite a work under the name recorded on the work itself. However, sometimes authors change their names during their careers or various publishers spell an author's name differently. Work-arounds may be needed for economy of citation, to provide useful information to the reader about authors or their canon of work, or to avoid a name an author no longer uses, when known.

[5.13] *Different spellings*

The name of an author may be spelled in various ways in works you consult (e.g., one edition of the *Aeneid* may list the author as *Virgil* and another as *Vergil*). The spelling of names from languages that do not use the Latin alphabet, like Chinese and Russian, may vary depending on the system of romanization used (e.g., *Zhuang Zhou, Zhuangzi*; *Dostoyevsky, Dostoevsky*). If the spelling or transliteration of an author's name varies, choose the variant preferred by your dictionary or another authoritative source and list all the works by the author under that variant in your works-cited list. Generally use the same form of the name in prose as you do in your works-cited list.

[5.14] *Pseudonyms and name changes*

Authors may write and publish under different names—for instance, by adopting pseudonyms or changing their names. When you are aware that an author has published under different names, consider whether it is useful for your reader to know that works published under different names are by the same person, clearer to use a well-known form of an author's name for easy recognition, or appropriate to avoid the former version of an author's name. Various solutions exist for presenting such works.

One technique is to list the work or works under the best-known form of the name. This might be suitable for especially well-known persons, even when the version of the work you are citing was published under a different form of the name. For example, if a letter by Mark Twain (a well-known pseudonym) was written and published under his real name, Samuel

Clemens, you can list a single entry under the better-known form of the name, allowing you to refer to that form in your prose and to avoid cumbersome in-text references. Likewise, when citing more than one work you can consolidate entries under the better-known form of the name. Consolidating makes it simpler for readers to locate all the works by an author in one place in your works-cited list.

> Twain, Mark. *Adventures of Huckleberry Finn*. William Collins, 2010.
>
> ———. Letter to Francis D. Clark. 5 Jan. 1876. *Mark Twain Project*, Regents of the University of California, 2017–20, www.marktwainproject.org.

Another technique is to add information to entries in square brackets. For example, when citing a single work by an author published under a less widely known pseudonym, you can list the entry under the pseudonym found on the work and annotate the entry using square brackets in the Author element after the pseudonym.

> Bachman, Richard [Stephen King]. *The Long Walk*. Signet, 1979.
>
> Clerk, N. W. [C. S. Lewis]. *A Grief Observed*. Faber and Faber, 1961.

Or, if you elect to list the work under the person's better-known, real name, provide the pseudonym in square brackets, preceded by *published as* in italics.

> King, Stephen [*published as* Richard Bachman]. *The Long Walk*. Signet, 1979.
>
> Lewis, C. S. [*published as* N. W. Clerk]. *A Grief Observed*. Faber and Faber, 1961.

Alternatively, you can place the better-known form of the name in brackets, indicating that it has been supplied by you, and not include the less-familiar form found on the work.

> [King, Stephen]. *The Long Walk*. Signet, 1979.
>
> [Lewis, C.S.]. *A Grief Observed*. Faber and Faber, 1961.
>
> [Twain, Mark]. Letter to Francis D. Clark. 5 Jan. 1876. *Mark Twain Project*, Regents of the University of California, 2017–20, www.marktwainproject.org.

When citing an author who has published under various names, you may list all works under one form of the name. Doing so allows you, in prose and in-text citations, to use the better-known form of the name or to avoid presenting a name no longer used by the author. It also allows readers to more easily locate all works by the author in your works-cited list, where the entries are grouped under one name. Place the name that appears on a given work in square brackets, preceded by *published as* in italics.

> Staley, Lynn. *Margery Kempe's Dissenting Fictions.* U of Pennsylvania P, 1994.
> ——— [*published as* Lynn Staley Johnson]. *The Voice of the Gawain-Poet.* U of Wisconsin P, 1984.
>
> Vivien, Renée [*published as* Paule Riversdale]. *L'être double.* Edited by Nicolas Berger, ErosOnyx, 2014.
> ——— [*published as* Pauline Tarn]. *Le langage des fleurs.* ErosOnyx, 2012.
> ———. *Lilith's Legacy: Prose Poems and Short Stories.* Translated by Brian Stableford, Snuggly Books, 2018.

Another option, if the works you are citing use only two forms of an author's name, is to separately list entries and provide cross-references.

> Penelope, Julia [*see also* Stanley, Julia P.]. "John Simon and the 'Dragons of Eden.'" *College English*, vol. 44, no. 8, Dec. 1982, pp. 848–54. *JSTOR*, https://doi.org/10.2307/377341.
> Stanley, Julia P. [*see also* Penelope, Julia]. "'Correctness,' 'Appropriateness,' and the Uses of English." *College English*, vol. 41, no. 3, Nov. 1979, pp. 330–35. *JSTOR*, https://doi.org/10.2307/376452.

Using brackets for supplied information: 5.122.

[5.15] When not to supply information, cross-reference, or use the published form of a name

If you are writing about or working directly with an author whose name changed and you know that they do not use their former name in references to their work—for example, for trans authors—list their works under the name they use, regardless of the name that appears in the source. Do not supply information about the name change or cross-reference entries, and avoid using the former name in your prose.

[5.16] *Online handles*

If an author's online handle differs from the author's account name (**fig. 5.13**), it may be helpful to supply the handle in square brackets after the name.

> Fogarty, Mignon [@GrammarGirl]. "Every once in a while, that Gmail notice asking if you meant to reply to a 5-day-old message is quite helpful." *Twitter*, 13 Feb. 2019, twitter.com/GrammarGirl/status/1095734401550303232.

When the handle and account name are similar (e.g., Angie Thomas, @angiethomas), you can usually omit the handle if you include the URL in your entry.

> Thomas, Angie. Photo of *The Hate U Give* cover. *Instagram*, 4 Dec. 2018, www.instagram.com/p/Bq_PaXKgqPw/.

If you do not include the URL—for instance, if you access the post from a mobile device or you follow the option presented in 5.84 to omit URLs— retain the handle since it is a useful finding aid.

> Nguyen, Viet Thanh [@viet_t_nguyen]. "I could put on my headphones at the Chinese restaurant or I could listen to @barrymanilow sing 'Mandy.' I choose Mandy." *Twitter*, 19 Feb. 2019.

URLs in the Location element: 5.95–5.98.

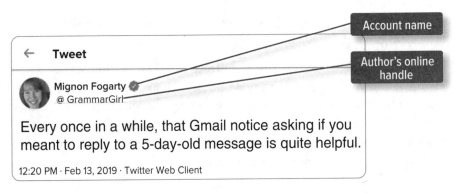

Fig. 5.13. A tweet. The author's online handle differs from the author's account name.

[5.17] Organizations, groups, and government authors

[5.18] *Listing by name*

Initial articles (*a*, *an*, *the*) should be omitted in the works-cited-list entry.

Incorrect

The Beatles. *Revolver.* EMI Records, 1966.

Beatles, The. *Revolver.* EMI Records, 1966.

Correct

Beatles. *Revolver.* EMI Records, 1966.

Alphabetize a name of an organization by the first word and do not reverse the name.

Incorrect

Nations, United. *Consequences of Rapid Population Growth in Developing Countries.* Taylor and Francis, 1991.

Correct

United Nations. *Consequences of Rapid Population Growth in Developing Countries.* Taylor and Francis, 1991.

[5.19] *Avoiding redundancy*

When a nongovernment organization is both author and publisher, you may skip the Author element and begin the entry with the work's title. List the organization only as publisher. (For an exception when citing government publications, see 5.22.)

Report to the Teagle Foundation on the Undergraduate Major in Language and Literature. Modern Language Association of America, 2009.

But when the author of a work is a division or committee of the organization, list the division or committee as the author and list the organization as the publisher. In the example below, the Association of Specialized and Cooperative Library Agencies is a subdivision of the American Library Association.

Association of Specialized and Cooperative Library Agencies. *Library Standards for Adult Correctional Institutions.* American Library Association, 1992.

[5.20] *Government authors*

Government publications emanate from many sources and so present special problems in citation. If you are working with many government sources, you may choose to standardize the names of government entities so that entries can be consolidated. But nonspecialists and writers working with very few government sources can usually treat them just like any other source written by an organization: record the name as presented by the source.

> U.S. Department of Labor. *Occupational Outlook Handbook, 2014–2015.*
> Skyhorse Publishing, 2014.

[5.21] Standardizing and supplying information

If the author of the document is not specified, is given in shorthand, or is otherwise unclear, or if you are writing in a specialist context, cite as the author the government agency that issued the document, listing the entities from largest to smallest—that is, state the name of the government first, followed by the name of the agency or agencies.

> United States, Congress, House. Improving Broadband Access for Veterans
> Act of 2016. *Congress.gov,* www.congress.gov/bill/114th-congress/
> house-bill/6394/text.

When standardizing entries, spell out the government name (*United States*) even if your source does not.

> Government agencies as publishers: 5.63.
> Government documents: 5.118.

[5.22] Consolidating entries

If you are citing two or more works by the same government or government entity, you have the option to consolidate the works by standardizing the government name and listing them under the government author, even when the author and publisher are the same. Organizing the works by author instead of title is particularly useful in specialized studies or long-form works like books and dissertations. Begin the entry with the name of the government, followed by a comma and the name of the agency. Between them, name any organizational units of which the agency is part (for example, the House of Representatives is part of Congress). All the names are arranged from the largest entity to the smallest.

Australia, Institute of Health and Welfare
California, Department of Industrial Relations
United States, Congress, House

Substitute three hyphens or three em dashes for any name repeated from the Author element in the previous entry (whichever mark you use, be consistent).

United States, Congress, House.
———, ———, Senate.
———, Department of Health and Human Services, Centers for Disease Control and Prevention.

> Ordering the works-cited list: 5.123–5.130.
> Government authors in in-text citations: 6.6.

[5.23] Title of Source: What It Is

In the Title of Source element, list the title of the work you are citing. In the example below, *Insurrecto* is the title of a novel by Gina Apostol.

Apostol, Gina. *Insurrecto*. Soho Press, 2018.

If the work does not have a title (**figs. 5.14, 5.15**), provide a concise but informative description of the work.

Advertisement for Upton Tea Imports. *Smithsonian*, Oct. 2018, p. 84.
Lizzo. Concert. Vega, 19 Nov. 2019, Copenhagen.
Mackintosh, Charles Rennie. Chair of stained oak. 1897–1900, Victoria and Albert Museum, London.
Ng, Celeste [@pronounced_ing]. Photo of a letter from Shirley Jackson. *Twitter*, 22 Jan. 2018, twitter.com/pronounced_ing/status/955528799357231104.

Fig. 5.14.
An advertisement without a title.
In the Title of Source element,
provide a description.

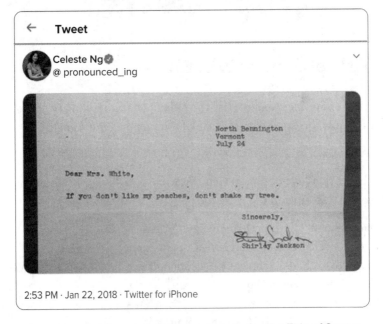

Fig. 5.15. A tweet containing a photograph of a letter. In the Title of Source
element, provide a description of the photograph.

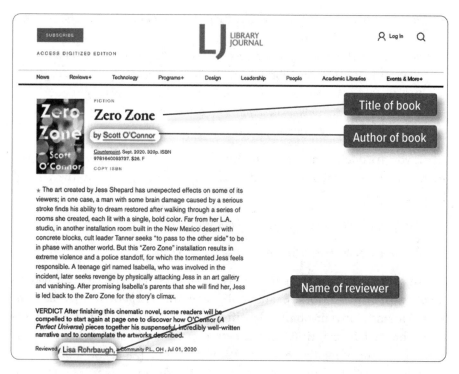

Fig. 5.16. A review of a book. In your entry, list the name of the reviewer in the Author element. In the Title of Source element, provide a description that includes the title of the reviewed book and its author. The title of the reviewed book, *Zero Zone*, is in italics, but the rest of the description is not.

The description might also include other pertinent information, such as the recipient of a letter or other type of message, the location of a performance featured in a program, the name of the work and author that are the subject of a review, and the artist whose exhibit is introduced in museum wall text. In some cases, the description may include the title of another work (**fig. 5.16**).

> Benton, Thomas Hart. Letter to Charles Fremont. 22 June 1847. John Charles Fremont Papers, Southwest Museum Library, Los Angeles. Manuscript.

Program for Arthur Miller's *The Crucible* at the Walter Kerr Theatre, New York
  City. Playbill, 2016.
Rohrbaugh, Lisa. Review of *Zero Zone*, by Scott O'Connor. *Library Journal*,
  1 July 2020, www.libraryjournal.com/?reviewDetail=zero-zone.
Wall text for *A Warrior's Story, Honoring Grandpa Blue Bird*, by Lauren Good
  Day Giago. *Unbound: Narrative Art of the Plains*, 12 Mar.–4 Dec. 2016,
  National Museum of the American Indian, New York City.

If you are documenting a communication you received, pertinent information includes a reference to yourself as *author* or by name in the Title of
Source element.

Zamora, Estelle. E-mail to the author. 3 May 2018.

Zamora, Estelle. E-mail to Penny Kinkaid. 3 May 2018.

In some cases, using text from the work itself is the clearest way to
identify an untitled work. Examples include untitled short works (like untitled poems, conventionally identified by the first line) and digital mes-
sages that lack formal titles (like tweets, e-mails, and texts). When a digital
message or social media post consists entirely of a photograph or a video,
provide a description for a title (see **fig. 5.15**). You may also choose to provide a description in place of text from the post itself when your discussion
focuses on a nontextual part of the post such as a photograph or a video.

Chaucer Doth Tweet [@LeVostreGC]. "A daye wythout anachronism ys lyke
  Emily Dickinson wythout her lightsaber." *Twitter*, 7 Apr. 2018, twitter
  .com/LeVostreGC/status/982829987286827009.
Hughes, Langston. "I look at the world." *Poetry Foundation*, www.poetry
  foundation.org/poetrymagazine/poems/52005/i-look-at-the-world.
MacLeod, Michael. Cover of *Space Cat and the Kittens*, by Ruthven Todd.
  Pinterest, 2020, www.pinterest.com/pin/565412928193207246/.
Wilson, Rebel. Video of tire-flipping exercise. *Snapchat*, 14 July 2020, www
  .snapchat.com/add/rebelwilsonsnap.

[5.24] Title of Source: Where to Find It

The title is usually prominently displayed in the work, often near the author's name (**figs. 5.17–5.21**).

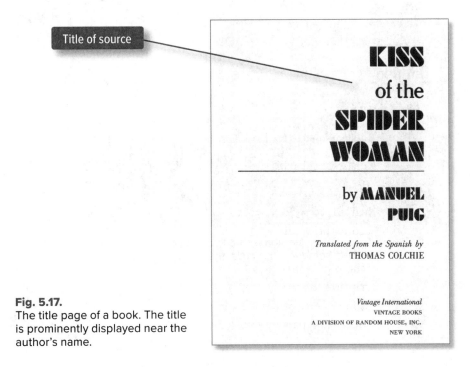

Fig. 5.17.
The title page of a book. The title is prominently displayed near the author's name.

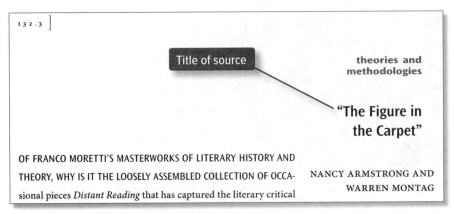

Fig. 5.18. Part of the first page of a journal article. The title is located above the authors' names.

Fig. 5.19. The cover of a music album. The title is displayed on the cover near the name of the author—in this case, the band that made the album.

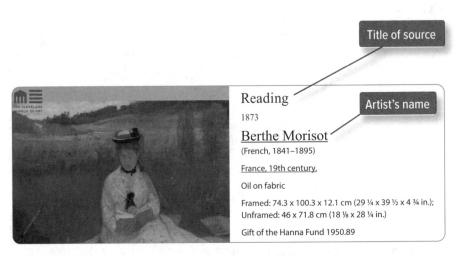

Fig. 5.20. A digitized image of a painting published on a website. The title is displayed above the artist's name.

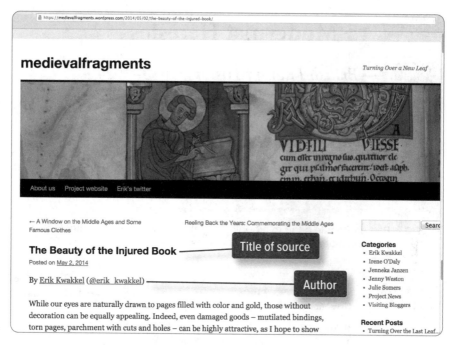

Fig. 5.21. A post on a website. The title of the post is displayed above the author's name.

Some works have subtitles. They are usually rendered less prominently than the title or indicated by punctuation—typically a colon but sometimes a dash (**figs. 5.22–5.24**).

If the design of a work makes distinguishing the title and subtitle difficult (**fig. 5.25**), corroborate the title by checking another authoritative location in the work such as the copyright page.

If the title of a web page and the title of the site it appears on are hard to distinguish, look for cues in the relative prominence of the titles, the design and layout, and the URL (**fig. 5.26**).

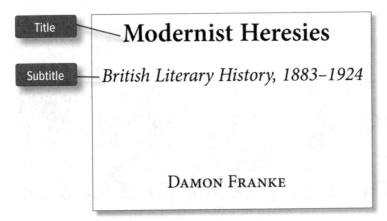

Fig. 5.22. Part of the title page of a book. The title and subtitle are distinguished from each other by different typefaces.

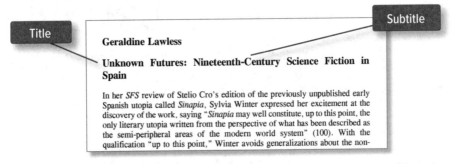

Fig. 5.23. Part of the first page of a journal article. The subtitle follows the title and is separated from it by a colon.

Fig. 5.24. An online news article. The subtitle follows the title and is separated from it by a colon.

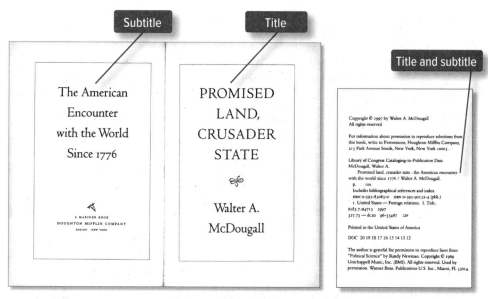

Fig. 5.25. The title of the book *Promised Land, Crusader State* is shown on the title page, and the facing page shows the subtitle. You can confirm the title and subtitle on the book's copyright page.

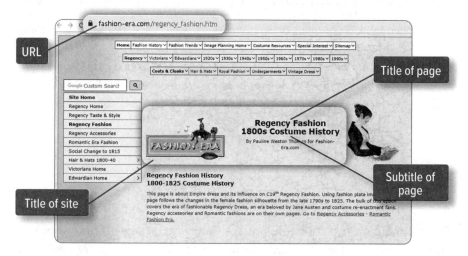

Fig. 5.26. A page on a website. The title of the site, *Fashion-Era*, and the title of the page, "Regency Fashion: 1800s Costume History," appear side by side. The title of the page appears near the author's name and is rendered in text, whereas the title of the site matches the URL and is displayed as a logo.

[5.25] Title of Source: How to Style It

Titles are given in the entry in full exactly as they are found in the source, except that capitalization, the punctuation between the main title and a subtitle, and the styling of titles that normally appear in italic typeface are standardized. The Title of Source element is followed by a period (unless the title ends in a question mark or an exclamation point). The examples in this section cover styling issues unique to the list of works cited and supplement the guidelines on titles given elsewhere in this handbook.

> Titles of works in prose: 2.89–2.125.

[5.26] Shortened titles

Very long titles can be shortened in the list of works cited. Be sure to include enough of the title to make identification of the work unambiguous, and use ellipses to indicate that a title has been shortened. If a period or comma is needed to mark the end of an element, insert it after the ellipsis.

> Bulwer, John. *Philocophus; or, The Deafe and Dumbe Mans Friend* . . . . Humphrey Moseley, 1648.
>
> Mander, Karel van. "The Life of Henricus Goltzius." *The Lives of the Illustrious Netherlandish and German Painters* . . . , edited and translated by Hessel Miedema, vol. 1, Davaco Publishers, 1994, pp. 384–407.

> Shortening very long titles in prose: 2.123.

[5.27] Sections of a work labeled generically

To document an introduction, preface, foreword, afterword, or other section of a work that is titled only with a generic label (**fig. 5.27**), capitalize the label just as you would a title but do not italicize it or enclose it in quotation marks.

> Felstiner, John. Preface. *Selected Poems and Prose of Paul Celan*, translated by Felstiner, W. W. Norton, 2001, pp. xix–xxxvi.

If the introduction, preface, foreword, afterword, or other similar section has a unique title in addition to a generic label (**fig. 5.28**), generally give only the unique title, enclosed in quotation marks (see 5.109 for an exception).

> Seyhan, Azade. "Novel Moves." *Tales of Crossed Destinies: The Modern Turkish Novel in a Comparative Context,* by Seyhan, Modern Language Association of America, 2008, pp. 1–22.

PREFACE

Would we, if somehow this were possible, trade Anne Frank's diary for her life, give up those salvaged pages to let her survive unscathed, in her seventies now? And would we forgo Charlotte Salomon's *Life or Theater?,* her 1941 autobiography in 760 watercolors, if in exchange she were not to perish in Auschwitz? Would we, in effect, do without such indispensable human documents, relinquish them so as to secure the undeflected lives their creators might have lived?

Fig. 5.27. Part of the first page of the preface to a book. The preface is labeled with a generic label.

CHAPTER 1

Introduction: Novel Moves

Poetry is the art of inner fortification. Language becomes the inner fortress of a nation, not when it is used for communication but when it becomes the material and texture of that fortress. As such, language is the very essence of a

Fig. 5.28. Part of the first page of the introduction to a book. The introduction has a unique title in addition to a generic label.

[5.28] Description in place of a title

When describing a work that lacks a title, capitalize the first word of the description. Then style the description just as you would a phrase in your prose: capitalize proper nouns and use punctuation when necessary. Do not enclose the description in quotation marks or italicize it.

> Beatles. Booklet. *The Beatles*, EMI Records, 1968.
>
> Mackintosh, Charles Rennie. Chair of stained oak. 1897–1900, Victoria and Albert Museum, London.
>
> Slide of Linus, Lucy, and Snoopy. English 204: Animals in Graphic Art, 4 Apr. 2016, Evergreen State College. Slide 2.
>
> Wall text for central Caribbean tripod vessel in the form of a spectacled owl. *Cerámica de los Ancestros: Central America's Past Revealed*, 18 Apr. 2015–Dec. 2017, National Museum of the American Indian, New York City.
>
> Young, Talia. E-mail to Standards Committee. 15 Jan. 2019.
>
> Zamora, Estelle. Text message to the author. 3 May 2018.

When the description includes the title of another work, style the title within the description according to the guidelines for styling titles in prose.

> Max the Pen. Comment on "Why They're Wrong." *The Economist*, 29 Sept. 2016, 6:06 p.m., www.economist.com/node/21707926/comments.
>
> Rohrbaugh, Lisa. Review of *Zero Zone*, by Scott O'Connor. *Library Journal*, 1 July 2020, www.libraryjournal.com/?reviewDetail=zero-zone.

> Styling titles in prose: 2.106–2.110.

[5.29] Quoted text in place of a title

When using text from the work itself to identify an untitled work, use the first line of the work (as for a poem), the full text (exactly as it appears in the source) if it is very short, or a short introductory fragment. Enclose the quoted text in quotation marks and conclude it with a period, placed inside the final quotation mark. Reproduce the text as written, styled, and capitalized in the source.

Dickinson, Emily. "I heard a Fly buzz—when I died—." *The Poems of Emily Dickinson*, edited by R. W. Franklin, Harvard UP, 1999, pp. 265–66.

Persiankiwi. "We have report of large street battles in east & west of Tehran now - #Iranelection." *Twitter*, 23 June 2009, twitter.com/persiankiwi/ status/2298106072.

Wyatt, Thomas. "They flee from me, that sometime did me seek." *The Columbia Anthology of British Poetry*, edited by Carl Woodring and James Shapiro, Columbia UP, 1995, p. 30.

To truncate short introductory fragments as well as those that conclude with nontextual elements like emojis, use an ellipsis at the end.

Smith, Clint. "Today is Frederick Douglass' 200th birthday . . . ." *Twitter*, 14 Feb. 2018, twitter.com/ClintSmithIII/status/963810866964639745.

[5.30] Translations of titles

In the works-cited list, translations of titles in languages other than English are usually unnecessary, especially if your audience is composed primarily of people who know the language (e.g., when you are writing a paper for a class studying the language or for a specialist journal).

Erpenbeck, Jenny. *Gehen, ging, gegangen.* Penguin Verlag, 2015.

If your audience is likely to include readers unfamiliar with the language, however, it may be helpful to provide a translation, placed in square brackets after the original title and with the same formatting as the original title (here, italics).

Erpenbeck, Jenny. *Gehen, ging, gegangen* [*Go, Went, Gone*]. Penguin Verlag, 2015.

For titles written in non-Latin characters, it may be useful to supply a transliteration in addition to a translation, especially if the list of works cited includes more than one work in the same non-Latin alphabet under the same author or title. Translations and transliterations of book titles are italicized, but titles written in non-Latin characters are styled roman. Separate a transliteration and translation with a semicolon.

Chreiteh, Alexandra [Shuraytiḥ, Aliksandrā]. عَلِيّ و أُمُّهُ الرُّوسِيّة [*'Alī wa-ummuhu al-Rūsīyah; Ali and His Russian Mother*]. Al-Dār al-ʿArabīyah lil-ʿUlūm Nāshirūn, 2009.

Alphabetize the titles according to the transliteration so that any in-text references in your prose using the transliterated title can be more easily identified in the works-cited-list entries by readers unfamiliar with the language.

> Translations of titles in prose: 2.125. Alphabetizing the works-cited list: 5.123–5.130.

[5.31] Title of Container: What It Is

On the MLA template of core elements (see **fig. 5.1**), a *container* is a work that contains another work. In the example below, the website *Guernica* contains the short story "Carrot Legs"; the website name appears in the Title of Container element.

> Chou, Elaine Hsieh. "Carrot Legs." *Guernica,* 12 Sept. 2019, www.guernicamag
> .com/carrot-legs/.

Examples of containers are shown in the following list and in **figure 5.29**:

- A periodical, such as a journal, magazine, or newspaper, is the container of an article published in it.
- A print anthology is the container of an essay, poem, or short story published in it.
- A website or database can be the container of a post, a comment, a review, a song or audio file, a video or film, an image, a digitized essay or book, or other media published or aggregated on it.
- A vinyl album or CD is the container of a song.
- Television series, podcasts, and radio programs are the containers of individual episodes.
- An art exhibit is the container of an artwork featured in it.

Container	Contained
journal, magazine, newspaper	article
anthology	essay, poem, or short story
blog	blog post
Twitter	tweet
website like *Facebook*	post or comment
website like *SoundCloud*	song
album	song
website like *YouTube*	video clip or movie
TV series, podcast, or radio program	individual episode
website like *Google Books*	digitized book
website or app like *Instagram*	photo or video clip
museum website	digital image of a painting
art exhibit	artwork
app like *Bible Gateway*	version of the Bible

Fig. 5.29. Examples of containers, works that contain another work.

[5.32] Works that are self-contained

Some works are self-contained, such as a print version of a novel and the original theatrical release of a film. The title of the work is listed in the Title of Source element. The Title of Container element is left blank, but any relevant publication details are provided in the container section of the template and in the entry.

> Austen, Jane. *Emma*. Penguin Books, 2011.
> *Moonlight*. Directed by Barry Jenkins, A24 / Plan B Entertainment / Pastel Productions, 2016.

[5.33] Works with more than one container

A container can be contained by another container. For example, an essay can appear in a print book and that book can be digitized on a website. In

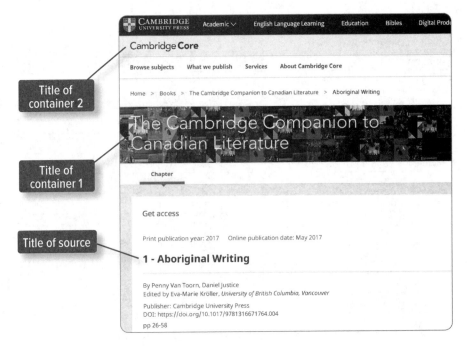

Fig. 5.30. An essay in a book collection digitized online.

this case, both the book and the website are containers: the book contains the essay, and the website contains the book (**fig. 5.30**).

> Toorn, Penny van, and Daniel Justice. "Aboriginal Writing." *The Cambridge Companion to Canadian Literature*, edited by Eva-Marie Kröller, Cambridge UP, 2017, pp. 26–58. *Cambridge Core*, https://doi.org/ 10.1017/9781316671764.004.

See 5.102 for examples of how to fill out the template of core elements for works with more than one container.

[5.34] Determining when a website is a container

As **figure 5.29** shows, websites can be containers. However, websites are not always containers. A website is a container when it serves as the platform of publication of the particular version of the work you consult; it is not a container when it is a passive conduit providing access to the work. **Figure 5.31** and the following examples illustrate this principle:

- If you click on a link on *Facebook* that takes you to a *New York Times* article, *Facebook* is not the container of the article; the *New York Times* website is. But when you read a comment posted by one of your friends on *Facebook*, then *Facebook* is the container of the comment.

- A learning management system, like *Blackboard*, is not a container if it links you to a work on an external website, like *Project Muse*. But if you read a class lecture on *Blackboard* and quote from that lecture in your paper, then *Blackboard* is the container because it is the platform of publication of the version of the lecture you quote from.

- An online store, like *Amazon*, is not the container of an e-book that you download from the store. But if you quote a review of the book posted by a customer on the *Amazon* website, the *Amazon* website is the container of the review.

- If you search for an image of the *Mona Lisa* through *Google Images* and the results page includes thumbnails of the painting, do not cite the results page as the container for one of the thumbnails. Choose a thumbnail from the search results and click through to the website hosting the image of the *Mona Lisa*. That website, not *Google Images*, is the container because it is the platform that published the image. But when *Google* publishes an original artwork, as it does when it features changes to its search bar with Google Doodles, *Google* is the container of the artwork.

	Not a container	A container
Blackboard	when it links you to another website	when something, like a lecture, is published on it
Amazon	when you download an e-book from it	when a customer review is published on the site
Google	when it displays snippets of text in the results page of a search	when it publishes an original artwork, such as a Google Doodle
Facebook	when you click on a link (e.g., a link to a news story) that takes you to another website	when a user publishes or comments on a link or post

Fig. 5.31. A website is a container only when it serves as the platform of publication of the particular version of the work you consult.

[5.35] Apps and databases

To determine whether an app or a database is a container, apply the same criteria as for a website.

When an app like *Bible Gateway* that is downloaded to your phone, tablet, or computer contains other works—in this case, different versions of the Bible—the app is a work containing other works, and thus it is a container. However, what is commonly referred to as an *app* is not always a work. For example, if you quote from a PDF of an article you downloaded and saved on the *Google Drive* app on your phone, the app is not a work and not the platform of publication for the work. It is simply software through which you accessed the work published elsewhere.

Similarly, online research databases and the platforms aggregating them sometimes, but not always, contain works in their entirety, not just previews or snippets. When you read, view, or listen to an entire work on such a site, it is the container of the work. Suppose, for example, that you search for articles on the role of literature in promoting literacy at public libraries on the *EBSCOhost* site (**fig. 5.32**) and then decide to read the article "The Latinx Family" by clicking on the PDF (**fig. 5.33**). The journal *Bilingual Review / La revista bilingüe* contains the article, and *EBSCOhost* is the container of the journal.

> Dávila, Denise, et al. "The Latinx Family: Learning *y La Literatura* at the Library." *Bilingual Review / La revista bilingüe*, vol. 33, no. 5, May 2017, pp. 33–49. *EBSCOhost*, search.ebscohost.com.

If, however, you search for an article on how teachers can provide helpful feedback on student papers and decide to read the article "Preparing Teacher Candidates for the Instruction of English Language Learners" (**fig. 5.34**), you are sent to the website eric.gov to read the article (**fig. 5.35**). Thus, the website titled *ERIC* (an abbreviation for *Education Resources Information Center*, so styled in capital letters) is the container of the article, not *EBSCOhost*.

> Gonzalez, Monica Marie. "Preparing Teacher Candidates for the Instruction of English Language Learners." *Networks: An Online Journal for Teacher Research*, vol. 18, no. 2, fall 2016. *ERIC*, eric.ed.gov/?id=EJ1152320.

Note that the search filters you apply on a database like *EBSCOhost* to find these articles (the MLA International Bibliography in the first example and ERIC in the second) are not containers.

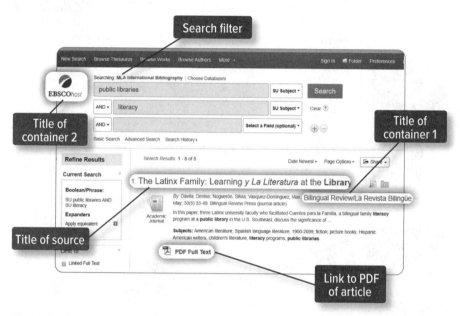

Fig. 5.32. Search results on *EBSCOhost*.

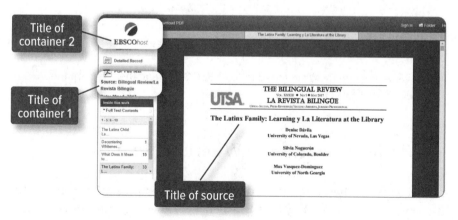

Fig. 5.33. A work that was searched for and viewed on *EBSCOhost*.

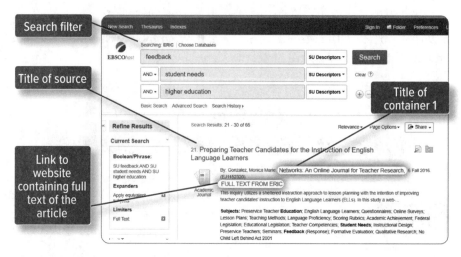

Fig. 5.34. Search results on *EBSCOhost*.

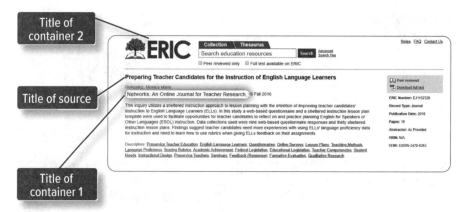

Fig. 5.35. A work that was searched for on *EBSCOhost* and then read on the website *ERIC*.

[5.36] Title of Container: Where to Find It

Like the title of the source, the title of the container is usually prominently displayed in the work. **Figures 5.36–5.43** show examples of container titles in a variety of source types.

Fig. 5.36. A print news article. The title of the container, *The New York Times*, appears at the top of the page.

Fig. 5.37. An online news article. The title of the container, *Los Angeles Times*, appears at the top of the page.

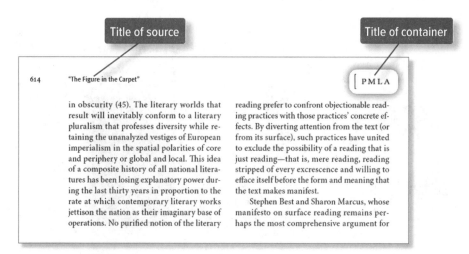

Fig. 5.38. An article in a print journal. The title of the container, *PMLA*, can be found in the running head, on the front cover of the issue, and on the journal's masthead.

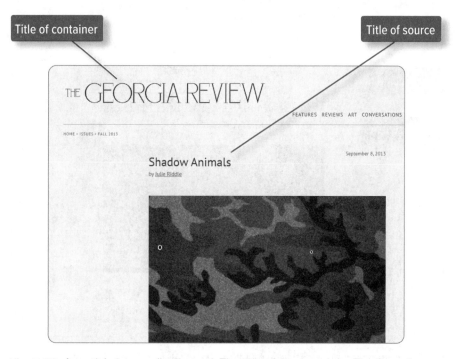

Fig. 5.39. An article in an online journal. The title of the container, *The Georgia Review*, is displayed prominently at the top of the page.

Fig. 5.40. A music recording on a website. The title of the container, *Rolling Stone*, appears at the top of the page.

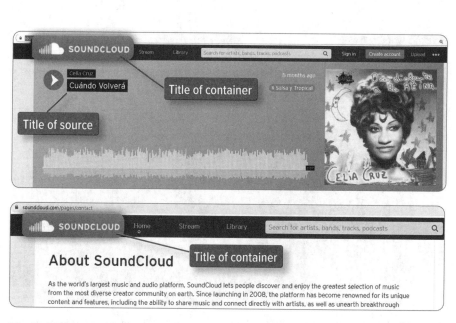

Fig. 5.41. A song on a website. The title of the container, *SoundCloud*, appears at upper left. It can also be found on the site's "About" page.

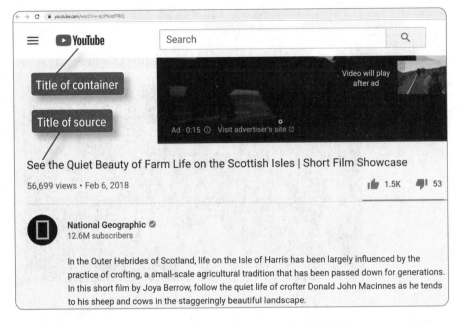

Fig. 5.42. A video on a website. The title of the container, *YouTube*, appears at the top of the page.

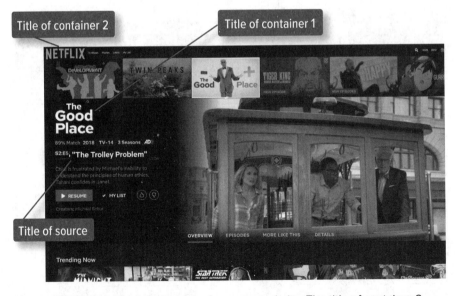

Fig. 5.43. An episode of a television show on a website. The title of container 2, *Netflix*, appears at the top of the landing page for each episode.

[5.37] Title of Container: How to Style It

Style the Title of Container element following the same guidelines as those for the Title of Source element. The title of the container is normally italicized and followed by a comma, since the information that comes next provides publication details for the work in the container.

> Quirk, Tom. "The Flawed Greatness of *Huckleberry Finn.*" *American Literary Realism*, vol. 45, no. 1, fall 2012, pp. 38–48. *JSTOR*, https://doi.org/ 10.5406/amerlitereal.45.1.0038.
>
> Sigmund, Paul E. "Chile." *Latin American Politics and Development*, edited by Howard J. Wiarda and Harvey F. Kline, 7th ed., Westview Press, 2011, pp. 168–99.

When a container is untitled, describe it. In the first example, "*Decision* magazine papers" has been supplied in the Title of Container element; the information that follows is the location (see 5.99).

> Auden, W. H., and Klaus Mann. Prospectus. *Decision* magazine papers, Yale U Library, Manuscripts and Archives, MS 176, box 1, folder 20.
>
> "Fall Publications Feature DC Heroes." Marketing newsletter, no. 6, Fantagraphics, 2016, pp. 1–2.
>
> Schimpf, K. D. "Quarterly Earnings Prompt Stock Split." Monthly newsletter of the Phillips Petroleum Company, Aug. 2008, www.philpet.com/ smartin/quarterly-split/.

> Titles of works in prose: 2.89–2.125.

[5.38] Contributor: What It Is

People, groups, and organizations can contribute to a work while not being its primary creator. This may be the case for works that have a primary author, whether specified or anonymous, and for ensemble works that are the product of many contributors but not of a single, primary creator. Key contributors should always be listed in your entry. Other kinds of contributors should be listed on a case-by-case basis in the Contributor element, as explained below. Whenever you list a contributor, include a label describing the role played.

[5.39] Key contributors

You should always list the following contributors in your entry, generally in the Contributor element:

- translators
- editors responsible for scholarly editions and anthologies of a primary author's works
- editors responsible for edited collections of works by various primary authors from which you cite an individual contribution

Other key contributors that should generally be listed in the Contributor element are film directors, music conductors, and performing groups like dance companies and choirs. The following examples show how you might indicate the participation of one or more key contributors in various types of works.

Translator of a work with a primary author

Chartier, Roger. *The Order of Books: Readers, Authors, and Libraries in Europe between the Fourteenth and Eighteenth Centuries.* Translated by Lydia G. Cochrane, Stanford UP, 1994.

Translator of an anonymous work

Beowulf. Translated by Stephen Mitchell, Yale UP, 2017.

Editors of an edition of a work with a primary author

Milton, John. *Paradise Lost.* Edited by Stephen Orgel and Jonathan Goldberg, Oxford UP, 2008.

Editor of an edition of an anonymous work

Lazarillo de Tormes. Edited by Stanley Appelbaum, Dover Publications, 2001.

Editor of an anthology from which an authored essay is cited

Sabau, Ana. "The Perils of Ownership: Property and Literature in Nineteenth-Century Mexico." *Mexican Literature in Theory*, edited by Ignacio M. Sánchez Prado, Bloomsbury Academic, 2018, pp. 33–54.

Editor of an anthology from which an anonymous poem is cited

"The Husband's Message." *The First Poems in English*, edited and translated by Michael Alexander, Penguin Classics, 2008, pp. 65–66.

Director of a film

Point of No Return. Directed by John Badham, Warner Bros., 1993.

Dance company that performed the work of a choreographer for a live event

Brown, Trisha. *Foray Forêt.* Performance by Trisha Brown Dance Company, 28 Sept. 2019, Fairmount Park, Philadelphia.

Music ensemble that performed the work of a composer for a recording

Schubert, Franz. *Piano Trio in E-flat Major D 929.* Performance by Wiener Mozart-Trio, unabridged version, Preiser Records, 2011. Vinyl LP.

Director of a performance of a play

Shaw, George Bernard. *Heartbreak House.* Directed by Robin Lefevre, Roundabout Theatre Company, 11 Oct. 2006, American Airlines Theatre, New York City.

Conductor and ensemble that performed a concert with no named composer

Sing Me the Universal: A Walt Whitman Bicentennial. Conducted by Mark Shapiro, performed by Cecilia Chorus of New York, 2 Mar. 2019, Church of Saint Francis Xavier, New York City.

[5.40] Key contributors in the Author element

Occasionally you may have reason to list a key contributor in the Author element. For example, if you are discussing a translated work and your discussion focuses on the translator's choices, you may place the translator in the Author element (followed by the label *translator*). If the work has a primary author, place the primary author's name in the Contributor element preceded by the label *by*.

Wall, Geoffrey, translator. *Madame Bovary.* By Gustave Flaubert, Penguin Books, 2003.

Likewise, if you are discussing a collaborative work but focusing on the contributions of a particular key contributor, you may place that contributor in the Author element followed by an appropriate label.

Johnson, Rian, director. *Star Wars: The Last Jedi.* Walt Disney Studios, 2017.

Placing key contributors like editors, translators, or directors in the Author element can be useful for long works-cited lists, such as those in books or dissertations, where organizing information efficiently is paramount. Doing so makes in-text citations more concise and allows readers to locate the corresponding works in the works-cited list more easily.

[5.41] Other types of contributors

It may be necessary to include other types of contributors if they shaped the overall presentation of the work, if your discussion focuses on their contribution, or if they are important for identifying a version of the work. For example, the person or organization responsible for uploading a video to a sharing site, the creator of a television show, the narrator of an audiobook, and a featured performer can be listed in the Contributor element. Unlike key contributors, they are generally not listed in the Author element.

Organization responsible for uploading a video to a sharing site
"2016 MLA-Prize-Winning Publications." *YouTube*, uploaded by
    ModernLanguageAssoc, 18 Jan. 2017, www.youtube.com/
    watch?v=zKROuhFF9dU.

Creator of a television show
"Strike Up the Band." *The Marvelous Mrs. Maisel*, created by Amy Sherman-
    Palladino, season 3, episode 1, Amazon Studios, 2019.

Audiobook narrator whose contribution is the focus of your discussion
Lee, Harper. *To Kill a Mockingbird*. Narrated by Sissy Spacek, audiobook ed.,
    unabridged ed., HarperAudio, 8 July 2014.

Singer whose contribution is the focus of your discussion
Rossini, Gioachino. *La Cenerentola*. Performance by Joyce DiDonato, 10 May
    2014, Metropolitan Opera House, New York City.

Actors whose contributions are the focus of your discussion
Star Wars: The Last Jedi. Directed by Rian Johnson, performances by Adam
    Driver and Carrie Fisher, Walt Disney Studios, 2017.

Actors who are important for identifying the version of a work
Othello. Directed by Stuart Burge, performances by Laurence Olivier et al.,
    BHE Films, 1965.

[5.42] Contributor: Where to Find It

The names of contributors, especially those who play key roles, are sometimes displayed near the name of the primary author, if there is one (see **fig. 5.5**). Other times the names of contributors are listed elsewhere in the source (**figs. 5.44–5.46**).

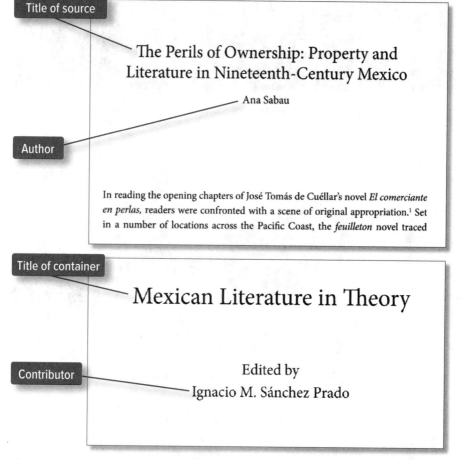

Title of source

The Perils of Ownership: Property and Literature in Nineteenth-Century Mexico

Ana Sabau

Author

In reading the opening chapters of José Tomás de Cuéllar's novel *El comerciante en perlas*, readers were confronted with a scene of original appropriation.[1] Set in a number of locations across the Pacific Coast, the *feuilleton* novel traced

Title of container

Mexican Literature in Theory

Edited by
Ignacio M. Sánchez Prado

Contributor

Fig. 5.44. An essay in an anthology. The name of the anthology's editor is shown on the title page of the volume. In your entry, list the name of the article's author in the Author element and the name of the anthology's editor in the Contributor element.

Fig. 5.45. A film still. The film director's name is shown in the credits. A film is a collaborative work, so the director's name is listed in the Contributor element.

Fig. 5.46. The title page of a graphic narrative showing the names of several contributors. The names of contributors who are important to your discussion can be listed in the Contributor element.

[5.43] Contributor: How to Style It

Names in the Contributor element are styled just like names in your prose. Note that, unlike names in the Author element, names in the Contributor element are not reversed for alphabetization, since this element does not begin the entry.

> Styling names in prose: 2.71–2.86.

[5.44] Labels describing the contributor's role

Introduce each name (or each group of names, if more than one person performed the same function) by describing the role that the person or group played in the creation of the work. Below are common descriptions.

adapted by	directed by	narrated by
choreographed by	edited by	performance by
conducted by	illustrated by	translated by
created by	introduction by	

The nature of the contribution may require you to develop a more specific label.

> *Othello.* Directed by Stuart Burge, Japanese subtitles by Shunji Shimizu, BHE Films, 1965.

When a work's author is listed in the Contributor element, precede the author's name with the label *by*.

> Eiland, Howard, and Kevin McLaughlin, translators. *The Arcades Project*, by Walter Benjamin, Belknap Press, 1999.

If the role played cannot be described using a phrase with *by*, specify the role with a noun or noun phrase surrounded by commas after the name, as for the general editor in the example below.

> Berger, André. "Climate Model Simulations of the Geological Past." *The Earth System: Physical and Chemical Dimensions of Global Environmental Change*, edited by Michael C. MacCracken and John S. Perry, pp. 296–301. *Encyclopedia of Global Environmental Change*, Ted Munn, general editor, 2nd ed., vol. 1, Wiley, 2002.

When a work uses terms such as *with* or *with the assistance of* instead of specifying the person's contribution, place the name in the Contributor element preceded by the term *with*.

>   Dydo, Ulla E. *Gertrude Stein: The Language That Rises, 1923–1934*. With William
>   Rice, Northwestern UP, 2003.

If a contributor has more than one role, precede the contributor's name by a label identifying each role.

>   Freud, Sigmund. *Civilization and Its Discontents*. Edited and translated by James
>   Strachey, W. W. Norton, 2005.

But do not indicate when an editor or translator has also written a preface, foreword, introduction, or other section of a work, even when your source does. Similarly, if the name of the author of a preface, introduction, or the like is given on the title page, do not include the name in the Contributor element. When citing a preface or an introduction, list its author in the Author element (**fig. 5.47**).

>   Flaubert, Gustave. *Madame Bovary*. Translated by Geoffrey Wall, rev. ed.,
>   Penguin Books, 2007.

Citing a section of a work labeled generically: 5.27.

Fig. 5.47. Part of the title page of a translated book. The title page indicates that the translator contributed an introduction and notes and that another person contributed a preface, but this information is not included in the works-cited-list entry.

[5.45] Capitalization of labels

The label describing the contributor's role should be lowercase (unless it is a proper noun). Note, however, that the initial word after the period that concludes an element should be capitalized. In the first example below, *edited* is lowercase because it is a word normally lowercase and appears after a comma. It is capitalized in the second example because it is placed after the period following the Title of Source element.

> Sabau, Ana. "The Perils of Ownership: Property and Literature in Nineteenth-Century Mexico." *Mexican Literature in Theory*, edited by Ignacio M. Sánchez Prado, Bloomsbury Academic, 2018, pp. 33–54.
>
> Wollstonecraft, Mary. *A Vindication of the Rights of Woman*. Edited by Deidre Shauna Lynch, Norton Critical Edition, 3rd ed., W. W. Norton, 2009.

[5.46] Multiple contributors in the same role

When a source has three or more contributors in the same role, list the name of the first contributor and follow it with the abbreviation *et al.* ("and others").

> Balibar, Étienne. *Politics and the Other Scene*. Translated by Christine Jones et al., Verso, 2002.

If you are listing more than one contributor in different roles, follow the order of the source or list contributors in order of prominence or importance to the work. But when you are including the author in the Contributor element, as in the example below, always list the author first.

> King, Martha, and Carol Lazzaro-Weis, translators. *"The Signorina" and Other Stories*. By Anna Banti, edited by Lazzaro-Weis, Modern Language Association of America, 2001.

[5.47] Repeated personal names in an entry

When a name appearing in the Contributor element has already been given in full in an entry, shorten it by listing the form that you would use for subsequent references in your prose.

> Bakhtin, M. M. *The Dialogic Imagination: Four Essays*. Edited by Michael Holquist, translated by Caryl Emerson and Holquist, U of Texas P, 1981.

Dung Kai-cheung. *Atlas: The Archaeology of an Imaginary City.* Translated by
Dung et al., Columbia UP, 2012.

If the author's name is included in the title of the work, the author's
name generally does not need to be listed in the Contributor element.

Harrison, James A., editor. *The Complete Works of Edgar Allan Poe.* Vol. 4,
Thomas Y. Crowell, 1902.

[5.48] Version: What It Is

If the source carries a notation indicating that it is a version of a work released in more than one form, identify the version in your entry. Books are
commonly issued in versions called *editions*. A revised version of a book may
be labeled *revised edition* or be numbered (*second edition*, etc.). Versions of
books are sometimes given other descriptions as well.

The Bible. Authorized King James Version, Oxford UP, 1998.
Cheyfitz, Eric. *The Poetics of Imperialism: Translation and Colonization from* The
Tempest *to* Tarzan. Expanded ed., U of Pennsylvania P, 1997.
Miller, Casey, and Kate Swift. *Words and Women.* Updated ed., HarperCollins
Publishers, 1991.
Newcomb, Horace, editor. *Television: The Critical View.* 7th ed., Oxford UP,
2007.

Works in other media, such as websites, apps, musical compositions, and
films, may also appear in versions.

Bible Gateway. Version 42, Bible Gateway / Zondervan, 2016.
Blade Runner. 1982. Directed by Ridley Scott, director's cut, Warner Bros.,
1992.
Minecraft. Java ed. for Mac, 2017.
Schubert, Franz. *Piano Trio in E-flat Major D 929.* Performance by Wiener
Mozart-Trio, unabridged version, Preiser Records, 2011.

You can also use the Version element to specify that you have used an e-book version of a printed book. (An e-book is defined here as a digital book that lacks a URL and that you use software to read on a personal electronic device.)

> Crystal, David. *Making a Point: The Persnickety Story of English Punctuation.* E-book ed., St. Martin's Press, 2015.
>
> *MLA Handbook.* 9th ed., e-book ed., Modern Language Association of America, 2021.

> Including e-book format as a final supplemental element: 5.112.

[5.49] Version: Where to Find It

For books, the edition is usually given on the title page (**fig. 5.48**).

For works in other media, the version may be given on an "About" page or other informational page, on a box or album cover containing the work, or in a booklet accompanying the work (**figs. 5.49, 5.50**).

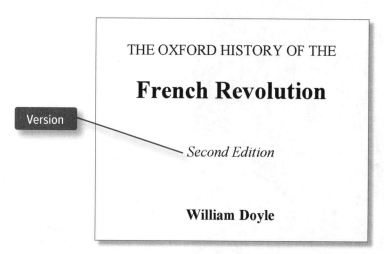

Fig. 5.48. Part of the title page of a book. The edition number is shown on the title page.

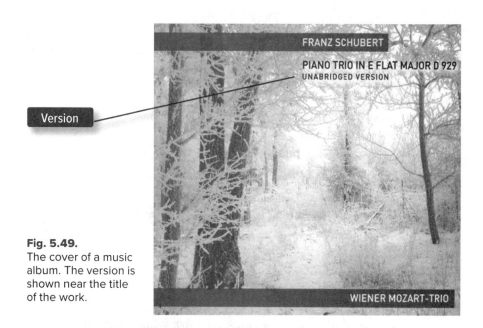

Fig. 5.49.
The cover of a music album. The version is shown near the title of the work.

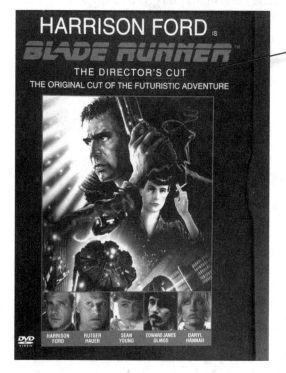

Fig. 5.50.
A box containing a film DVD. The version, director's cut, is shown below the title of the film.

[5.50] Version: How to Style It

When citing versions in the works-cited list, write ordinal numbers with arabic numerals and no superscript (*2nd, 10th*). Abbreviate *revised* (*rev.*) and *edition* (*ed.*).

> Parker, William Riley. *The MLA Style Sheet.* Rev. ed., Modern Language Association of America, 1962.
>
> Rampersad, Arnold. *The Life of Langston Hughes.* 2nd ed., Oxford UP, 2002. 2 vols.

Descriptive terms for versions, such as *expanded ed.*, are written lower-cased, but an initial letter directly following a period is capitalized (**figs. 5.51, 5.52**).

> Cheyfitz, Eric. *The Poetics of Imperialism: Translation and Colonization from* The Tempest *to* Tarzan. Expanded ed., U of Pennsylvania P, 1997.
>
> Rumi, Jalal al-Din. *The Essential Rumi.* Translated by Coleman Barks, with Reynold Nicholson et al., new expanded ed., HarperCollins Publishers, 2010.

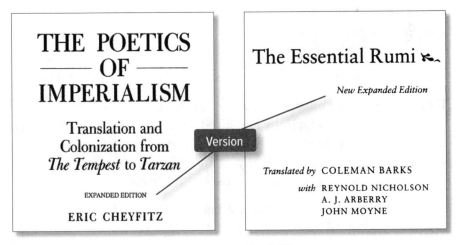

Fig. 5.51.
Part of the title page of a book. The title page lists a named version in all capital letters. In your entry, standardize the capitalization.

Fig. 5.52.
Part of the title page of a book. The title page lists a named version with each word capitalized. In your entry, standardize the capitalization.

Names like Authorized King James Version and Norton Critical Edition are proper nouns (names of unique things) and are therefore capitalized like titles. Such names are not abbreviated.

> *The Bible.* Authorized King James Version, Oxford UP, 1998.
> Wollstonecraft, Mary. *A Vindication of the Rights of Woman.* Edited by Deidre
>   Shauna Lynch, Norton Critical Edition, 3rd ed., W. W. Norton, 2009.

> Common abbreviations used in the works-cited
> list: appendix 1.

[5.51] Number: What It Is

The source you are documenting may be part of a sequence, like a numbered volume, issue, episode, or season. If your source uses a numbering system, include the number in your entry, preceded by a common abbreviation or term that identifies the kind of division the number refers to (see appendix 1 for commonly abbreviated terms).

A text too long to be printed in one book, for instance, is issued in multiple volumes, which may be numbered. If you consult one volume of a numbered multivolume set and each volume is titled the same, indicate the volume number.

> Rampersad, Arnold. *The Life of Langston Hughes.* 2nd ed., vol. 2, Oxford UP, 2002.
> Wellek, René. *A History of Modern Criticism, 1750–1950.* Vol. 5, Yale UP, 1986.

If each volume has a unique title, see the guidance in 5.117.

Journal issues are typically numbered. Some journals use both volume and issue numbers. In general, the issues of a journal published in a single year compose one volume. Usually, volumes are numbered sequentially, while the numbering of issues starts over with 1 in each new volume.

> Young, Vershawn Ashanti. "Should Writers Use They Own English?" *Iowa
>   Journal of Cultural Studies,* vol. 12, no. 1, 2010, pp. 110–18.

Some journals do not use volume numbers but instead number all the issues in sequence.

> Kafka, Ben. "The Demon of Writing: Paperwork, Public Safety, and the Reign
>   of Terror." *Representations,* no. 98, 2007, pp. 1–24.

Comic books are commonly numbered like journals—for instance, with issue numbers.

Clowes, Daniel. *David Boring. Eightball*, no. 19, Fantagraphics, 1998.

The seasons of a television series are typically numbered, as are the episodes in a season. Both numbers should be recorded in the works-cited list if they are available.

"Hush." *Buffy the Vampire Slayer*, created by Joss Whedon, season 4, episode 10, Mutant Enemy, 1999.

[5.52] Number: Where to Find It

The number of a work can be found in various places. The volume number of a book is typically located on its title page (**fig. 5.53**) or cover, as for a graphic narrative (**fig. 5.54**). Volume and issue numbers for journals appear variously on the cover of the journal, in a header or footer to each article, on the landing page of the database where the article was retrieved, or on the cover page of the PDF downloaded from a database (**figs. 5.55–5.57**).

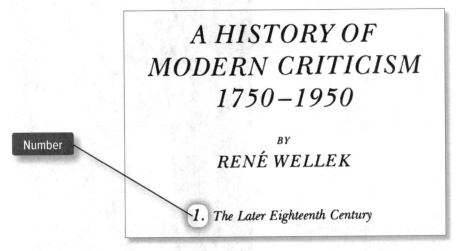

Fig. 5.53. Part of the title page of a book. The title page lists the volume number.

Fig. 5.54.
The cover of a graphic narrative. The cover and spine list the volume number.

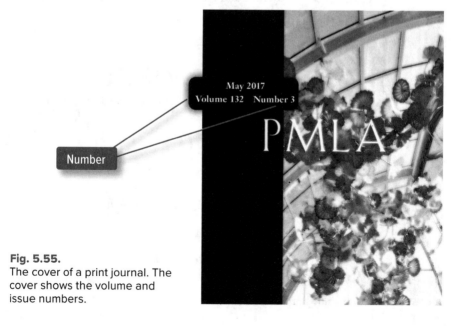

Fig. 5.55.
The cover of a print journal. The cover shows the volume and issue numbers.

Fig. 5.56. The landing page for a journal article in a database. The landing page lists the volume and issue numbers for the article. The format "30.3" refers to volume 30, number 3.

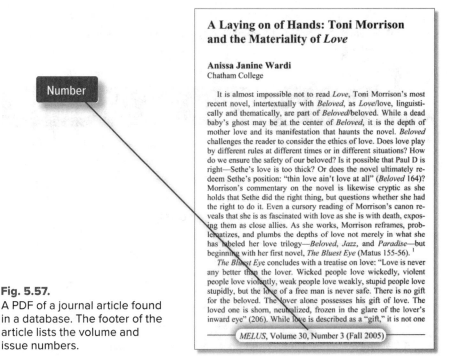

Fig. 5.57.
A PDF of a journal article found in a database. The footer of the article lists the volume and issue numbers.

The season and episode numbers of a television show will usually not be apparent when you are watching the show live; when you are streaming the show, the navigation menu or landing page sometimes indicates this information (**fig. 5.58**). Similarly, podcasts and other audiovisual sources published online or streamed through apps will indicate the number alongside other publication information (**figs. 5.59, 5.60**).

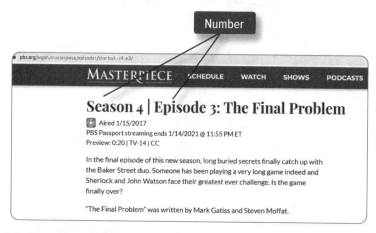

Fig. 5.58. Streamed episode of a television show showing season and episode numbers.

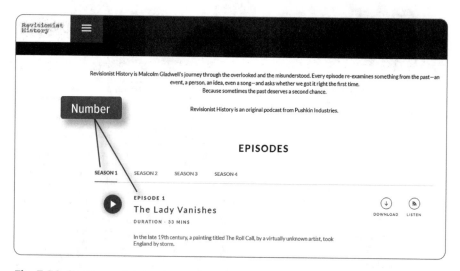

Fig. 5.59. Season and episode numbers from a podcast streamed on the web.

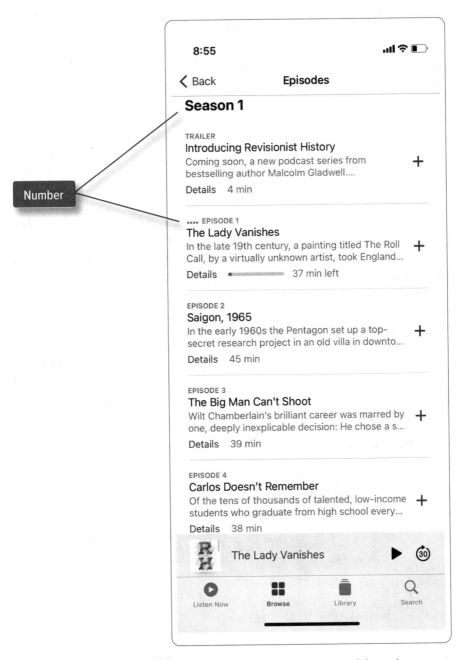

Fig. 5.60. Season and episode numbers from a podcast accessed through an app.

[5.53] Number: How to Style It

Use arabic numerals in the Number element. Convert roman numerals in the source to arabic numerals; numbers that are spelled out in the source should also be rendered as arabic numerals.

In the source	In the Number element
Volume Two	vol. 2
Number XXIX	no. 29

Precede the number with a label, often abbreviated, identifying the type of division it is. Some works require more than one component in the Number element: for example, a journal that publishes issues in volumes and numbers or a television show or podcast that produces numbered episodes and seasons. When your source uses more than one number, show both components, each with an appropriate label. Separate two components in the Number element with a comma.

> Baron, Naomi S. "Redefining Reading: The Impact of Digital Communication Media." *PMLA*, vol. 128, no. 1, Jan. 2013, pp. 193–200.
>
> "Hush." *Buffy the Vampire Slayer*, created by Joss Whedon, season 4, episode 10, Mutant Enemy, 1999.

If the label follows a comma, use an initial lowercase letter. If the label follows a period, use an initial capital letter.

> Dettmar, Kevin, and Jennifer Wicke, editors. *The Longman Anthology of British Literature*. Vol. 2C, Longman, 1999.

> Numbers in prose: 2.126–2.139. Common abbreviations used in the works-cited list: appendix 1.

[5.54] Publisher: What It Is

The publisher is the entity primarily responsible for producing the work or making it available to the public. In the example below, Oxford

University Press is the publisher of the book *"Who Set You Flowin'?" The African-American Migration Narrative.*

> Griffin, Farah Jasmine. *"Who Set You Flowin'?" The African-American Migration Narrative.* Oxford UP, 1996.

The Publisher element may include the following:

- the publisher of a book
- the studio, company, distributor, or network that produced or broadcast a film or television show
- the institution responsible for creating the content of a website
- the theater company that put on a play
- the agency or department that printed or produced a government publication

A publisher's name may be omitted when, by convention, the publisher need not be given or there is no publisher. Examples include the following:

- periodicals (works whose publication is ongoing, like journals, magazines, and newspapers)
- works published by their authors or editors (that is, self-published works)
- websites whose titles are essentially the same as the names of their publishers (e.g., the Modern Language Association publishes a website of the same name)
- websites not involved in producing the works they make available (e.g., a service where users upload and manage their own content, like *WordPress* or *YouTube*, or a platform that aggregates previously published content, like *JSTOR*; if the contents of an aggregated site are organized into a whole, as the contents of *YouTube* and *JSTOR* are, the site is named in the Container element)

Containers: 5.31.

[5.55] Publisher: Where to Find It

[5.56] Books

To determine the publisher of a book, first check the title page (**fig. 5.61**). If no publisher's name appears there, look on the copyright page (in print, usually the reverse of the title page). If the name of the parent company is listed along with one or more divisions (**fig. 5.62**), consult *WorldCat*, the *Library of Congress Catalog*, or another reputable resource to determine which entity has primary responsibility for the work (**fig. 5.63**).

Copublishers: 5.61.

Fig. 5.61.
The title page of a book listing the publisher's name.

Fig. 5.62.
The title page of a book that lists both "Liveright Publishing Corporation" and "W. W. Norton & Company." In your entry, give only the division, Liveright Publishing.

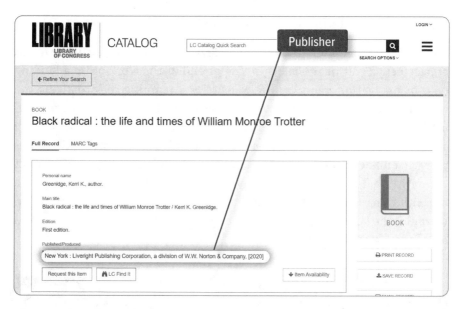

Fig. 5.63. The Library of Congress record for *Black Radical* shows Liveright Publishing as the entity primarily responsible for having published the work. Liveright is named as a division of W. W. Norton.

[5.57] Websites

Websites are published by individuals and various kinds of organizations, including media companies, corporations, governments, museums, libraries, and universities and their departments. The publisher's name can often be found in a copyright notice at the bottom of the home page or on a page that gives information about the site (**fig. 5.64**).

Fig. 5.64. A copyright notice at the bottom of a web page showing the publisher's name, Modern Language Association of America.

[5.58] **Audio and visual media**

Publication information for films and television series can usually be found on a screen credit near the beginning or end of the work or on a landing page or navigation menu on the website or streaming service airing the work (**fig. 5.65**). Films and television shows are often produced and distributed by several companies performing different tasks. When documenting a work in film or television, you should generally cite the production company that made the show or the network that broadcast it (**fig. 5.66**). Select the entity that is most prominently displayed or, if you know that one of the entities had primary overall responsibility for the show, cite that entity. It would not be wrong, however, to cite both a production company and broadcast network as copublishers (see 5.61).

Fig. 5.65.
Publication details
from a television show
on a streaming service.
The information
includes the name of
the network that
broadcast the show.

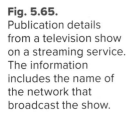

Fig. 5.66. The network that released a television show appears on the screen. The network and production company appear in the show's credits.

[5.59] Publisher: How to Style It

Record the name of the publisher—including its punctuation—as presented in the work you are citing (**figs. 5.67, 5.68**). Exceptions are noted in 5.60–5.66.

> Drabble, Margaret. *The Pattern in the Carpet: A Personal History with Jigsaws.*
>   Houghton Mifflin Harcourt, 2009.
> Ghosh, Amitav. *Gun Island.* Farrar, Straus and Giroux, 2019.

[5.60] Capitalization

Standardize the capitalization of publishers' names according to the guidelines for capitalizing the names of organizations (see 2.87).

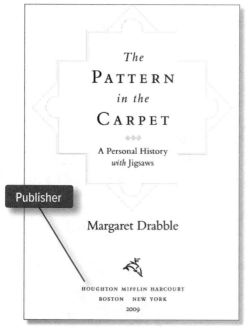

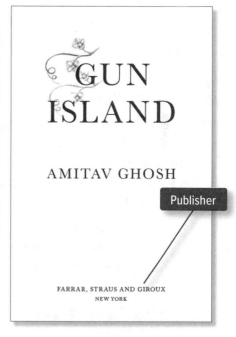

Fig. 5.67.
The title page of a book. Render the publisher's name without punctuation, as it appears in the source.

Fig. 5.68.
The title page of a book. No serial comma is used in the publisher's name, so do not add one in your works-cited-list entry.

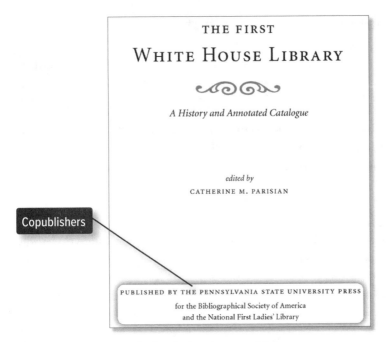

Fig. 5.69. A title page of a book showing copublishers.

[5.61] **Copublishers**

If two or more independent organizations are named in the source and they seem equally responsible for the work (**fig. 5.69**), include each of them in the Publisher element, separating the names with a forward slash (/). But if you know that one of the organizations had primary responsibility for the work, list it alone.

> Parisian, Catherine M., editor. *The First White House Library: A History and Annotated Catalogue.* Pennsylvania State UP / Bibliographic Society of America / National First Ladies' Library, 2010.

[5.62] **Divisions of nongovernment organizations as publishers**

When a work is published by a division of a nongovernment organization, list the entities from largest to smallest and separate them with commas. The following example shows three copublishers—U of Texas, U of Oxford, and the Folger Shakespeare Library—two of which have multiple entities ordered from largest to smallest: U of Texas, Austin, Harry Ransom Center, and U of Oxford, Bodleian Libraries.

> *Manifold Greatness: The Creation and Afterlife of the King James Bible.* U of Texas, Austin, Harry Ransom Center / U of Oxford, Bodleian Libraries / Folger Shakespeare Library, 2016, manifoldgreatness.org.

[5.63] Government agencies as publishers

If the government agency as it appears in the source has many component parts, you can truncate the name, keeping only the name of the government and the primary agency (**fig. 5.70**).

> Durose, Matthew R., et al. *Multistate Criminal History Patterns of Prisoners Released in Thirty States.* U.S. Dept. of Justice, Sept. 2015, www.bjs.gov/content/pub/pdf/mschpprts05.pdf.

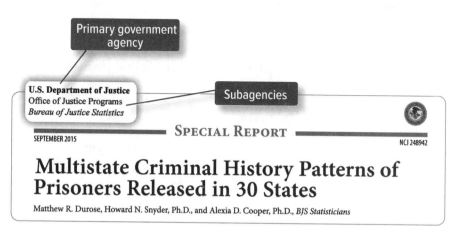

> Standardizing entries for government documents: 5.21. Consolidating entries for government documents: 5.22.

Primary government agency

U.S. Department of Justice
Office of Justice Programs
Bureau of Justice Statistics

Subagencies

SEPTEMBER 2015 ▬▬ SPECIAL REPORT ▬▬ NCJ 248942

Multistate Criminal History Patterns of Prisoners Released in 30 States

Matthew R. Durose, Howard N. Snyder, Ph.D., and Alexia D. Cooper, Ph.D., *BJS Statisticians*

Fig. 5.70. A government report. The agency that released the report is composed of the government (U.S.), primary agency (Department of Justice), and two subagencies (Office of Justice Programs and Bureau of Justice Statistics). The subagencies can be omitted from the Publisher element.

[5.64] Terms omitted from publishers' names

When you give publishers' names in the list of works cited, include the word
Publishing or *Publishers* (e.g., Workman Publishing) or *Pictures* (e.g., Dream-
Works Pictures) if it appears, but omit words denoting the type of legal
corporate entity the publisher is, like *Company (Co.)*, *Corporation (Corp.)*, *Incorporated (Inc.)*, and *Limited (Ltd.)*. Also omit initial articles (*The*).

[5.65] Common abbreviations in publishers' names

If the name of an academic press contains the words *University* and *Press* or
a foreign language equivalent, use the abbreviation *UP* or the equivalent in
the publisher's name.

In the source	In your entry
Oxford University Press	Oxford UP
SUNY Press *or* State University of New York Press	State U of New York P
Presses Universitaires de Grenoble	PU de Grenoble

If the word *University* or a foreign language equivalent does not appear in
the name of the press but the word *Press* does, spell out *Press*.

Academic Press	Feminist Press	New Press
Belknap Press	MIT Press	

[5.66] Ampersands and plus signs in publishers' names

As you do for publishers' names in prose, change an ampersand or a plus
sign to *and* in a publisher's name in your list of works cited.

In the source	In your entry
Farrar & Rinehart	Farrar and Rinehart

[5.67] City of publication

The traditional practice of citing the city where the publisher of a book
was located usually serves little purpose today. There remain a few circumstances in which the city of publication may matter, however.

Books published before 1900 are conventionally associated with their cities of publication. In an entry for a pre-1900 work, you may give the city of publication in place of the publisher. Spell the name of the city according to the source: for example, if the source shows *Firenze*, do not render it as *Florence*.

> Goethe, Johann Wolfgang von. *Conversations of Goethe with Eckermann and Soret*. Translated by John Oxenford, new ed., London, 1875.
>
> Segni, Bernardo, translator. *Rettorica et poetica d'Aristotile*. Firenze, 1549.

A publisher with offices in more than one country may release a novel in two versions—perhaps with different spelling and vocabulary. If you read an unexpected version of a text (such as the British edition when you are in the United States), stating the city of publication will help your readers understand your source. Place the name of the city, followed by a comma, before that of the publisher.

> Rowling, J. K. *Harry Potter and the Philosopher's Stone*. London, Bloomsbury, 1997.

[5.68] Publication Date: What It Is

The Publication Date element tells your reader when the version of the work you are citing was published. In the example below, 2018 is the publication date of the novel *There There*.

> Orange, Tommy. *There There*. Alfred A. Knopf, 2018.

In addition to an actual date of publication, this element may include the following:

- the date of composition for unpublished material (such as letters)
- the date of revision or upload if that is more pertinent (e.g., the date a wiki post was last updated rather than the date it was started)
- the label *forthcoming* for works not yet published
- the date on which a source was viewed or heard firsthand (e.g., the date that you attended the performance of a play)

The Publication Date element may include one or more of the following components:

- a year
- a day and month
- a season
- a time stamp
- a range of dates or years

Works may be associated with more than one publication date. You should record the publication date provided by the version of the source you consult.

[5.69] Publication Date: Where to Find It

[5.70] Books

First, look for the publication date on a book's title page. If the title page lacks a date, check the book's copyright page (usually the reverse of the title page) and use the most recent copyright date listed on it (**fig. 5.71**).

Ellison, Ralph. *Invisible Man*. 2nd Vintage International ed., Random House, 1995.

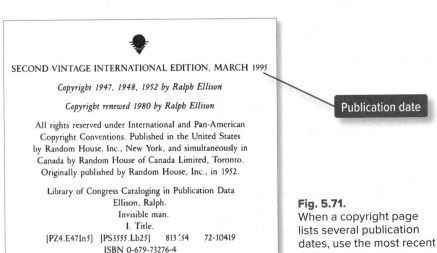

Fig. 5.71.
When a copyright page lists several publication dates, use the most recent date.

Generally avoid taking the publication dates of books from an outside re-source—such as a bibliography, a published review, or an online catalog or bookstore—since the information there may be inaccurate (**fig. 5.72**).

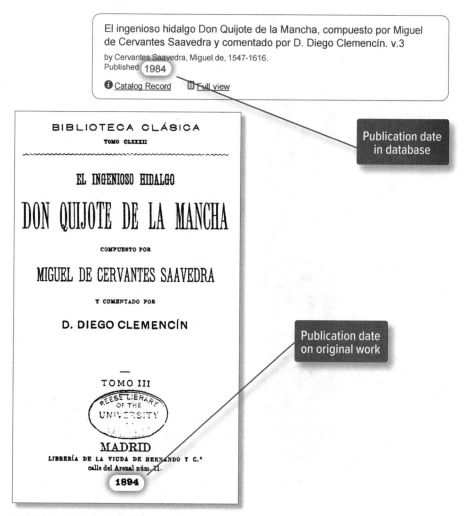

Fig. 5.72. Differing publication dates for a book shown in an online database and on the book's title page. Use the date on the book's title page in the Publication Date element.

[5.71] E-books

The publication date of a book rendered in e-book format can appear on the copyright page, which is usually placed at either the beginning or the end of the e-book (**fig. 5.73**). The copyright page may include a month and a year for an e-book's publication date, but in your entry give the year only.

> Crystal, David. *Making a Point: The Persnickety Story of English Punctuation.* E-book ed., St. Martin's Press, 2015.

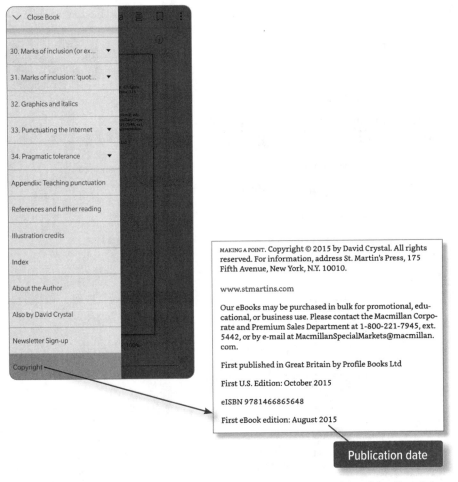

Fig. 5.73. The copyright page at the end of an e-book showing the publication date. When you select the copyright page you can view publication details including the publication date.

[5.72] News articles

The publication date for a print news article generally appears on the front page of the periodical (**fig. 5.74**).

> Hunter, Marjorie. "Johnson Antipoverty Bill Approved in House, 228-190, but Foes Balk Final Vote." *The New York Times,* 8 Aug. 1964, pp. 1+.

The publication date for an online news article is generally near the name of the author and title of the article (**fig. 5.75**).

> Hoekstra, Gordon. "Historic Opportunity to Push Forward Rights and Recognition: Assembly of First Nations." *Vancouver Sun*, 24 July 2018, vancouversun.com/news/local-news/historic-opportunity-to-push-forward-rights-and-recognition-assembly-of-first-nations.

"All the News That's Fit to Print"

The New York Times.

LATE CITY EDITION

NEW YORK, SATURDAY, AUGUST 8, 1964.

TEN CENTS

CONGRESS BACKS PRESIDENT ON SOUTHEAST ASIA MOVES; KHANH SETS STATE OF SIEGE

RESOLUTION WINS

Senate Vote Is 88 to 2 After House Adopts Measure, 416-0

TURKS SEND JETS TO WARN CYPRUS; STRAFING ALLEGED

KENNEDY WEIGHS RACE FOR SENATE; HE SEES WAGNER

JOHNSON ANTIPOVERTY BILL APPROVED IN HOUSE, 228-190, BUT FOES BALK FINAL VOTE

Goldwater Sees a Victory If He Takes 5 Big States

Asserts California, Texas, Illinois, Ohio and Indiana and Smaller 'States Already for Me' Could Beat Johnson

CRITICS REPULSED

Size of Victory Margin Surprises Backers—Action Due Today

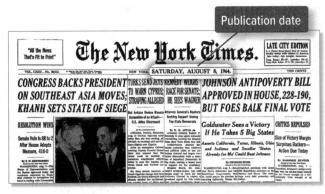

Fig. 5.74.
The front page of a newspaper. The publication date is given below the newspaper name.

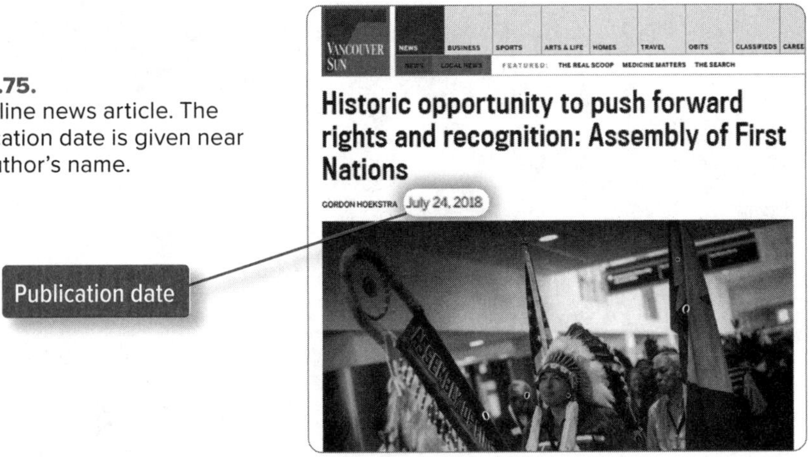

Fig. 5.75.
An online news article. The publication date is given near the author's name.

[5.73] Journal articles

If you are citing a print article, you can usually find the date on the title page of the journal or in the header or footer of the article.

> Riddle, Julie. "Shadow Animals." *The Georgia Review*, vol. 67, no. 3, fall 2013, pp. 424–47.

If you access a digitized version of the print article online, you can usually find the date in the publication information supplied by the website or on a cover sheet accompanying the PDF download (**fig. 5.76**).

> Riddle, Julie. "Shadow Animals." *The Georgia Review*, vol. 67, no. 3, fall 2013, pp. 424–47. *JSTOR*, www.jstor.org/stable/43492249.

If you access an HTML version of the article from the website of the journal, you can usually find the date at the top of the article web page, near the author's name and the article's title. If there is more than one date, use the more specific one (**fig. 5.77**).

> Riddle, Julie. "Shadow Animals." *The Georgia Review*, 8 Sept. 2013, thegeorgiareview.com/posts/shadow-animals.

Note in these examples that the publication date of the print and digitized print versions differs from that of the HTML version. Always provide the date of the version you are citing.

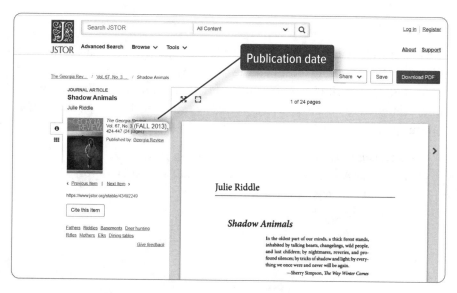

Fig. 5.76. A journal article in an online archive. The publication date is shown on the landing page for the article.

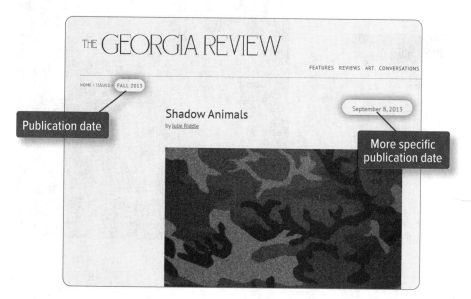

Fig. 5.77. An article from a journal's website. The site lists two dates—fall 2013 and September 8, 2013. The more specific date should be given in the works-cited-list entry.

[5.74] Music

The publication date for an audio recording in a physical format, like a vinyl album or CD, is usually found on the cover, on the album itself, or in an accompanying booklet (**fig. 5.78**). The information provided about a song or album listened to on a website, app, or streaming service can be supplied in various places (**fig. 5.79**).

> Odetta. *One Grain of Sand*. Vanguard Recording Society, 1963. Vinyl.
> Odetta. "Sail Away, Ladies." *One Grain of Sand*, Vanguard Records, 1 Jan. 2006. *Spotify* app.

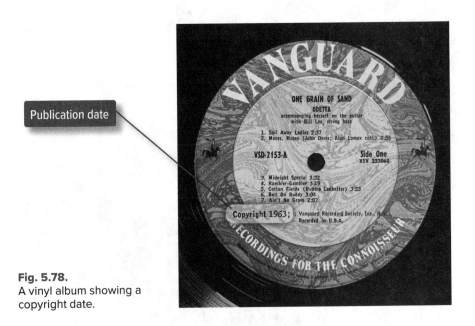

Fig. 5.78.
A vinyl album showing a copyright date.

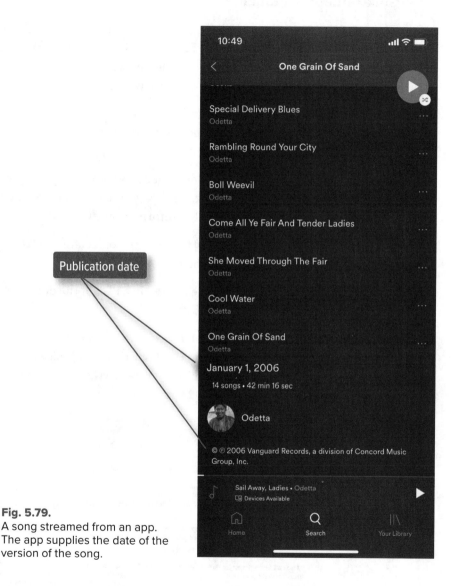

Publication date

Fig. 5.79.
A song streamed from an app.
The app supplies the date of the
version of the song.

[5.75] Government documents

The publication date for a printed government document can generally be found on the title page of the work (**fig. 5.80**). Provide only the year even if your source includes a more specific date, following the principle for publication dates of e-books and other nonperiodical works.

> United States, Congress, House, Permanent Select Committee on Intelligence. *Al-Qaeda: The Many Faces of an Islamist Extremist Threat.* Government Printing Office, 2006.

The publication date for a government document found online might be located on the website itself, either on the same page as the document or on another page indicating the currency of the information (**fig. 5.81**).

> United States, Congress, House, Office of the Law Revision Counsel. *United States Code*, 8 Nov. 2019, uscode.house.gov.

Alternatively, the publication date may be located in a PDF of the document that you download from the site (**fig. 5.82**).

> United States, Congress. Public Law 111-1. *United States Statutes at Large*, vol. 123, part 1, 2011, United States Government Printing Office, pp. 3480–82. *U.S. Government Publishing Office*, www.gpo.gov/fdsys/pkg/STATUTE-123/pdf/STATUTE-123.pdf.

Government authors: 5.20–5.22.

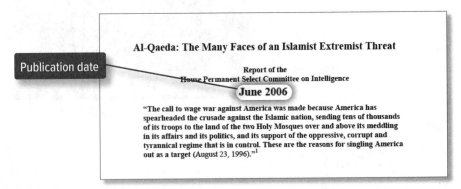

Fig. 5.80. Part of the title page of a printed government document showing the publication date.

Fig. 5.81.
An online government
document. The publication
date is shown on the
"Currency and Updating"
page.

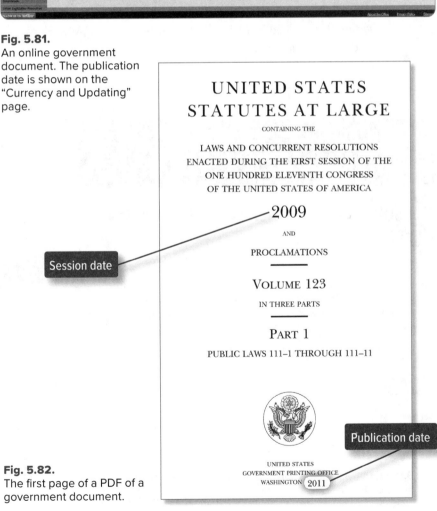

Fig. 5.82.
The first page of a PDF of a
government document.

[5.76] Television episodes

The publication date for a television episode you access through a streaming service or website can generally be found on the page from which you download the episode (**fig. 5.83**).

> "The Final Problem." *Sherlock*, created by Steven Moffat and Mark Gatiss, season 4, episode 3, BBC, 15 Jan. 2017. *Masterpiece*, WGBH Educational Foundation, 2019, www.pbs.org/wgbh/masterpiece/episodes/ sherlock-s4-e3/.
>
> "Manhattan Vigil." Directed by Jean de Segonzac. *Law and Order: Special Victims Unit*, created by Dick Wolf, season 14, episode 5, Wolf Films, 24 Oct. 2012. *Netflix*, www.netflix.com.

Fig. 5.83. A television episode streamed from a website showing the date of the episode.

[5.77] Publication Date: How to Style It

Use the day-month-year style to minimize commas in your entry. Generally provide the most specific date you can find in your source. Thus, include the day, month, and year if your source does.

> Merrill, Stephen. "Teaching through a Pandemic: A Mindset for This Moment." *Edutopia*, 19 Mar. 2020, www.edutopia.org/article/teaching-through-pandemic-mindset-moment.

> Dates: 2.138.

[5.78] Year

If your source presents roman numerals for the year, convert them to arabic numerals (e.g., MCMXCII in the credits of a television show should appear as 1992 in your entry). If a range is needed, style it as you would in prose.

[5.79] Season

Lowercase seasons of the year when they are part of a publication date in the works-cited list, just as you would in prose.

> Belton, John. "Painting by the Numbers: The Digital Intermediate." *Film Quarterly*, vol. 61, no. 3, spring 2008, pp. 58–65.

[5.80] Time

When a time is given and helps define and locate the work, include it. Times should be expressed in whatever form you find them in the source: the twelve-hour-clock form (2:00 p.m.) or the twenty-four-hour-clock form (14:00). Include time zone information when provided and pertinent.

> Max the Pen. Comment on "Why They're Wrong." *The Economist*, 29 Sept. 2016, 6:06 p.m., www.economist.com/node/21707926/comments.

> Abbreviating time zones: 2.138.

[5.81] Date range

When documenting a nonperiodical work that is ongoing—namely, a multi-volume set of books—leave a space after the en dash (or hyphen, if used instead) that follows the beginning date.

> Caro, Robert A. *The Years of Lyndon Johnson.* Vintage Books, 1982– .

Do not use this technique for websites, journals, television or streaming series, and other works published on an episodic or periodic basis.

For works with a clear beginning and end date, such as a museum exhibition, a completed date range may be provided in the Publication Date element. (If you are citing a live performance, however, cite the specific date you attended it, because performances can vary during the run of a play or a concert tour, for example.)

> Kwang Young Chun. *Aggregations.* 16 Nov. 2018–28 July 2019, Brooklyn Museum, New York City.

[5.82] Approximate date given in source

If your source or the archive, museum, or other institution holding it gives an approximate date (e.g., *circa 1400–10* or *early 15th century*), record the date as given, but spell out phrases normally spelled out in prose, like *fifteenth century*, even if numerals are given in the source. Capitalize or lowercase the term just as you would in prose, unless a period precedes it, in which case capitalize the term.

> Chaucer, Geoffrey. *The Canterbury Tales.* Circa 1400–10, British Library, London, Harley MS 7334.
> ———. *The Canterbury Tales.* Early fifteenth century, U of Oxford, Bodleian Libraries, Corpus Christi College MS 198.

[5.83] Uncertain date given in source

If your source or the institution holding it indicates that the date is uncertain (e.g., *probably 1870, possibly 1870, 1870?*), list the date followed by a question mark.

Dickinson, Emily. "Distance - is not the Realm of Fox." 1870?, Pierpont Morgan Library, New York City. Manuscript.

> Citing physical locations: 5.99.
> Supplied publication information: 5.122.

[5.84] Location: What It Is

How to specify a work's location depends on the format of the work (**fig. 5.84**). For paginated print or similar fixed-format works (like PDFs) that are contained in another work (e.g., an essay in a print anthology or the PDF of an article in a journal), the location is the page range.

Copeland, Edward. "Money." *The Cambridge Companion to Jane Austen*, edited by Copeland and Juliet McMaster, Cambridge UP, 1997, pp. 131–48.
Soyinka, Wole. "Twice Bitten: The Fate of Africa's Culture Producers." *PMLA*, vol. 105, no. 1, Jan. 1990, pp. 110–20.

In rare cases, additional information may need to be included with the page numbers so that the work can be found. In the example below, for a print newspaper, the section title is included in the Location element along with the page number. Include a section name only if it is needed to locate the work.

Akabas, Shoshana. Letter. *The New York Times*, 5 Apr. 2020, Sunday Review sec., p. 8.

Format	Location	Examples
Paginated print or similar fixed-format works contained in another work	Page range	Essay in a print anthology; PDF of an article in a journal
Online works	DOI, permalink, or URL	Article on a news website; essay in journal
Unique or ephemeral works viewed or heard firsthand	Place where the work was viewed or heard	Performance; lecture; artwork; manuscript in an archive
Physical media other than paginated print works	Numbering system provided by the source	Numbered disc in a DVD set

Fig. 5.84. Source formats and their locations.

For online works, the location, in order of preference, is the DOI, permalink, or URL. A DOI (digital object identifier) is an identifier permanently assigned to a source by the publisher. DOIs are more reliable locators than URLs (uniform resource locators), the web addresses that appear in your browser window, because DOIs remain attached to their sources even if the URLs change, and DOIs are often more concise. When a DOI is available and specified by the publisher, include it in the works-cited-list entry instead of a URL or permalink (a URL intended to be permanent). Although URLs, even when obsolete or leading to gated material, can provide readers with information about where the work was found and can link your reader directly to your sources when presented in a digital project, they have disadvantages: they cannot be clicked on in print, often clutter the works-cited list, and do not always offer access to the work being cited. Therefore, in deciding when to include a URL, follow the preferences of your instructor, institution, or publisher (see also 5.96 for guidance on shortening URLs).

For unique or ephemeral works viewed or heard firsthand—like a performance, lecture, artwork, or manuscript in an archive—the location is the place where the work was viewed or heard.

For physical media other than paginated print works, use the numbering system provided by the source (e.g., the location of a television episode in a DVD set may be indicated by the disc number). Do not include a numbering system if it is specific to your version of the source, as is the case for a location number for an e-book read on a personal device.

Page numbers do not need to be specified in your works-cited-list entry for a paginated work, like a novel, that is not contained in another work—even when that work is digitized on a website. For example, the Location element for a print copy of *Pride and Prejudice* is left blank; for a copy digitized by *HathiTrust Digital Library*, the Location element lists the permalink.

Austen, Jane. *Pride and Prejudice*. Harcourt, Brace and World, 1962.

Austen, Jane. *Pride and Prejudice*. Harcourt, Brace and World, 1962. *HathiTrust Digital Library*, hdl.handle.net/2027/osu.32435004226296.

A library can sometimes be the location of a rare work seen or heard firsthand, because archives and special collections curate, assess, and preserve unique collections of works like manuscripts, letters, and other media. But a library should not be placed in the Location element for a published or widely available work borrowed from it. Similarly, the online store where you purchased an e-book should not appear in the Location element.

[5.85] Location: Where to Find It

[5.86] Page numbers

Check the first and last page number in the work itself. Do not rely on a contents listing at the beginning of the work or online (**fig. 5.85**).

[5.87] Online works

URLs should be copied directly from the address bar in a browser window (**fig. 5.86**), as should DOIs and permalinks when you use them to directly access a work. Even if you initially access a work through a URL, when the publisher indicates (typically on the landing page of the work) that a DOI or permalink is associated with the work, list it in your entry instead (**figs. 5.87, 5.88**).

[5.88] Location: How to Style It

[5.89] Inclusive pages

When a work contained in another work is paginated, provide the entire page range for the contained work, not just the page or pages you used from the work. If the contained work appears on a single page and the work is paginated, provide the page number. Style page numbers and ranges just as you would in prose.

Boggs, Colleen Glenney. "Public Reading and the Civil War Draft Lottery." *American Periodicals*, vol. 26, no. 2, 2016, pp. 149–66.

> Number ranges: 2.139.

132.3

theories and
methodologies

"The Figure in the Carpet"

OF FRANCO MORETTI'S MASTERWORKS OF LITERARY HISTORY AND
THEORY, WHY IS IT THE LOOSELY ASSEMBLED COLLECTION OF OCCA-
sional pieces *Distant Reading* that has captured the literary critical
spotlight? Why now, just when enrollments in the humanities are
plummeting, new technologies for storing and distributing information are revolutionizing interpersonal communication and scientific
methods, and *global* is well on its way to replacing *interdisciplinary*
as the descriptor favored by university administrators? Moretti is not
alone in attempting to reconfigure a discipline that tends to favor the
singular text and national literary traditions for a generation of students who apparently could not care less about either. In his effort
to adapt literary history and form to the conditions of globalization
that make them seem irrelevant—to start instead considering how certain
forms of literature made the quantum leap from nation to world and
what formal changes they underwent in doing so. This project he
warns, will require us to "unlearn" how to read a literary text and
to question the assumption that "world literature" is an object to be
known: "We must think of it as a problem that asks for a new critical
method" (46). He famously exposes this problem by staging various
encounters between literary form and quantitative analysis.

If it was already hard to master a single literary tradition, not to
mention the three national literatures that originally constituted the
object of comparative literature, any effort to assemble an archive of
all the modern literatures produced throughout the world is obviously doomed from the start. No matter how much information one
or several researchers can master, the task will eventually surpass
their respective abilities and lifetimes. They will have to fall back on
secondary sources, and the archive thus assembled will be no more
than "a patchwork of other people's research, *without a single direct
textual reading*" (46). Never mind that this research will necessarily
attend to certain literary texts more than others, leaving "the great
unread" (a term Moretti borrows from Margaret Cohen) to languish

NANCY ARMSTRONG AND
WARREN MONTAG

NANCY ARMSTRONG is Gilbert, Louis,
and Edward Lehrman Professor of Trin-
ity College at Duke University and editor
of the journal *Novel: A Forum on Fiction*.
Her most recent books include *How Novels Think: The Limits of Individualism,
1719–1900* (Columbia UP, 2005) and *Novels in the Time of Democratic Writing* (U of
Pennsylvania P, 2017).

WARREN MONTAG is the Brown Family Professor of Literature at Occidental
College in Los Angeles. His most recent
books include the collection (coedited
with Hanan Elsayed) *Balibar and the Citi-
zen Subject* (Edinburgh UP, 2017), *Althusser
and His Contemporaries* (Duke UP, 2013),
and *The Other Adam Smith* (Stanford UP,
2014). Montag is also the editor of *Décal-
ages*, a journal on Althusser and his circle,
and translator of Étienne Balibar's *Identity
and Difference: John Locke and the Inven-
tion of Consciousness* (Verso, 2013).

PMLA 132.3 (2017), published by the Modern Language Association of America

613

Location

132.3

Works Cited

Althusser, Louis, and Étienne Balibar. *Reading Capital*.
  Translated by Ben Brewster, New Left Books, 1970.
Augustine. *De doctrina Christiana*. Edited and translated
  by R. P. H. Green, Oxford UP, 1995.
Best, Stephen, and Sharon Marcus. "Surface Reading: An
  Introduction." *Representations*, vol. 108, no. 1, 2009,
  pp. 1–21.
Braudel, Fernand. *The Perspective of the World*. Trans-
  lated by Siân Reynolds, U of California P, 1992. Vol. 3

of *Civilization and Capitalism: Fifteenth–Eighteenth
  Century*.
Casanova, Pascale. *The World Republic of Letters*.
  Translated by M. B. Debevoise, Harvard UP, 2004.
Macherey, Pierre. *A Theory of Literary Production*. Trans-
  lated by Geoffrey Wall, Routledge and Kegan Paul,
  1978.
Moretti, Franco. *Distant Reading*. Verso, 2013.
Schwarz, Roberto. "Former Colonies: Local or Univer-
  sal?" *Novel: A Forum on Fiction*, vol. 43, no. 1, 2010,
  pp. 100–06.

theories and methodologies

Fig. 5.85. The first and last pages of an essay in a journal.

Fig. 5.86. A post on a website. Copy the URL directly from the address bar in the browser window.

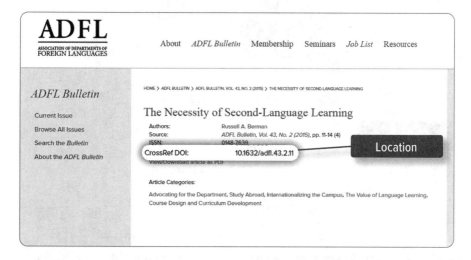

Fig. 5.87. The landing page for a journal article on a website. The page shows the DOI for the article.

Fig. 5.88. A web page that provides a permalink, a stable URL that the publisher promises not to change.

[5.90] Descriptive label before page numbers

Precede a page number or range with the abbreviation *pp.* (for *pages*) and a single page number with *p.* (for *page*).

> Adichie, Chimamanda Ngozi. "On Monday of Last Week." *The Thing around Your Neck*, by Adichie, Alfred A. Knopf, 2009, pp. 74–94.
>
> Marvell, Andrew. "The Mower's Song." *The Norton Anthology of English Literature*, M. H. Abrams, general editor, 4th ed., vol. 1, W. W. Norton, 1979, p. 1368.

[5.91] Numerals for page numbers

Use the same numeric symbols for page numbers that your source does (e.g., arabic, roman, alphanumeric) and the same case, whether lowercase roman numerals (*i, ii, iii*), uppercase roman numerals (*I, II, III*), or upper- or lowercase alphabetic letters (*A1, 89d*).

> Felstiner, John. Preface. *Selected Poems and Prose of Paul Celan*, translated by Felstiner, W. W. Norton, 2001, pp. xix–xxxvi.
>
> Magra, Iliana, and Andrea Zaratemay. "Hikers' Love of a Rarity in the Andes Takes a Toll." *The New York Times*, 3 May 2018, p. A7.
>
> Richards, Marla. "Digital Literacy Lessons for High School Students." *Teaching Today*, 8 Mar. 2020, pp. A11–A12.
>
> Woolf, Virginia. "How Should One Read a Book?" *The Essays of Virginia Woolf, 1929–1932*, edited by Stuart N. Clarke, Houghton Mifflin Harcourt, 2009, pp. 572–93. Vol. 5 of *The Essays of Virginia Woolf*.

[5.92] Plus sign with page number

If a work in a periodical (journal, magazine, newspaper) is not printed on consecutive pages—if, for example, after beginning on page 1 it skips to page 10—include only the first page number and a plus sign, leaving no intervening space.

> Williams, Joy. "Rogue Territory." *The New York Times Book Review*, 9 Nov. 2014, pp. 1+.

[5.93] **DOIs**

A DOI is a string of numbers and letters that typically begins with the number 10 (**fig. 5.89**). If the DOI is not preceded by http:// or https:// in your source, precede the DOI in your entry with the following:

https://doi.org/

Doing so will allow others to call up the source in a browser window.

> Bockelman, Brian. "Buenos Aires *Bohème*: Argentina and the Transatlantic Bohemian Renaissance, 1890–1910." *Modernism/Modernity*, vol. 23, no. 1, Jan. 2016, pp. 37–63. *Project Muse*, https://doi.org/10.1353/mod.2016.0011.

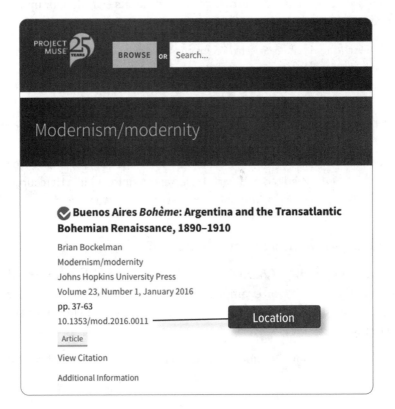

Fig. 5.89. A DOI on the landing page for a journal article.

[5.94] Permalinks

If your source offers a URL that it identifies as stable, permanent, or persistent (sometimes called a *permalink*), use it in your entry instead of the URL that appears in your browser, and copy it directly from the source (see **fig. 5.88**).

[5.95] URLs

URLs have a few basic components (**fig. 5.90**):

- the protocol (what precedes //)
- the double forward slash
- the host (which encompasses the domain—like *www*)
- the path

In addition, sometimes file-specific information or a query string is appended.

> https://style.mla.org/files/2016/04/practice-template.pdf
>
> https://www.mla.org/search/?query=pmla

When including a URL, copy it in full from your browser. Omit a query string when possible. Some URLs display *www* but others do not.

[5.96] *Truncating*

You can usually omit *http://* or *https://* from URLs unless you want to hyperlink them and are working in a software program that does not allow

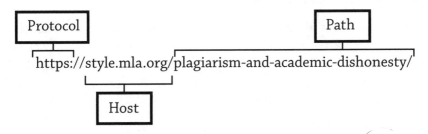

Fig. 5.90. The components of a URL.

hyperlinking without the protocol (but include *https://* with DOIs). In professionally designed and typeset fixed-format works like print and PDF, the protocol can always be omitted.

If a URL runs more than three full lines or is longer than the rest of the entry, truncate it. When truncating, always retain at least the host. For example, the following URL runs more than three full lines:

go.galegroup.com/ps/retrieve.do?sort=RELEVANCE&docType=Journal+article
&tabID=T003&prodId=MLA&searchId=R1&resultListType=RESULT_LIST&
searchType=BasicSearchForm&contentSegment=&currentPosition=3&search
ResultsType=SingleTab&inPS=true&userGroupName=mla&docId=GALE%
7CN2810522710&contentSet=GALE%7CN2810522710

It could be shortened to the following:

go.galegroup.com/ps

Avoid citing URLs produced by shortening services (like bit.ly), since they obfuscate information when not clickable (as in a print paper) and since such a URL may stop working if the service that produced it disappears.

[5.97] *Breaking*

When giving a URL in your paper, never introduce a hyphen or space in it (turn off your word processing software's automatic hyphenation feature). Do not worry about uneven line breaks: the accurate display of the URL is more important than its appearance. Professionally typeset publications in fixed formats, like print or PDF, normally follow rigorous conventions for breaking URLs to avoid ambiguity or uneven line breaks.

[5.98] *Including terminal slash*

Whether omitting the terminal slash—a forward slash at the end of a URL—will disable the link depends on how the URL is set up. The most cautious approach for writers is to test the link with and without the slash and use the shortest form that works (i.e., use the slash-free URL if it works). When editing a work, do not delete or add a slash; use what the writer has provided.

[5.99] Physical locations and events

For a physical object or event that you experienced firsthand (not in a reproduction), such as a work of art in a museum, an artifact in an archive, a conference presentation, or a performance, give the name of the institution and a sufficient amount of information to identify where it is located—whether the city alone, city and state, or city and country.

> Alÿs, Francis. *Cuando la fe mueve montañas.* 11 Apr. 2002, Lima, Peru.
>
> Bhatia, Rafiq. Concert. 10 Feb. 2018, Mass MOCA, North Adams.
>
> Knapp, David. *Beneath the Smokestacks.* 15 July–29 Nov. 2020, Springfield Museum of Art, Springfield, Ohio.
>
> Rankine, Claudia. Interview. By Synne Rifbjerg, 23 Aug. 2019, Louisiana Literature Festival, Louisiana Museum of Modern Art, Humlebaek, Denmark.

Other information may be used to identify archival materials held in a physical location—for example, a shelf mark (in the example below, Harley MS 7334). Such information should generally be recorded exactly as found.

> Chaucer, Geoffrey. *The Canterbury Tales.* Circa 1400–10, British Library, London, Harley MS 7334.

[5.100] The Three Most Common Types of Entries

Below are examples showing the filled-out template and corresponding works-cited-list entry for the three most common types of entries: works that use one container, works that use two containers, and works that are self-contained.

To create an entry, assess the work you are citing and determine whether the elements apply to it. List each pertinent element in the order it appears on the template, followed by the punctuation shown. Omit an element that is absent from or not relevant to the work being documented. The exception is Title of Source: because you must identify each work that you cite, substitute a description for a work that lacks a title.

[5.101] Works in One Container

The works listed in the Title of Source element in **figures 5.91–5.93** are contained in another work.

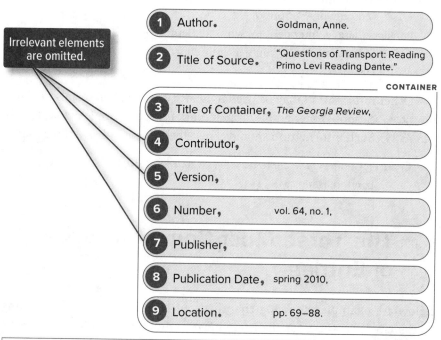

Goldman, Anne. "Questions of Transport: Reading Primo Levi Reading Dante." *The Georgia Review*, vol. 64, no. 1, spring 2010, pp. 69–88.

Fig. 5.91. A work in one container: an article from a print journal. The article is contained in the journal.

Fig. 5.92.
A work in one container: an episode from a series watched on broadcast television. The series contains the episode.

1. Author.
2. Title of Source. "I Don't Want to Be Free."

CONTAINER

3. Title of Container, *Killing Eve*,
4. Contributor,
5. Version,
6. Number, season 1, episode 7,
7. Publisher, BBC America
8. Publication Date, 20 May 2018.
9. Location.

> If the episode was watched on the original air date, the full date can be given. Otherwise, the year alone is sufficient.

"I Don't Want to Be Free." *Killing Eve*, season 1, episode 7, BBC America, 20 May 2018.

Fig. 5.93.
A work in one container: a short story contained in a multivolume edition.

1. Author. Poe, Edgar Allan.
2. Title of Source. "The Masque of the Red Death."

CONTAINER

3. Title of Container, *The Complete Works of Edgar Allan Poe*,
4. Contributor, edited by James A. Harrison,
5. Version,
6. Number, vol. 4,
7. Publisher, Thomas Y. Crowell,
8. Publication Date, 1902,
9. Location. pp. 250–58.

> Contributors' names are preceded by a label.

Poe, Edgar Allan. "The Masque of the Red Death." *The Complete Works of Edgar Allan Poe*, edited by James A. Harrison, vol. 4, Thomas Y. Crowell, 1902, pp. 250–58.

[5.102] **Works in Two Containers**

Because a work containing another work can itself be contained in a work—such as an article published in a journal and contained in a database—sometimes you will need to use two containers. Fill out the template again from Title of Container to Location, listing all elements that apply to the second container (**fig. 5.94**). The works listed in the Title of Source element in **figures 5.95–5.97** are contained in another work, which is itself contained in a work.

Fig. 5.94.
The MLA template of core elements with two containers.

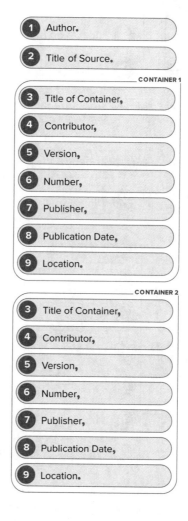

1 Author.

2 Title of Source.

CONTAINER 1

3 Title of Container,

4 Contributor,

5 Version,

6 Number,

7 Publisher,

8 Publication Date,

9 Location.

CONTAINER 2

3 Title of Container,

4 Contributor,

5 Version,

6 Number,

7 Publisher,

8 Publication Date,

9 Location.

Fig. 5.95.
A work in two containers: an article from a print journal in an online database. The database contains the journal, which in turn contains the article.

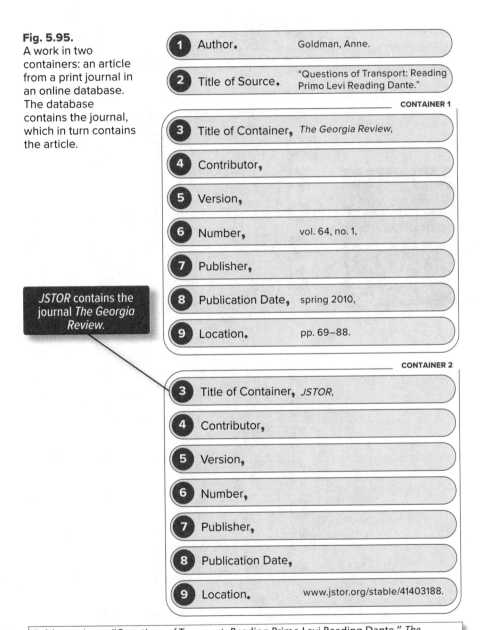

1. Author.   Goldman, Anne.

2. Title of Source.   "Questions of Transport: Reading Primo Levi Reading Dante."

CONTAINER 1

3. Title of Container,   *The Georgia Review,*

4. Contributor,

5. Version,

6. Number,   vol. 64, no. 1,

7. Publisher,

8. Publication Date,   spring 2010,

9. Location.   pp. 69–88.

JSTOR contains the journal *The Georgia Review.*

CONTAINER 2

3. Title of Container,   *JSTOR,*

4. Contributor,

5. Version,

6. Number,

7. Publisher,

8. Publication Date,

9. Location.   www.jstor.org/stable/41403188.

Goldman, Anne. "Questions of Transport: Reading Primo Levi Reading Dante." *The Georgia Review,* vol. 64, no. 1, spring 2010, pp. 69–88. *JSTOR,* www.jstor.org/stable/41403188.

Fig. 5.96.
A work in two containers: an episode of a television series watched on a streaming service. The streaming service contains the series.

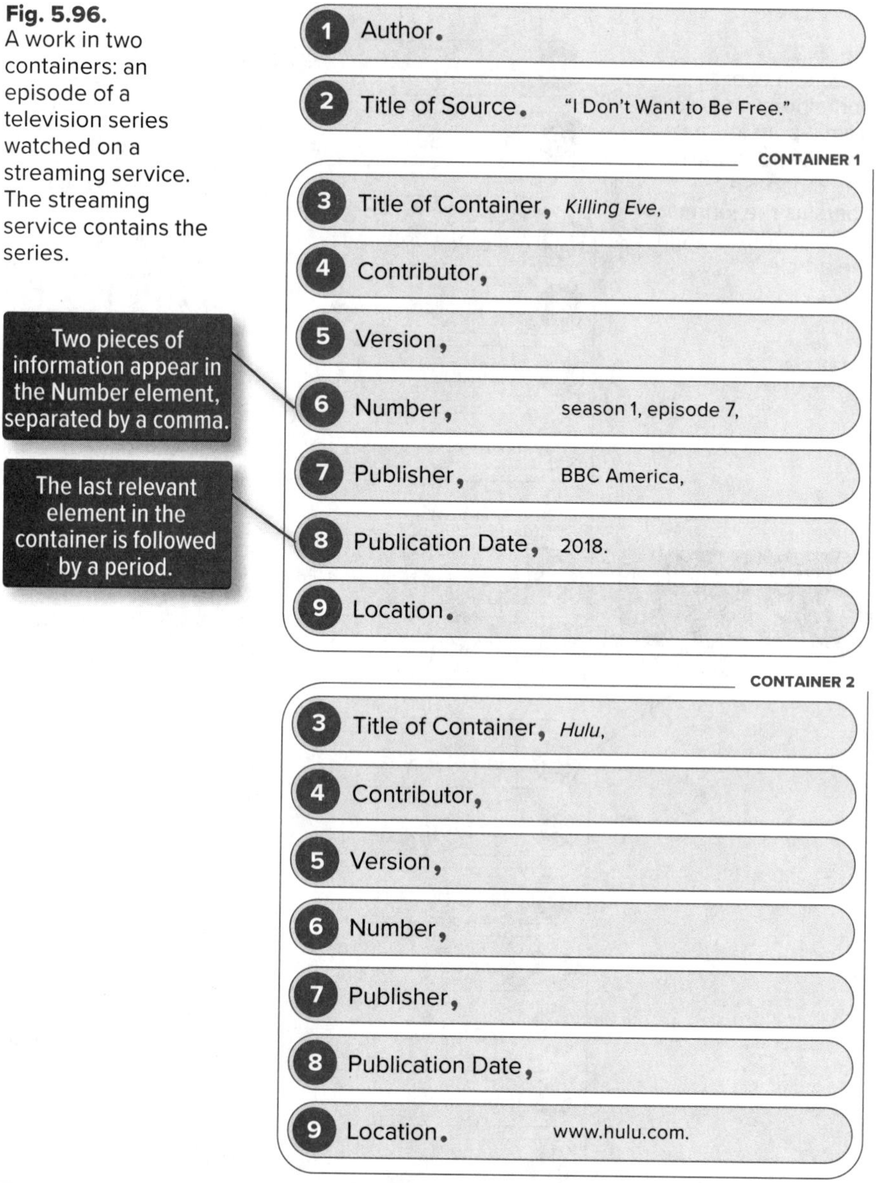

1 Author.

2 Title of Source.   "I Don't Want to Be Free."

CONTAINER 1

3 Title of Container, *Killing Eve,*

4 Contributor,

5 Version,

6 Number,   season 1, episode 7,

7 Publisher,   BBC America,

8 Publication Date,   2018.

9 Location.

Two pieces of information appear in the Number element, separated by a comma.

The last relevant element in the container is followed by a period.

CONTAINER 2

3 Title of Container, *Hulu,*

4 Contributor,

5 Version,

6 Number,

7 Publisher,

8 Publication Date,

9 Location.   www.hulu.com.

"I Don't Want to Be Free." *Killing Eve,* season 1, episode 7, BBC America, 2018. *Hulu,* www .hulu.com.

Fig. 5.97.
A work in two containers: a short story from a multivolume work contained on a website.

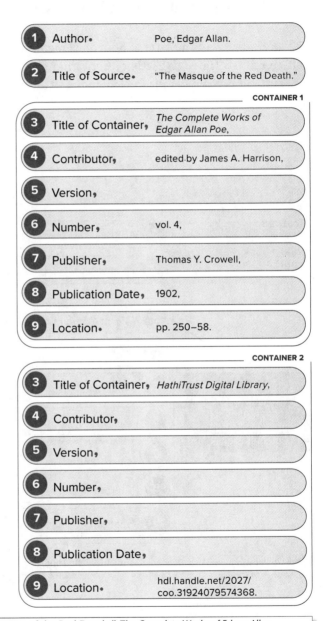

1. Author. Poe, Edgar Allan.
2. Title of Source. "The Masque of the Red Death."

CONTAINER 1

3. Title of Container, *The Complete Works of Edgar Allan Poe,*
4. Contributor, edited by James A. Harrison,
5. Version,
6. Number, vol. 4,
7. Publisher, Thomas Y. Crowell,
8. Publication Date, 1902,
9. Location. pp. 250–58.

CONTAINER 2

3. Title of Container, *HathiTrust Digital Library,*
4. Contributor,
5. Version,
6. Number,
7. Publisher,
8. Publication Date,
9. Location. hdl.handle.net/2027/ coo.31924079574368.

Poe, Edgar Allan. "The Masque of the Red Death." *The Complete Works of Edgar Allan Poe*, edited by James A. Harrison, vol. 4, Thomas Y. Crowell, 1902, pp. 250–58. *HathiTrust Digital Library*, hdl.handle.net/2027/coo.31924079574368.

[5.103] **Works That Are Self-Contained**

The works listed in the Title of Source element in **figures 5.98–5.101** are self-contained. Thus, the Title of Container element is left blank, but any relevant publication details in elements 4–9 are provided.

Fig. 5.98.
A self-contained work: a book read in print.

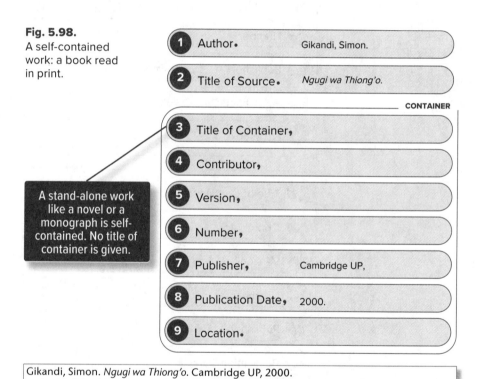

Gikandi, Simon. *Ngugi wa Thiong'o.* Cambridge UP, 2000.

Fig. 5.99.
A self-contained work: a movie watched in a theater.

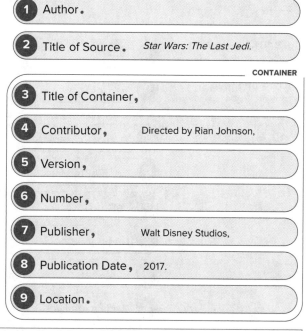

1 Author.

2 Title of Source. *Star Wars: The Last Jedi.*

CONTAINER

3 Title of Container,

4 Contributor, Directed by Rian Johnson,

5 Version,

6 Number,

7 Publisher, Walt Disney Studios,

8 Publication Date, 2017.

9 Location.

Star Wars: The Last Jedi. Directed by Rian Johnson, Walt Disney Studios, 2017.

Fig. 5.100.
A self-contained work: a manuscript read in person.

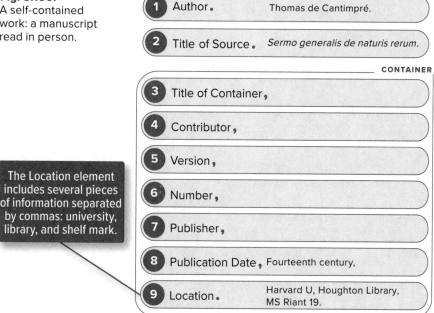

1 Author. Thomas de Cantimpré.

2 Title of Source. *Sermo generalis de naturis rerum.*

CONTAINER

3 Title of Container,

4 Contributor,

5 Version,

6 Number,

The Location element includes several pieces of information separated by commas: university, library, and shelf mark.

7 Publisher,

8 Publication Date, Fourteenth century,

9 Location. Harvard U, Houghton Library, MS Riant 19.

Thomas de Cantimpré. *Sermo generalis de naturis rerum.* Fourteenth century, Harvard U, Houghton Library, MS Riant 19.

Fig. 5.101.
A self-contained
work: a performance
of a play attended
in person.

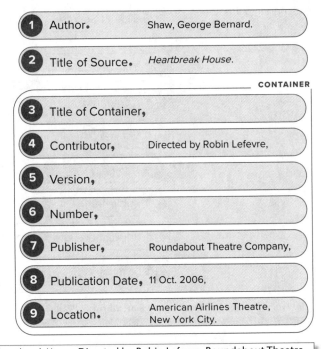

CONTAINER

1. Author. — Shaw, George Bernard.
2. Title of Source. — *Heartbreak House.*
3. Title of Container,
4. Contributor, — Directed by Robin Lefevre,
5. Version,
6. Number,
7. Publisher, — Roundabout Theatre Company,
8. Publication Date, — 11 Oct. 2006,
9. Location. — American Airlines Theatre, New York City.

Shaw, George Bernard. *Heartbreak House.* Directed by Robin Lefevre, Roundabout Theatre Company, 11 Oct. 2006, American Airlines Theatre, New York City.

[5.104] One Work Cited Different Ways

When, where, and how you access a work will dictate the publication information you supply in your entry. You should record the publication information given by the version of the source you consult. The example below, for a journal article first published online ahead of the full journal issue and, later, as part of an issue, shows how the same work can be cited in different ways depending on the version accessed because different publication information is supplied by the source (e.g., date of publication, page numbers, volume and issue numbers).

Published ahead of Issue Online, in HTML

Groot Kormelink, Tim, and Irene Costera Meijer. "Material and Sensory Dimensions of Everyday News Use." *Media, Culture, and Society*, 5 Feb. 2019. *Sage Journals*, https://doi.org/10.1177/0163443718810910.

Published in a Print Issue

Groot Kormelink, Tim, and Irene Costera Meijer. "Material and Sensory Dimensions of Everyday News Use." *Media, Culture, and Society*, vol. 41, no. 5, 1 July 2019, pp. 637–53.

Published in an Issue Online, in HTML

Groot Kormelink, Tim, and Irene Costera Meijer. "Material and Sensory Dimensions of Everyday News Use." *Media, Culture, and Society*, vol. 41, no. 5, 1 July 2019. *Sage Journals*, https://doi.org/10.1177/01634437 18810910.

Published in an Issue Online, in PDF

Groot Kormelink, Tim, and Irene Costera Meijer. "Material and Sensory Dimensions of Everyday News Use." *Media, Culture, and Society*, vol. 41, no. 5, 1 July 2019, pp. 637–53. *Sage Journals*, https://doi .org/10.1177/0163443718810910.

[5.105] Supplemental Elements

Works-cited-list entries in MLA style are based on the template of core elements. Each element should generally be included in your works-cited-list entry when relevant to the work you are documenting. Sometimes, however, you may need or want to supply additional information about a work. You can do so by adding supplemental elements to the template.

A supplemental element should be inserted after the Title of Source element if it does not pertain to the entry as a whole. Otherwise, it should be inserted at the end of the entry (**fig. 5.102**). Exceptionally, it may be placed between containers if it applies only to the preceding container and not to the container following it.

A period should be placed after a supplemental element. As with core elements, you can include more than one item of information as a supplemental element. List them in whatever order you prefer and separate them with a comma.

[5.106] **Placement after Title of Source**

Three pieces of information—contributors other than an author, the original publication date, and generically labeled sections—are the most likely to appear in the middle supplemental element.

[5.107] **Contributor**

Use the middle supplemental element to identify a contributor who played an important role in a work contained in another work. While in some cases the

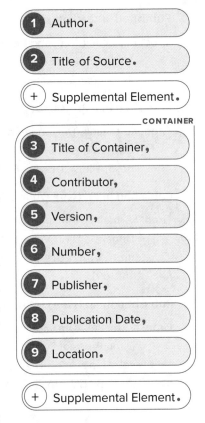

Fig. 5.102.
Placement of supplemental elements in the template of core elements.

information you include as a supplemental element is optional, in other cases the information is necessary for defining a work. A contributor given in this position provides additional information that applies not to the whole container but to the information in the Author and Title of Source elements. In the examples below, the insertion of the contributors' roles and names after the Title of Source element tells your reader that Leila El Khalidi and Christopher Tingley translated only *The Singing of the Stars*, not all the other works in *Short Arabic Plays*, and that Diri I. Teilanyo conducted the interview "English Is the Hero."

> Fagih, Ahmed Ibrahim al-. *The Singing of the Stars*. Translated by Leila El Khalidi and Christopher Tingley. *Short Arabic Plays: An Anthology*, edited by Salma Khadra Jayyusi, Interlink Books, 2003, pp. 140–57.
>
> Saro-Wiwa, Ken. "English Is the Hero." Interview by Diri I. Teilanyo. *No Condition Is Permanent: Nigerian Writing and the Struggle for Democracy*, edited by Holger Ehling and Claus-Peter Holste-von Mutius, Rodopi, 2001, pp. 13–19.

> Contributor element: 5.38–5.47.

[5.108] Original publication date

For a work contained in another work, sometimes the only date you can supply pertains to the Title of Source element and not to the work it is contained in. In this case you must use the supplemental element for the publication date. In the first example below, the date of composition of a letter is placed in the middle supplemental element to indicate that the date applies to the letter and not to the archive containing the letter. In the second example, placing the date in the middle supplemental element tells readers that it is the date of the decision, not the date of online publication, for which no date is given by the source.

> Benton, Thomas Hart. Letter to Charles Fremont. 22 June 1847. John Charles Fremont Papers, Southwest Museum Library, Los Angeles. Manuscript.
>
> United States, Supreme Court. *Brown v. Board of Education*. 17 May 1954. *Legal Information Institute*, Cornell Law School, www.law.cornell.edu/supremecourt/text/347/483.

Although you should record the publication date of the version of the source you consult, giving the original publication date can provide readers with insight into the work's creation or relation to other works. While this information is not required and may not be found in the source itself, writers with specialist knowledge of the work may sometimes find that providing the original date is helpful to readers.

> *Blade Runner.* 1982. Directed by Ridley Scott, director's cut, Warner Bros.,
>   1992.
> Larsen, Nella. *Passing.* 1929. Penguin Classics, 2020.
> Smith, Patti. "Because the Night." 1978. *Easter,* Arista Records, 1996.
>   *Spotify* app.

> Publication dates: 5.68–5.83.

[5.109] Section of a work labeled generically

If the introduction, preface, foreword, afterword, or other section of a work has a unique title as well as a generic label, you can use the middle supplemental element to provide the generic description if you think it will be important for your reader (**fig. 5.103**). In general, however, omit the label.

> Seyhan, Azade. "Novel Moves." Introduction. *Tales of Crossed Destinies: The
>   Modern Turkish Novel in a Comparative Context,* by Seyhan, Modern
>   Language Association of America, 2008, pp. 1–22.

> Sections of a work labeled generically: 5.27.

[5.110] Placement at End of Entry

The final supplemental element is used to clarify something about the entry as a whole, and it should be used judiciously.

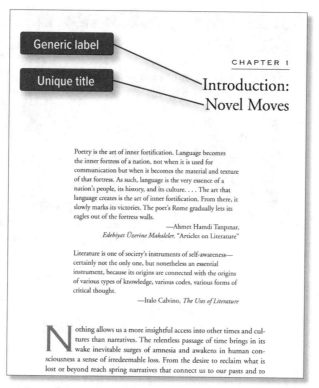

Generic label

Unique title

CHAPTER 1

Introduction:
Novel Moves

Poetry is the art of inner fortification. Language becomes the inner fortress of a nation, not when it is used for communication but when it becomes the material and texture of that fortress. As such, language is the very essence of a nation's people, its history, and its culture. . . . The art that language creates is the art of inner fortification. From there, it slowly marks its victories. The poet's Rome gradually lets its eagles out of the fortress walls.

—Ahmet Hamdi Tanpınar,
Edebiyat Üzerine Makaleler, "Articles on Literature"

Literature is one of society's instruments of self-awareness—certainly not the only one, but nonetheless an essential instrument, because its origins are connected with the origins of various types of knowledge, various codes, various forms of critical thought.

—Italo Calvino, *The Uses of Literature*

Nothing allows us a more insightful access into other times and cultures than narratives. The relentless passage of time brings in its wake inevitable surges of amnesia and awakens in human consciousness a sense of irredeemable loss. From the desire to reclaim what is lost or beyond reach spring narratives that connect us to our pasts and to

Fig. 5.103. An introduction with a unique title as well as a generic label.

[5.111] Date of access

An access date for an online work should generally be provided if the work lacks a publication date or if you suspect that the work has been altered or removed. (In the example that follows, the website no longer exists.)

> "Orhan Pamuk: Un écrivain turc à succès." *Orhan Pamuk Site,* İletişm Publishing, orhanpamuk.net/book.aspx?id=10&lng=eng. Accessed 25 Oct. 2015.

[5.112] Medium of publication

Include the medium of publication as a final supplemental element when more than one version of a source is accessible on the same landing page

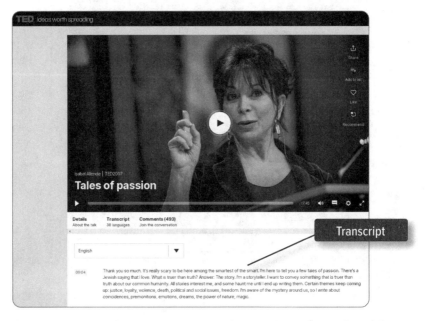

Fig. 5.104. The transcript of a talk available on a website alongside a video of the talk.

and you are citing a version that is not the default version (that is, the user must select a version).

For example, if you are citing the transcript of a talk found on a web page that features an audio clip of the talk as the default version, include *Transcript* as a supplemental element (**fig. 5.104**). Similarly, if you cite the printed lyrics of a song available alongside a video of the song, include *Transcript of lyrics* or some similar indicator as a supplemental element. This tells your reader that you are quoting from text, not transcribing audio yourself. And if you view a file type, such as a PDF, other than the one presented as the default version of the work on a page where other versions of the work are available, include *PDF download, supplementary material*, or a similar description in the supplemental element. There may be small differences among the available versions; in the case of data sets and other supplementary materials, you need to direct your reader to such materials.

Allende, Isabel. "Tales of Passion." *TED*, Mar. 2007, www.ted.com/talks/isabel_allende_tells_tales_of_passion/transcript?language=en. Transcript.

Beyoncé. "Pretty Hurts." *Beyoncé*, Parkwood Entertainment, 2013, www.beyonce.com/album/beyonce/lyrics. Transcript of lyrics.

Moskowitz, Daniel J. "Local News, Information, and the Nationalization of U.S. Elections." *American Political Science Review*, vol. 115, no. 1, Feb. 2021, pp. 114–29. *Cambridge Core*, https://doi:10.1017/S0003055420000829. Moskowitz supplementary material.

National Academy of Sciences and the Royal Society. *Climate Change: Evidence and Causes: Update 2020*. National Academies Press, 2020, https://doi.org/10.17226/25733. PDF download.

Generally cite the final published version whenever possible. If you are citing the draft version of a work, including one submitted for publication (sometimes called a *preprint*, which often indicates that the work has not yet been peer reviewed or edited), indicate this in the final supplemental element.

Glass, Erin Rose, and Micah Vandegrift. "Public Scholarship in Practice and Philosophy." *CORE*, 2018, https://doi.org/10.17613/g64d-gd16. PDF download, draft of working paper.

The final supplemental element can be used to indicate the medium of publication for a work whose format would otherwise be ambiguous.

Rushkoff, Douglas. "Team Human: Find the Others." 92nd Street Y, New York City, 21 May 2019. Lecture.

The final supplemental element can also be used to specify the file type for an electronic edition of a work when that information conveys essential information—for example, if you know that the display of a work varies by the file format or that the content you are citing is uniquely produced by a platform.

Lopez, Jennifer. "Vivir mi vida." Sony Music Latin, 2017. *Spotify* app.

MLA Handbook. 8th ed., e-book ed., Modern Language Association of America, 2016. EPUB.

Using the Version element for e-book editions: 5.48.

[5.113] Dissertations and theses

The institution conferring the degree and the type of thesis or dissertation (BA, MA, or PhD) are essential to defining the work and should appear as a final supplemental element.

> Njus, Jesse. *Performing the Passion: A Study on the Nature of Medieval Acting.* 2010. Northwestern U, PhD dissertation.

[5.114] Publication history

Although you should generally avoid providing details about a source's publication history in a works-cited-list entry, there may be times when those writing for a specialist audience find it is important to give additional information about a source. In such instances, the core elements should provide publication details for the version of the source used; any relevant information about the original publication context can be given in the supplemental element at the end of the entry.

> Johnson, Barbara. "My Monster / My Self." *The Barbara Johnson Reader: The Surprise of Otherness*, edited by Melissa Feuerstein et al., Duke UP, 2014, pp. 179–90. Originally published in *Diacritics*, 1982.

If you use the original version of a source and it was subsequently published in a new version, do not supply information about the later version.

[5.115] Book series

Publishers sometimes publish books in series, and for some specialist audiences, the name of a series may be meaningful. Series information, when relevant, can be given as a final supplemental element.

> d'Aragona, Tullia. *Dialogue on the Infinity of Love.* Edited and translated by Rinaldina Russell and Bruce Merry, U of Chicago P, 1997. The Other Voice in Early Modern Europe.
> Neruda, Pablo. *Canto general.* Translated by Jack Schmitt, U of California P, 1991. Latin American Literature and Culture 7.

[5.116] Columns, sections, and other recurring titled features

A column title, section title, or other recurring titled feature in a periodical publication like a magazine or website organizes or brands information but usually does not need to be included in a works-cited-list entry (unless, as with titled sections of print newspapers, it is needed to locate the work). When including inessential column or section information, provide it as a final supplemental element.

> "How Do I Style the Names of Fictional Characters?" *MLA Style Center*, Modern Language Association of America, 18 Oct. 2017, style.mla .org/2017/10/18/names-of-fictional-characters/. Ask the MLA.
> Kuperberg, Ethan. "Nuclear Mindfulness." *The New Yorker*, 9 Oct. 2017, p. 31. Shouts and Murmurs.

> Styling of columns, sections, and other recurring features: 2.110. Titled sections of newspapers in the Location element: 5.84.

[5.117] Multivolume works

The total number of volumes for a multivolume work cited as a whole can be included as a final supplemental element.

> Rampersad, Arnold. *The Life of Langston Hughes*. 2nd ed., Oxford UP, 2002. 2 vols.

When an individual volume of a multivolume work has a unique title, give the title of the work as a whole as a final supplemental element.

> Caro, Robert A. *The Passage of Power*. Vintage Books, 2012. Vol. 4 of *The Years of Lyndon Johnson*.

When an individual volume of a multivolume work that does not have a unique title provides the scope of the volume (usually, the period or portion of work covered) on the title page, the scope should generally be omitted; the volume number is sufficient to distinguish the work.

> Dettmar, Kevin, and Jennifer Wicke, editors. *The Longman Anthology of British Literature*. Vol. 2C, Longman, 1999.

Poe, Edgar Allan. *The Complete Works of Edgar Allan Poe.* Edited by James A.
Harrison, vol. 4, Thomas Y. Crowell, 1902.

If, however, you elect to include the scope, treat it as part of the title. The
volume number and title of the work as a whole must also be included as a
final supplemental element; other information (total number of volumes,
general editors, a date range for the work as a whole) can be supplied
there too.

Benet, Juan. *Herrumbrosas lanzas, libros 8–12.* Alfaguara, 1986. Vol. 3 of
Herrumbrosas lanzas, 3 vols., 1983–86.

Dettmar, Kevin, and Jennifer Wicke, editors. *The Longman Anthology of
British Literature: The Twentieth Century.* Longman, 1999. Vol. 2C of *The
Longman Anthology of British Literature,* 6 vols.

Woolf, Virginia. *The Essays of Virginia Woolf, 1929–1932.* Edited by Stuart N.
Clarke, Houghton Mifflin Harcourt, 2009. Vol. 5 of *The Essays of Virginia
Woolf.*

[5.118] Government documents

At the end of entries for legislative documents, you may want to provide
the number and session of Congress, the chamber (Senate or House of Representatives), and the type and number of the publication. Types of con-
gressional publications include bills, resolutions, reports, and documents.

Poore, Benjamin Perley, compiler. *A Descriptive Catalogue of the Government
Publications of the United States, September 5, 1774–March 4, 1881.*
Government Printing Office, 1885. 48th Congress, 2nd session,
Miscellaneous Document 67.

United States, Congress, House. Improving Broadband Access for Veterans
Act of 2016. *Congress.gov,* www.congress.gov/bill/114th-congress/
house-bill/6394/text. 114th Congress, 2nd session, House Resolution
6394, passed 6 Dec. 2016.

———, ———, ———, Permanent Select Committee on Intelligence. *Al-Qaeda:
The Many Faces of an Islamist Extremist Threat.* Government Printing
Office, 2006. 109th Congress, 2nd session, House Report 615.

> Consolidating entries for government authors: 5.22.

[5.119] Placement between Containers

In an entry with two or more containers, a supplemental element that supplies information relevant only to one container may be placed after the container it pertains to. In the example below, the information "Indiana U, PhD dissertation" is placed after the first container, which contains only the date of the work; the information does not apply to the second container, the online repository *CORE*.

> Sewell, Amanda. *A Typology of Sampling in Hip-Hop*. 2018. Indiana U, PhD dissertation. *CORE*, https://doi.org/10.17613/M6P850.

[5.120] Punctuation of Entries

Periods are used after the Author element, after the Title of Source element, at the end of each container string, and at the end of each entry. Commas are used mainly between elements within each container and between the surname and the first name when the name in the Author element is inverted.

> Formatting entries in the works-cited list: 5.1.

[5.121] More Than One Item in an Element

If an element contains more than one piece of information, use a comma to separate the pieces of information.

> Abdo, Diya, and Maria Bobroff. "Cross-Disciplinary Teaching of Mariama Bâ's *So Long a Letter*." *ADFL Bulletin*, vol. 45, no. 1, 2018, pp. 171–83, https://doi.org/10.1632/adfl.45.1.171.
>
> *MLA Handbook*. 9th ed., e-book ed., Modern Language Association of America, 2021.

But use a hyphen to join seasons or months in the Publication Date element. If you use hyphens in number ranges, use a hyphen to join two issue numbers in the Number element. But if you use en dashes in number ranges, as this handbook does, use an en dash to join issue numbers in the Number element.

> Dungy, Camille T. "Is All Writing Environmental Writing?" *The Georgia Review*, fall-winter 2018, thegeorgiareview.com/posts/is-all -writing-environmental-writing/.
>
> Fisher, Margaret. "The Music of Ezra Pound." *Yale University Library Gazette*, vol. 80, nos. 3–4, Apr. 2006, pp. 139–60. *JSTOR*, www.jstor.org/ stable/40859548.

When citing an essay in a journal that contains two volumes, use *and* to join the volumes, issues, and dates of the volumes.

> Govan, Sandra Y. "*Fledgling* by Octavia Butler." *Obsidian III: Literature in the African Diaspora,* vol. 6, no. 2, fall-winter 2005 and vol. 7, no. 1, spring-summer 2006, pp. 40–43.

Another exception to the use of the comma occurs when more than one publisher is listed on a work: use a slash between the names of co-publishers in the Publisher element.

Supplemental elements follow the same general pattern: a period concludes the element, and commas are used to separate multiple pieces of information supplied as supplemental elements.

Copublishers: 5.61.

[5.122] Supplied Publication Information

When a source does not indicate necessary facts about its publication, such as the name of the publisher, the date of publication, or an author's full name, writers, especially scholars who possess working familiarity with their sources, may be able to supply missing information. Use square brackets to show that the information was supplied. If you are uncertain about the accuracy of the information that you supply, add a question mark.

> "The Famous Sea-Fight between Captain Ward and the Rainbow." London, [1650].
>
> Bauer, Johann. *Kafka und Prag.* Belser, [1971?].

If the city of publication is not included in the name of a locally published newspaper, add the city, not italicized, in square brackets after the name.

> Beecher, Thomas K. "Brother Anderson." *Herald and Presbyter* [Cincinnati],
>   19 Sept. 1872, p. 3.

You need not add the city of publication to the name of a nationally published newspaper (e.g., *The Wall Street Journal*, *The Chronicle of Higher Education*).

> Uncertain date given in source: 5.83.

[5.123] Ordering the List of Works Cited

The works-cited list is arranged in alphabetic order by the part of the author's name that comes first in each entry or, for works listed by title, the first eligible word in the Title of Source element.

[5.124] Alphabetizing: An Overview

Use the letter-by-letter system of alphabetization, in which entries are ordered by the part of the name, title, or description beginning the entry. For reversed names of authors or for corporate authors (i.e., organizations) or government authors consisting of administrative units separated by commas, alphabetize up to the comma; the letters following the comma are considered in alphabetization only when two or more names begin in an identical way. Other punctuation marks and spaces are ignored in alphabetizing titles, descriptions, and corporate names. When alphabetizing titles, ignore initial articles (*A*, *An*, *The*, or the equivalent in other languages) and omit them for corporate authors (e.g., the *Beatles*, the *Modern Language Association*, the *United Nations*).

Accents and other diacritical marks should be ignored in alphabetization: for example, *é* is treated the same as *e*.

Germanists writing for a specialist audience may treat an umlauted vowel as if the letter were followed by an *e*; thus, *Götz* would be alphabetized as *Goetz* and would precede *Gott* in an alphabetic listing. Nonspecialists, however, and many libraries in English-speaking countries, alphabetize such words without regard to the umlaut; for publications addressed primarily to speakers of English, this is the recommended practice.

The following list shows letter-by-letter alphabetization.

Achebe, Chinua

Beatles

Beowulf

Christine de Pizan

Descartes, René

De Sica, Vittorio

Duong Thu Huong

Executive summary

Film Crit Hulk

Gott

Götz

MacDonald, George

McCullers, Carson

MLA Handbook

Modern Language Association

Moonlight

Morris, Robert

Morris, William

Morrison, Toni

Saint-Exupéry, Antoine de

The Second Shepherds' Play

St. Denis, Ruth

United Nations

United States, Congress, House, Permanent Select Committee on Intelligence

United States, Department of Health and Human Services, Centers for Disease Control and Prevention

[5.125] Alphabetizing by Author

Ordering multiple works by one author, multiple works by two authors, and multiple works by more than two authors requires special consideration.

> Surnames: 2.73–2.81. Styling the Author element in works-cited-list entries: 5.5–5.11.

[5.126] Multiple works by one author

To document two or more works by the same author, give the author's name in the first entry only. Thereafter, in place of the name, type three em dashes (or, if using hyphens, three hyphens). The three em dashes or hyphens stand for exactly the same name as in the preceding entry and are usually followed by a period and then by the source's title.

> Borroff, Marie. *Language and the Poet: Verbal Artistry in Frost, Stevens, and Moore.* U of Chicago P, 1979.
> ———. "Sound Symbolism as Drama in the Poetry of Robert Frost." *PMLA,* vol. 107, no. 1, Jan. 1992, pp. 131–44. *JSTOR,* https://doi.org/10.2307/462806.

If the person named performed a role other than creating the work's main content, however, place a comma after the three dashes or hyphens and enter a term describing the role (*editor, translator, director*) before recording the title. Multiple sources by the same person are alphabetized by their titles; terms describing the person's roles are not considered in alphabetization.

> Borroff, Marie. *Language and the Poet: Verbal Artistry in Frost, Stevens, and Moore.* U of Chicago P, 1979.
> ———, translator. Pearl: *A New Verse Translation.* W. W. Norton, 1977.
> ———. "Sound Symbolism as Drama in the Poetry of Robert Frost." *PMLA,* vol. 107, no. 1, Jan. 1992, pp. 131–44. *JSTOR,* https://doi.org/10.2307/462806.
> ———, editor. *Wallace Stevens: A Collection of Critical Essays.* Prentice-Hall, 1963.

[5.127] **Multiple works by two authors**

If two or more entries citing coauthors begin with the same name, alphabetize them by the surnames of the second authors listed.

> Scholes, Robert, and Robert Kellogg
>
> Scholes, Robert, and Eric S. Rabkin

To document two or more works by the same coauthors whose names appear in a consistent order in the works, give the names in the first entry only. Thereafter, in place of the names, type three em dashes (or, if using hyphens, three hyphens), followed by a period and the title. The three dashes or hyphens stand for exactly the same names, in the same order, as in the preceding entry.

> Gilbert, Sandra M., and Susan Gubar, editors. *The Female Imagination and the Modernist Aesthetic.* Gordon and Breach Science Publishers, 1986.
>
> ———. "Sexual Linguistics: Gender, Language, Sexuality." *New Literary History*, vol. 16, no. 3, spring 1985, pp. 515–43. *JSTOR*, https://doi.org/10.2307/468838.

If the coauthors' names do not appear in the same order in the source works, record the names as found in the works and alphabetize the entries accordingly.

[5.128] **Multiple works by more than two authors**

If the works-cited list contains works by the same lead author and the same coauthors listed in the work in the same order, you may order the entries according to the method described above for multiple works by two authors: give the lead author's name followed by *et al.* in the first entry and use three em dashes or three hyphens in the Author element for the subsequent entry or entries.

> Perry, John, et al. *Introduction to Philosophy: Classical and Contemporary Readings.* 7th ed., Oxford UP, 2015.
>
> ———. *Introduction to Philosophy: Classical and Contemporary Readings.* 8th ed., Oxford UP, 2018.

If the works-cited list contains works by the same lead author and different coauthors (or works by the same set of coauthors whose names appear in a different order), the names cannot be replaced with three em dashes or three hyphens in listings after the first. Each entry must list the lead author's name followed by *et al.* to indicate that the author teams are different (or that their names are differently ordered). Alphabetize more than one work by the same author plus *et al.* by title.

Horner, Bruce, et al., editors. *Cross-Language Relations in Composition.* Southern Illinois UP, 2010.

Horner, Bruce, et al. "Language Difference in Writing: Toward a Translingual Approach." *College English*, vol. 73, no. 3, Jan. 2011, pp. 304–21.

[5.129] Multiple works by a single author and coauthors

When citing a work written by a single author and then another work by that same author and coauthors, repeat the single author's name in full and do not substitute three em dashes or three hyphens. Order the individually authored work or works before the cowritten work. If there is more than one coauthored work by that author in the list of works cited, order the entries alphabetically by the first unique coauthor's surname, as listed in your source. Order works written by two authors before any works by more than two authors.

Tannen, Deborah. *Talking Voices: Repetition, Dialogue, and Imagery in Conversational Discourse.* 2nd ed., Cambridge UP, 2007. Studies in Interactional Sociolinguistics 26.

———. *You're Wearing That? Understanding Mothers and Daughters in Conversation.* Ballantine Books, 2006.

Tannen, Deborah, and Roy O. Freedle, editors. *Linguistics in Context: Connecting Observation and Understanding.* Ablex Publishing, 1988.

Tannen, Deborah, and Muriel Saville-Troike, editors. *Perspectives on Silence.* Ablex Publishing, 1985.

Tannen, Deborah, et al., editors. *Family Talk: Discourse and Identity in Four American Families.* Oxford UP, 2007.

Citing two or more works by the same author or authors: 6.8.

[5.130] Alphabetizing by Title

The alphabetization of an entry is based on the work's title when

- the entry lacks an author
- there is more than one work listed by the same author (see the Borroff examples in 5.126)
- there is more than one work by the same coauthors listed in the same order (see the Gilbert and Gubar examples in 5.127)
- there is more than one work by the same lead author plus *et al.* (see the Horner et al. examples in 5.128)

If two works have the same title, list them chronologically, either earliest to latest or latest to earliest. Use a consistent order for all such entries in your works-cited list.

Alphabetize titles letter by letter, ignoring any initial *A*, *An*, or *The* or the equivalent in other languages. For example, the title *An Encyclopedia of the Latin American Novel* would be alphabetized under *e* rather than *a*, and the title *Le théâtre en France au Moyen Âge* under *t* rather than *l*. If, however, you are unfamiliar with the language, alphabetize by the first word.

If the title begins with a numeral, alphabetize the title as if the numeral were spelled out. For instance, *1914: An Anonymous Diary on the Eve of World War I* should be alphabetized as if it began with *Nineteen Fourteen*.

The Guns of August

1914: An Anonymous Diary on the Eve of World War I

The Representation of War in German Literature

As an aid to readers, make exceptions to this practice for separately titled works in which the numbers represent a sequence or chronological ordering.

Henry IV

Henry V

Star Trek II: The Wrath of Khan

Star Trek III: The Search for Spock

[5.131] Cross-References

To avoid unnecessary repetition in citing two or more sources from a collection of works such as an anthology, you may create a complete entry for the collection and cross-reference individual pieces to that entry. In a cross-reference, first give the author and the title of the source. Follow this with a reference to the collection's full entry, usually consisting of the name or names starting the entry, followed by a short form of the collection's title, if needed—that is, if the list includes two or more works by the author or authors of the collection (see Baker examples below). Then give a comma, followed by the inclusive page or reference numbers. Cross-references are not needed if you are citing multiple works by the same author in a single collection of that author's works—edited or not. You may generally cite the collection as a whole in your works-cited list and refer to the individual works in your text.

Agee, James. "Knoxville: Summer of 1915." Oates and Atwan, pp. 171–75.

Angelou, Maya. "Pickin Em Up and Layin Em Down." Baker, *Norton Book*, pp. 276–78.

Atwan, Robert. Foreword. Oates and Atwan, pp. x–xvi.

Baker, Russell, editor. *The Norton Book of Light Verse*. W. W. Norton, 1986.

———, editor. *Russell Baker's Book of American Humor*. W. W. Norton, 1993.

Hurston, Zora Neale. "Squinch Owl Story." Baker, *Russell Baker's Book*, pp. 458–59.

Kingston, Maxine Hong. "No Name Woman." Oates and Atwan, pp. 383–94.

Lebowitz, Fran. "Manners." Baker, *Russell Baker's Book*, pp. 556–59.

Lennon, John. "The Fat Budgie." Baker, *Norton Book*, pp. 357–58.

Oates, Joyce Carol, and Robert Atwan, editors. *The Best American Essays of the Century*. Houghton Mifflin, 2000.

Rodriguez, Richard. "Aria: A Memoir of a Bilingual Childhood." Oates and Atwan, pp. 447–66.

Walker, Alice. "Looking for Zora." Oates and Atwan, pp. 395–411.

Cross-references are not suitable for ongoing works, like periodicals and websites, or works in a nonbook series, like podcasts and television shows, since information about the larger, ongoing series can change over time.

[5.132] Annotated Bibliographies

Style a source in an annotated bibliography just as you would one in a list of works cited, and then append an annotation to the end of the entry, indented an inch from the start of the entry (to distinguish it from the half-inch hanging indent of entries composed of more than one line).

Annotations describe or evaluate sources or do both. They should not rehash minor details, cite evidence, quote the author, or recount steps in an argument. Annotations are generally written as succinct phrases.

> Moore, Nicole. *The Censor's Library: Uncovering the Lost History of Australia's Banned Books*. U of Queensland P, 2012.
>> Comprehensive history of Australian print censorship, with discussion of this history's implications for questions of transnationalism and the construction of the reader.

But annotations can also be given as complete sentences.

> Moore, Nicole. *The Censor's Library: Uncovering the Lost History of Australia's Banned Books*. U of Queensland P, 2012.
>> The book provides a comprehensive history of Australian print censorship and discusses its implications for questions of transnationalism and the construction of the reader.

In an annotated bibliography, the annotations should generally be no more than one paragraph. If, however, you need several paragraphs, indent each one but do not add an extra space between paragraphs. Follow your instructor's guidelines on the use of phrases or full sentences and the length of annotations.

The list should be titled Annotated Bibliography or Annotated List of Works Cited. Writers may organize the bibliography alphabetically by author or title (as for a normal list of works cited), by date of publication, or by subject.

6. Citing Sources in the Text

[6.1] In-Text Citations

In-text citations are brief, unobtrusive references that direct readers to the works-cited-list entries for the sources you consulted and, where relevant, to the location in the source being cited.

[6.2] Overview

An in-text citation begins with the shortest piece of information that directs your reader to the entry in the works-cited list. Thus, it begins with whatever comes first in the entry: the author's name or the title (or description) of the work. The citation can appear in your prose or in parentheses.

Citation in prose

Naomi Baron broke new ground on the subject.

Parenthetical citation

At least one researcher has broken new ground on the subject (Baron).

Work cited

Baron, Naomi S. "Redefining Reading: The Impact of Digital Communication Media." *PMLA*, vol. 128, no. 1, Jan. 2013, pp. 193–200.

Citation in prose

According to the article "Bhakti Poets," female bhakti poets "faced overwhelming challenges through their rejection of societal norms and values."

Parenthetical citation

The female bhakti poets "faced overwhelming challenges through their rejection of societal norms and values" ("Bhakti Poets").

Work cited

"Bhakti Poets: Introduction." *Women in World History,* Center for History and New Media, chnm.gmu.edu/wwh/modules/lesson1/lesson1.php?s=0. Accessed 20 Sept. 2020.

When relevant, an in-text citation also has a second component: if a specific part of a work is quoted or paraphrased and the work includes a page number, line number, time stamp, or other indicator of the place in the work where the information can be found, that location marker must be included in parentheses.

Parenthetical citations

According to Naomi Baron, reading is "just half of literacy. The other half is writing" (194). One might even suggest that reading is never complete without writing.

Reading at Risk notes that despite an apparent decline in reading during the same period, "the number of people doing creative writing—of any genre, not exclusively literary works—increased substantially between 1982 and 2002" (3).

The author or title can also appear alongside the page number or other location marker in parentheses.

Parenthetical citations

Reading is "just half of literacy. The other half is writing" (Baron 194). One might even suggest that reading is never complete without writing.

Despite an apparent decline in reading during the same period, "the number of people doing creative writing—of any genre, not exclusively literary works—increased substantially between 1982 and 2002" (*Reading* 3).

Works cited

Baron, Naomi S. "Redefining Reading: The Impact of Digital Communication Media." *PMLA*, vol. 128, no. 1, Jan. 2013, pp. 193–200.
Reading at Risk: A Survey of Literary Reading in America. National Endowment for the Arts, June 2004.

All in-text references should be concise. Avoid, for instance, providing the author's name or title of a work in both your prose and parentheses.

Citations (incorrect)

According to Naomi Baron, reading is "just half of literacy. The other half is writing" (Baron 194).

Reading at Risk notes that despite an apparent decline in reading during the same period, "the number of people doing creative writing—of any genre, not exclusively literary works—increased substantially between 1982 and 2002" (*Reading* 3).

Citations (correct)

According to Naomi Baron, reading is "just half of literacy. The other half is writing" (194).

Reading at Risk notes that despite an apparent decline in reading during the same period, "the number of people doing creative writing—of any genre, not exclusively literary works—increased substantially between 1982 and 2002" (3).

In parenthetical citations, use only the part of an author's name—usually the surname only—necessary to find the entry in the list of works cited (on surnames, see 2.73–2.81).

Citation (incorrect)

At least one researcher has broken new ground on the subject (Naomi S. Baron).

Citation (correct)

At least one researcher has broken new ground on the subject (Baron).

Use shortened titles in parenthetical citations. See 6.10–6.14 for guidance on shortening titles in parenthetical citations.

In prose	In parenthetical citations	In works-cited list
Reading at Risk	*Reading*	*Reading at Risk: A Survey of Literary Reading in America*

For concision, do not precede a page number in a parenthetical citation with *p.* or *pp.*, as you do in the list of works cited (where such abbreviations lend clarity). If you cite a number other than a page number in a parenthetical citation, precede it with a label such as *chapter* or *section* (often abbreviated in parentheses) or *line* or *lines* (do not abbreviate). Otherwise, your reader is to assume that the numeral refers to a page number.

In prose	In parenthetical citations
chapter 2	(ch. 2)
line 110	(line 110)
scene 4	(sc. 4)

> Punctuation of works-cited-list entries: 5.120–5.122. Shortening titles in parenthetical citations: 6.10–6.14. Page numbers and other divisions of works: 6.16–6.29. Common abbreviations used in the works-cited list: appendix 1.

[6.3] What to Include and How to Style It

[6.4] Citing a work listed by author

If the works-cited-list entry begins with an author's name and you are citing the author in your prose, give the full name at first mention and the surname alone thereafter (see 2.74). If the entry includes the author's middle initial, you may omit it in your prose.

Citation in prose

Naomi Baron broke new ground on the subject. Although many scholars have explored the influence of computers on reading habits, Baron's work helps us understand how reading will continue to evolve.

Parenthetical citation (surname only)

At least one researcher has broken new ground on the subject (Baron).

Work cited

Baron, Naomi S. "Redefining Reading: The Impact of Digital Communication Media." *PMLA*, vol. 128, no. 1, Jan. 2013, pp. 193–200.

Surnames in some languages, like Chinese, Japanese, and Korean, usually precede given names. In your prose, provide both the surname and the given name at first reference. Thereafter, refer to the author by surname alone. Use the surname alone in parenthetical citations since only the surname is needed to find the corresponding entry in the works-cited list.

Citation in prose

According to Gao Xingjian, "Literature in essence is divorced from utility" (7). Gao adds, however, that the market for publishing works is constricted by politics (13).

Parenthetical citation (surname only)

Literature's aesthetic and social roles have been debated in the West at least since Plato. The global landscape in which so much literary production takes place, however, has revealed just how diminished—if not "wretched" (Gao 15)—the individual creator has become.

Work cited

Gao Xingjian. *Aesthetics and Creation*. Cambria Press, 2012.

When you refer to people who lived before or during the Renaissance who are conventionally referred to by their given name, the given name alone is sufficient to point to the corresponding entry in the works-cited list.

Citation in prose

Christine de Pizan's *Livre des trois vertus* (*Book of Three Virtues*) may be understood without extensive knowledge of late medieval society or politics. Christine says she hopes her work will be read widely, "en tous païs" ("in all countries"; 225; my trans.).

Parenthetical citation (given name only)

The author knew Bureau de la Rivière, another of Charles V's executors (Christine 192).

Work cited

Christine de Pizan. *Le livre des trois vertus*. Edited by Charity Cannon Willard and Eric Hicks, Champion, 1989.

> Names in Asian languages: 2.80.
> Premodern names: 2.81.

[6.5] *Coauthors*

If the entry in the works-cited list begins with the names of two authors, include both names in your citation. If you are mentioning the authors for the first time in your prose, include both first names and surnames. In a parenthetical citation connect the two surnames with *and*.

Citation in prose

Others, like Jay Lemery and Paul Auerbach, note that doctors have not yet adequately explained the effects climate change will have on human health (4–5). Lemery and Auerbach's book focuses on the human, not the environmental, risks.

Parenthetical citation (surnames only)

Others note that doctors have not yet adequately explained the effects climate change will have on human health (Lemery and Auerbach 4–5).

Work cited

Lemery, Jay, and Paul Auerbach. *Enviromedics: The Impact of Climate Change on Human Health*. Rowman and Littlefield, 2017.

If the source has three or more authors, the entry in the works-cited list begins with the first author's name followed by *et al.* If you refer to the coauthors in your prose rather than in a parenthetical citation, you may list all the names or provide the name of the first collaborator followed by "and others" or "and colleagues." In a parenthetical citation, list the surname of the first author and *et al.*

Citation in prose

Raymond Nickerson and colleagues argue that the truth value of statements—their premises and conclusions—is one factor that affects how people are persuaded by arguments (135).

Parenthetical citation

The authors argue that the truth value of statements—their premises and conclusions—is one factor that affects how people are persuaded by arguments (Nickerson et al. 135).

Work cited

Nickerson, Raymond S., et al. "Validity and Persuasiveness of Conditional Arguments." *The American Journal of Psychology*, vol. 132, no. 2, summer 2019, pp. 131–47.

Only italicize *et al.* if it is referred to as a term, as the example in this sentence shows. In parenthetical citations and works-cited-list entries, the abbreviation should be set roman (i.e., not italicized).

[6.6] *Corporate authors*

For concision, when a corporate author (i.e., an organization) is named in a parenthetical citation, shorten the name to the shortest noun phrase. For example, the American Historical Association consists entirely of a noun phrase (a noun, *association*, preceded by two modifiers) and would not be shortened. By contrast, the Modern Language Association of America can be shortened to its initial noun phrase, *Modern Language Association*. If possible, give the first noun and any preceding adjectives, while excluding any initial article: *a, an, the*.

Citation in prose

According to a study by the National Academy of Sciences and the Royal Society, the "speed of warming is more than ten times that at the end of an ice age, the fastest known natural sustained change on a global scale" (9).

Parenthetical citation

According to one study of climate change, the "speed of warming is more than ten times that at the end of an ice age, the fastest known natural sustained change on a global scale" (National Academy 9).

Work cited

National Academy of Sciences and the Royal Society. *Climate Change: Evidence and Causes: Update 2020*. National Academies Press, 2020, https://doi .org/10.17226/25733. PDF download.

If more than one entry appears in the works-cited list for different administrative units of the same organization or government author, in the parenthetical citation give only as much of the name as is needed to locate the entry.

Parenthetical citations

A recent case held that "the immunity enjoyed by foreign governments is a general rather than specific reference" (United States, Supreme Court).

One delegation noted that "Chinese authorities clearly remain concerned about the possibility of a resurgence of social unrest in Tibet" (United States, Senate 2).

Works cited

United States, Supreme Court. *Jam v. International Finance Corp.* 27 Feb. 2019. *Legal Information Institute*, Cornell Law School, www.law.cornell.edu/ supremecourt/text/17-1011.

———, Senate, Committee on Foreign Relations. *Tibet: Seeking Common Ground on the Rooftop of the World: A Trip Report from Staff of the Senate Foreign Relations Committee*. Mar. 2011, www.foreign.senate.gov/imo/ media/doc/Tibet.pdf.

[6.7] *Two authors with the same surname*

If you borrow from works by more than one author with the same surname (e.g., Jaimie Baron and Naomi Baron), use the first name of each author in prose, even after the first reference to the author, to eliminate ambiguity. In a parenthetical citation, add the author's first initial.

Citation in prose

Having read Naomi Baron's argument that writing is the "other half" of literacy (194), one might even suggest that reading is never complete without writing.

Parenthetical citation

Reading is "just half of literacy. The other half is writing" (N. Baron 194). One might even suggest that reading is never complete without writing.

Works cited

Baron, Jaimie. *Reuse, Misuse, Abuse: The Ethics of Audiovisual Appropriation in the Digital Era.* Rutgers UP, 2020.

Baron, Naomi S. "Redefining Reading: The Impact of Digital Communication Media." *PMLA*, vol. 128, no. 1, Jan. 2013, pp. 193–200.

If the authors' first names begin with the same initial, use first names in parenthetical citations.

Parenthetical citations

As one scholar notes, reading is "just half of literacy. The other half is writing" (Naomi Baron 194). Scientists must be able to successfully communicate why their research matters—and not just with one another. A recent study argues that the way scientists have been trained to communicate "leaves policymakers out of the loop" (Nancy Baron 90). Training scientists to write for a general audience is therefore just as important as promoting science literacy among our political leaders.

Works cited

Baron, Nancy. *Escape from the Ivory Tower: A Guide to Making Your Science Matter.* Island Press, 2010.

Baron, Naomi S. "Redefining Reading: The Impact of Digital Communication Media." *PMLA*, vol. 128, no. 1, Jan. 2013, pp. 193–200.

[6.8] *Two or more works by the same author or authors*

If two or more works appear under the same author name or names in the works-cited list, you must add a title to your in-text citation so that your reader knows which work you are citing. You may do this in one of three ways.

Author's name in prose and title in parenthetical citation

Morrison writes, "Places, places are still there. If a house burns down, it's gone, but the place—the picture of it—stays" (*Beloved* 35).

Author's name and title in prose

As Morrison writes in *Beloved*, "Places, places are still there. If a house burns down, it's gone, but the place—the picture of it—stays" (35).

Author's name and title in parenthetical citation

The character Sethe notes, "Places, places are still there. If a house burns down, it's gone, but the place—the picture of it—stays" (Morrison, *Beloved* 35).

Works cited

Morrison, Toni. *Beloved*. Alfred A. Knopf, 1987.

———. *Playing in the Dark: Whiteness and the Literary Imagination*. Harvard UP, 1992.

Use these same techniques when there is more than one work in the works-cited list under a particular author's name followed by *et al.* Distinguish the sources by including a short form of the title.

Author's name in prose and title in parenthetical citation

According to Horner and colleagues, "Growing numbers of U.S. teachers and scholars of writing recognize that traditional ways of understanding and responding to language differences are inadequate to the facts on the ground" ("Language Difference" 304).

Author's name and title in prose

In "Language Difference in Writing," Horner and colleagues suggest that "[g]rowing numbers of U.S. teachers and scholars of writing recognize that traditional ways of understanding and responding to language differences are inadequate to the facts on the ground" (304).

Author's name and title in parenthetical citation

According to a recent article, "Growing numbers of U.S. teachers and scholars of writing recognize that traditional ways of understanding and responding to language differences are inadequate to the facts on the ground" (Horner et al., "Language Difference" 304).

Works cited

Horner, Bruce, et al., editors. *Cross-Language Relations in Composition*. Southern
Illinois UP, 2010.

Horner, Bruce, et al. "Language Difference in Writing: Toward a Translingual
Approach." *College English*, vol. 73, no. 3, Jan. 2011, pp. 304–21.

[6.9] Citing a work listed by title

When an entry in the works-cited list begins with the title of the work, the
title may appear in prose or in parentheses.

Citation in prose

Reading at Risk notes that despite an apparent decline in reading during the
same period, "the number of people doing creative writing—of any genre, not
exclusively literary works—increased substantially between 1982 and 2002" (3).

Parenthetical citation

Despite an apparent decline in reading during the same period, "the number
of people doing creative writing—of any genre, not exclusively literary
works—increased substantially between 1982 and 2002" (*Reading* 3).

Work cited

Reading at Risk: A Survey of Literary Reading in America. National Endowment for
the Arts, June 2004.

[6.10] Shortening titles of works

For concision, when a title is needed in a parenthetical citation, shorten the
title if it is longer than a noun phrase. For example, *Faulkner's Southern Novels*
consists entirely of a noun phrase (a noun, *novels*, preceded by two modifiers)
and would not be shortened. By contrast, *Faulkner's Novels of the South* can
be shortened to its initial noun phrase, *Faulkner's Novels*. If possible, give the
first noun and any preceding adjectives, while excluding any initial article
(*a, an, the*). For foreign language titles that begin with an article, you may include or exclude the article, but do so consistently for all such titles you cite.

Full titles	Shortened titles
L'archéologie du savoir	*L'archéologie* (or *Archéologie*)
The Double Vision: Language and Meaning in Religion	*Double Vision*
"Traveling in the Breakdown Lane: A Principle of Resistance for Hypertext"	"Traveling"
"You Say You Want a Revolution? Hypertext and the Laws of Media"	"You"

If the title is short, especially if it forms a rhetorical unit, you can give the full title, even if it extends beyond the noun.

"Is Nothing Sacred?"

If the title does not begin with a noun phrase, stop at the first punctuation mark or at the end of the first phrase or clause.

Full titles	Shortened titles
How to Avoid Huge Ships	*How to Avoid*
In the Time of the Butterflies	*In the Time*
So Long, and Thanks for All the Fish	*So Long*

> Alphabetizing works-cited-list entries by title: 5.130.

[6.11] *Titles in quotation marks that start with a title in quotation marks*

In parenthetical citations, if you need to shorten a title within quotation marks that begins with a title in quotation marks, use the title within the title as the short form. Retain the single quotation marks within double quotation marks, but omit the initial article.

Citation

Karen Ford argues that Charlotte Perkins Gilman's "The Yellow Wallpaper" is "replete with contradictions" ("'Yellow Wallpaper'" 311).

Work cited

Ford, Karen. "'The Yellow Wallpaper' and Women's Discourse." *Tulsa Studies in Women's Literature*, vol. 4, no. 2, fall 1985, pp. 309–14.

> Titles within titles: 2.116.

[6.12] *Titles in quotation marks that start with a quotation*

If you need to shorten a title enclosed in quotation marks that begins with a quotation, use the quotation within the title as the short form and retain the single quotation marks within double quotation marks.

Citation

As Barry Menikoff shows, the novels of Robert Louis Stevenson were influenced by the author's relation to the South Seas ("'These Problematic Shores'").

Work cited

Menikoff, Barry. "'These Problematic Shores': Robert Louis Stevenson in the South Seas." *The Ends of the Earth, 1876–1918*, edited by Simon Gatrell, Ashfield Press, 1992, pp. 141–46.

When the introductory quotation is extremely long, truncate it.

Citation

Although Pamela is accepted into Mr. B.'s family, Charlotte Sussman argues that this outcome is tempered by the "precarious nature of Pamela's 'happiness,'" which is "hemmed in by the threat of physical punishment" as depicted in the narrative references to Sally Godfrey ("'I Wonder'" 97).

Work cited

Sussman, Charlotte. "'I Wonder Whether Poor Miss Sally Godfrey Be Living or Dead': The Married Woman and the Rise of the Novel." *Diacritics*, vol. 20, no. 1, 1990, pp. 88–102.

> Quotations within titles: 2.115.

[6.13] *Using abbreviations for titles of works*

As an alternative method to using shortened titles in parenthetical citations, you may use abbreviations for works or parts of works. Some works have conventional abbreviations (see appendix 1 for a list). For other works, devise simple, unambiguous abbreviations—generally, the first syllable for single-word titles, followed by a period, or the first letter of each capitalized word for titles of more than one word, omitting initial articles and ignoring punctuation. It is usually best to introduce an abbreviation in parentheses immediately after the first use of the full title in the text.

> The narrator in Viet Thanh Nguyen's *The Sympathizer* (*Sym.*) smugly asserts that liars have the fullest understanding of the world around them: "For just a moment I saw the truth in her eyes, and the truth was that she hated me for what she thought I was, the agent of an oppressive regime" (*Sym.* 9–10).

> In Shakespeare's *A Midsummer Night's Dream* (*MND*) the couples' many troubles exemplify Lysander's remark that "[t]he course of true love never did run smooth" (*MND* 1.1.134).

Abbreviating titles is appropriate, for example, if you repeatedly cite a variety of works by the same author. In such a discussion, abbreviations can make for more concise parenthetical documentation than the standard practice of shortening titles would.

Do not use abbreviations in prose. Instead, use a shortened title, such as *Midsummer* for *Midsummer Night's Dream*.

> Shortened titles in prose: 2.120–2.124.
> Abbreviations for titles of works: appendix 1.

[6.14] *Shortening descriptions used in place of titles*

If a descriptive phrase appears in the Title of Source element in your works-cited-list entry, in your parenthetical citation shorten the description to the first noun or noun phrase, as you would shorten a title.

In works-cited list	In the parenthetical citation
Letter to Charles Fremont	Letter
Advertisement for Upton Tea Imports	Advertisement

Capitalize the first letter of the first word, just as in the entry, and neither italicize the description nor enclose it in quotation marks. If a description begins with a generic term (like *review*), in prose that term should be low-ercased and then repeated and capitalized in the parenthetical citation so that it clearly points to the works-cited-list entry.

Citation

A review of Megan Abbott's *You Will Know Me* calls the author "a master of fingernails-digging-into-your-palms suspense" (Review).

Work cited

Review of *You Will Know Me*, by Megan Abbott. *Kirkus Reviews*, 5 May 2016, www.kirkusreviews.com/book-reviews/megan-abbott/ you-will-know-me/.

> Description in place of a title: 5.28.

[6.15] When author and title are not enough

If two or more works by an author have the same title or if works listed by title have the same title, additional information is needed in the citations so that the reference will lead clearly to the works-cited-list entry. Include either the first unique piece of information from the entry or the information that is most important to your discussion. This information might be the editor, translator, edition number, publisher, or publication date. Whichever piece of information you use, use it consistently for all works in your project. Insert the information in square brackets after the title.

Citation

The dedication is preserved in only three manuscripts (Christine, *Livre* [Willard and Hicks] 3–4).

Works cited

Christine de Pizan. *Le livre des trois vertus.* Translated by Liliane Dulac. *Voix de femmes au Moyen Âge*, edited by Danielle Régnier-Bohler, Robert Laffont, 2006, pp. 543–698.

———. *Le livre des trois vertus.* Edited by Charity Cannon Willard and Eric Hicks, Champion, 1989.

[6.16] Page numbers and other divisions of works

When you cite pages from a paginated work, use the same style of numerals as in the source—whether roman (traditionally used in the front matter of books), arabic, or a specialized style, like alphanumeric (e.g., *A1*). Use arabic numerals in all your other references to divisions of works (volumes, sections, books, chapters, acts, scenes, etc.), even if the numbers appear otherwise in the source. Do not precede a page number with *p.* or *pp.*, as you do in the list of works cited.

> (Drabble xi–xii)

> (Werner 622)

> (Richards A11)

[6.17] *One-page works*

If a work is only one page long, do not give the page number in your in-text citation.

Citation

The intellectual and political vision of the K-pop band BTS is especially evident in its song "Dionysus," according to one analysis, since this Greek god "forces his followers to abandon rigid patterns of thought or behavior that threaten to thwart their development" ("K-pop's Intellectuals").

Work cited

"K-pop's Intellectuals." *The Economist*, 11 Apr. 2020, p. 7.

[6.18] *Quotations spanning two or more pages of a work*

If a quotation starts at the bottom of one page and continues onto the next page (**fig. 6.1**), include the page span in your parenthetical citation.

Citation

The narrator smugly asserts that liars have the fullest understanding of the world around them: "For just a moment I saw the truth in her eyes, and the truth was that she hated me for what she thought I was, the agent of an oppressive regime" (Nguyen 9–10).

Work cited

Nguyen, Viet Thanh. *The Sympathizer*. Grove Press, 2015.

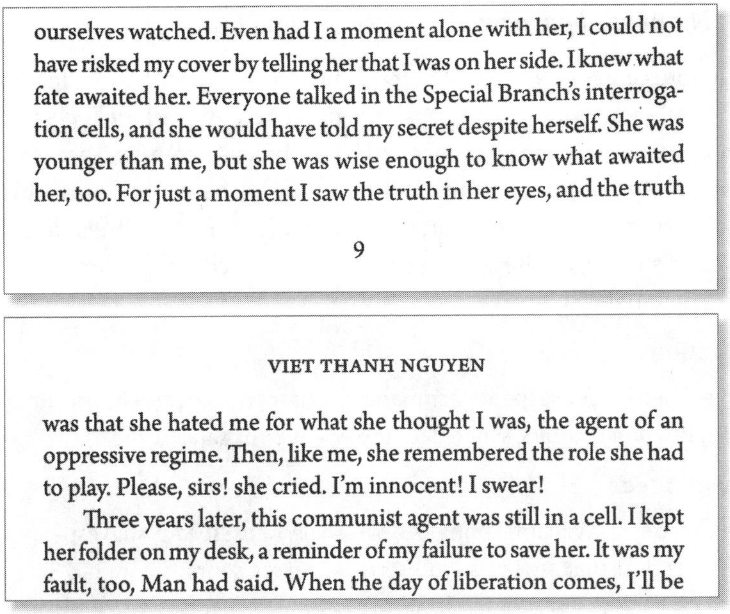

ourselves watched. Even had I a moment alone with her, I could not have risked my cover by telling her that I was on her side. I knew what fate awaited her. Everyone talked in the Special Branch's interrogation cells, and she would have told my secret despite herself. She was younger than me, but she was wise enough to know what awaited her, too. For just a moment I saw the truth in her eyes, and the truth

9

VIET THANH NGUYEN

was that she hated me for what she thought I was, the agent of an oppressive regime. Then, like me, she remembered the role she had to play. Please, sirs! she cried. I'm innocent! I swear!

Three years later, this communist agent was still in a cell. I kept her folder on my desk, a reminder of my failure to save her. It was my fault, too, Man had said. When the day of liberation comes, I'll be

Fig. 6.1. Cite a page span when the material you quote begins on one page and continues on the next page in your source.

[6.19] *Quotations from a nonconsecutively paginated work*

When the work you are citing is not printed on consecutive pages, include specific page numbers in the in-text citation even when they are represented by a plus sign in the works-cited-list entry. Present nonconsecutive page numbers in the same order as the quotations to which they refer.

Citation

Louis Menand notes that we have "very little hard information" and that "data on graduate education are notoriously difficult to come by" (29, 28).

Work cited

Menand, Louis. "The PhD Problem." *Harvard Magazine*, vol. 112, no. 2, Nov.–Dec. 2009, pp. 27+.

Number ranges: 2.139. Plus sign with page number: 5.92.

[6.20] *Numbered paragraphs, sections, and lines*

If your source uses explicit paragraph numbers rather than page numbers, give the relevant number or numbers, preceded by the label *par.* or *pars.* Do not, however, apply numbers not indicated by your source. Change the label appropriately if another kind of part is numbered in the source instead of pages, such as sections (*sec.*, *secs.*), chapters (*ch.*, *chs.*), or lines (*line*, *lines*). If the author's name begins such a citation, place a comma after the name and before the label.

Citation

In sonnet 73, Shakespeare compares the branches of trees in late autumn to "[b]are ruined choirs, where late the sweet birds sang" (line 4).

Work cited

Shakespeare, William. Sonnet 73. *The Folger Shakespeare*, shakespeare.folger
.edu/shakespeares-works/shakespeares-sonnets/sonnet-73/.

An e-book (that is, a work formatted for reading on an electronic device) may include a numbering system that tells readers their location in the work. Because such numbering usually varies from one device to another, do not use such numbering in a citation unless you know that it appears consistently to other users. If the work is divided into stable numbered sections like chapters, the numbers of those sections may be cited, with a label identifying the type of part that is numbered.

Citation

"What is it about us human beings that we can't let go of lost things?" asks the author (Silko, ch. 2).

Work cited

Silko, Leslie Marmon. *The Turquoise Ledge: A Memoir*. E-book ed., Viking Books, 2010.

Works without numbered pages or divisions: 6.26.

[6.21] *Commonly cited works*

Commonly studied literary works are frequently available in more than one edition. When you cite a work available in multiple editions, you can provide division numbers in addition to, or instead of, page numbers so readers can find your references in any edition of the work.

[6.22] Verse works

Editions of commonly studied poems and verse plays sometimes provide line numbers in the margins. Generally omit page numbers altogether and cite by division (act, scene, canto, book, part) and line, separating the numbers with periods. The example below refers to act 1, scene 5, lines 35–37 of Shakespeare's play *Hamlet*.

(*Hamlet* 1.5.35–37)

The division must be included if each begins anew with line 1. If you are citing only line numbers, do not use the abbreviation *l.* or *ll.*, which can be confused with numerals; instead, use the word *line* or *lines*. When it has been established that the numbers designate lines, you can give only the numbers.

Citation

Dressed as a beggar as he plots his return to power, Odysseus observes that "[o]f all the creatures / that live and breathe and creep on earth, we humans / are weakest" (bk. 18, lines 129–31), suggesting that an awareness of one's vulnerability is key to overcoming it.

Work cited

Homer. *The Odyssey.* Translated by Emily Wilson, W. W. Norton, 2018.

Citation

One of Shakespeare's protagonists seems resolute at first when he asserts, "Haste me to know't, that I, with wings as swift / As meditation . . . / May sweep to my revenge" (*Hamlet* 1.5.35–37), but he soon has second thoughts; another tragic figure, initially described as "too full o' th' milk of human kindness" (*Macbeth* 1.5.17), quickly descends into horrific slaughter.

Works cited

Shakespeare, William. *The Tragedy of Hamlet, Prince of Denmark. The Riverside Shakespeare,* edited by G. Blakemore Evans et al., Houghton Mifflin, 1974, pp. 1135–97.

———. *The Tragedy of Macbeth. The Riverside Shakespeare,* edited by G. Blakemore Evans et al., Houghton Mifflin, 1974, pp. 1306–42.

If you do not mention the author's name, title, or both in your prose and therefore must include such information in the parenthetical citation, separate with a comma the author's name or title from the word designating the division of the work being cited.

(*Beowulf*, lines 145–46)

(Homer, bk. 18, lines 129–31)

Do not count lines manually if no line numbers are present in the source; doing so would obligate your reader to do the same. Instead, cite page numbers or another explicit division numbering, if available (e.g., *canto 12*). Short poems in print sources can usually be cited by page number.

[6.23] Prose works

In a reference to a commonly studied modern prose work, such as a novel or a play in prose, give the page number first, followed by other identifying information, using appropriate abbreviations. Separate the page number from the other information with a semicolon.

Citation

In *A Vindication of the Rights of Woman*, Mary Wollstonecraft recollects many "women who, not led by degrees to proper studies, and not permitted to choose for themselves, have indeed been overgrown children" (185; ch. 13, sec. 2).

Work cited

Wollstonecraft, Mary. *A Vindication of the Rights of Woman*. Edited by Deidre Shauna Lynch, Norton Critical Edition, 3rd ed., W. W. Norton, 2009.

Citation

Willy Loman admits to his wife, "I have such thoughts, I have such strange thoughts" (Miller 9; act 1).

Work cited

Miller, Arthur. *Death of a Salesman*. Penguin Books, 1976.

[6.24] Ancient and medieval works

Works in prose and verse from ancient Greece and Rome, as well as some medieval texts, tend not to be cited by page number alone. You should supply the division numbers given by the work, which are often unique to it. For example, Aristotle's works are commonly cited by the page, column, and line in a landmark edition of the Greek text published in 1831. Thus, *1453a15–16* in a parenthetical citation refers to lines 15–16 of the left-hand column (*a*) on page 1453 of the 1831 edition. These indicators appear in the margins of modern editions of Aristotle's works.

[6.25] Scripture

When documenting scripture, provide an entry in the works-cited list for the edition you consulted. The names of scripture such as Bible, Talmud, and Koran are not italicized, but when these terms appear in full and shortened titles of specific editions of these works they are italicized (*The New Jerusalem Bible*). The first time you borrow from a work of scripture in your paper, state in your prose or in a parenthetical citation the element that begins the entry in the works-cited list. Identify the borrowing by divisions of the work—for the Bible, give the name of the book, usually abbreviated, as well as chapter and verse numbers—rather than by a page number. Subsequent citations of the same edition may provide divisions and numbers alone.

Citation

In one of the most vivid prophetic visions in the Bible, Ezekiel saw "what seemed to be four living creatures" (*New Jerusalem Bible*, Ezek. 1.5). John of Patmos echoes this passage when describing his vision (Rev. 4.6–8).

Work cited

The New Jerusalem Bible. Henry Wansbrough, general editor, Doubleday, 1985.

> Titles with no formatting: 2.110. Using abbreviations for titles of works: 6.13. Common academic abbreviations: appendix 1.

[6.26] *Works without numbered pages or divisions*

When a source has no page numbers or any other kind of part number, no number should be given in a parenthetical citation. Do not count unnumbered paragraphs or other parts.

Citation

"Small changes in your eating habits can lower your risk for many of the diseases associated with aging" (Parker-Pope), so it's never too early to evaluate your diet.

Work cited

Parker-Pope, Tara. "How to Age Well." *The New York Times*, 2 Nov. 2017, www.nytimes.com/guides/well/how-to-age-well.

When you quote from a work or paraphrase a passage from a work that has no page or part numbers, no parenthetical citation is needed if your prose mentions what comes first in the works-cited-list entry (that is, the author's name or, for a work that lacks a named author, the title or description).

Citation

As Tara Parker-Pope notes, "Small changes in your eating habits can lower your risk for many of the diseases associated with aging."

Work cited

Parker-Pope, Tara. "How to Age Well." *The New York Times*, 2 Nov. 2017, www.nytimes.com/guides/well/how-to-age-well.

Numbered paragraphs, sections, and lines: 6.20.

[6.27] *Volume numbers for multivolume nonperiodical works*

If you borrow from only one volume of a multivolume work that does not have a unique title, the number of the volume is specified in the entry in the works-cited list and does not need to be included in the in-text citation.

Citation

"In a few short months," Rampersad explains, "Hughes had become virtually the house poet of the most important journal in black America" (48).

Work cited

Rampersad, Arnold. *The Life of Langston Hughes*. 2nd ed., vol. 1, Oxford UP, 2002.

If you borrow from more than one volume, include a volume number and page number in the in-text citation, separating the two with a colon and a space. It is not necessary to use the words *volume* and *page* or their abbreviations. The functions of the numbers in such a citation are understood.

Citation

"The contributions to criticism of semantics, sociology, psychoanalysis, and anthropology are largely new," writes Wellek, acknowledging that the problems addressed by criticism in the modern era have historical specificity, too (1: 5). Ultimately, he asserts, "An evolutionary history of criticism must fail. I have come to this resigned conclusion" (5: xxii).

Work cited

Wellek, René. *A History of Modern Criticism, 1750–1950*. Yale UP, 1955–92. 8 vols.

If you refer parenthetically to an entire volume of a multivolume work, place a comma after the author's name and include the abbreviation *vol.*

Citation

During World War II, Eleanor and Franklin Roosevelt experienced marital troubles (Cook, vol. 3).

Work cited

Cook, Blanche Wiesen. *Eleanor Roosevelt*. Penguin Books, 1992–2016. 3 vols.

[6.28] *Time stamps*

For works in time-based media, such as audio and video recordings, cite the relevant time or time span if it is displayed. Give the numbers of the hours, minutes, and seconds as displayed in your media player, separating the numbers with colons, with no space on either side.

Citation

Buffy's promise that "there's not going to be any incidents like at my old school" is obviously not one that she can keep ("*Buffy*" 00:03:16–17).

Work cited

"*Buffy the Vampire Slayer*: Unaired Pilot 1996." *YouTube*, uploaded by Brian Stowe, 28 Jan. 2012, www.youtube.com/watch?v=WR3J-v7QXXw.

[6.29] *Numbered notes in your source*

Cite a numbered note or notes in a parenthetical citation by giving the page number or numbers followed by the abbreviation *n* (for *note*) or *nn* (*notes*) and the note number or *un* (for *unnumbered note*). If you cite one numbered note or multiple consecutive notes, no spaces are needed. But if the notes are nonconsecutive or unnumbered, use spaces as shown.

(77n5)

(77nn5–6)

(77 nn 5, 6, 8)

(3 un)

[6.30] **Punctuation in the parenthetical citation**

No punctuation is used between the author's name or the title (or description) and a page number.

(Baron 194)

When the citation includes a title in addition to the author's name, place a comma between the name of the author and the title.

(Wollstonecraft, *Vindication* 185)

If the number in a citation is not a page number, it is usually preceded by a label identifying the type of part that is numbered. A comma separates such a reference from the author's name or from the title (or description). For line numbers, once it has been established that the numbers designate lines, you can give only the numbers.

(Chan, par. 41)

(Hemans, lines 5–6)

(*Player's Handbook*, ch. 2)

In a citation of commonly studied literature, a semicolon separates a page number from references to other parts. The references to other parts are separated by a comma.

(Wollstonecraft 185; ch. 13, sec. 2)

When parenthetical citations are more complex, they must be additionally punctuated for clarity. Citations of multiple sources in a single parenthesis are separated by semicolons.

(Baron 194; Jacobs 55)

Citations of different locations in a single source are separated by commas.

(Baron 194, 200, 197–98)

In a citation of multiple works by the same author, the titles (shortened if necessary) are joined by *and* if there are two; otherwise, they use the serial comma and *and*.

(Glück, "Ersatz Thought" and "For")

(Glück, "Ersatz Thought," "For," and Foreword)

Your explanation of how you altered a quotation is separated from the citation by a semicolon.

(Baron 194; my emphasis)

If a parenthetical citation falls in the same place in your text as another kind of parenthesis, do not put the two parentheses side by side. Instead, enclose both pieces of information in a single parenthesis, placing the more immediately relevant one first and enclosing the other in square brackets.

> In *The American Presidency*, Sidney M. Milkis and Michael Nelson describe how "the great promise of the personal presidency was widely celebrated" during Kennedy's time in office—a mere thousand days (20 January 1961–22 November 1963 [325]).

Usually, however, the best option is to rewrite.

> In *The American Presidency*, Sidney M. Milkis and Michael Nelson describe how "the great promise of the personal presidency was widely celebrated" during Kennedy's time in office—a mere thousand days, from 20 January 1961 to 22 November 1963 (325).

Use square brackets for information supplied to distinguish works-cited-list entries from one another. For example, if two or more works are listed under the same author and title or two works listed by title have the same title and you need to specify which one you are citing, provide an additional element from the entry, such as an edition number or the name of a contributor like an editor.

> (*Curse* [3rd ed.] 45)

> (Christine, *Livre* [Willard and Hicks] 3–4)

Guidance on how to punctuate a quotation and its source from a non-English-language work given bilingually is covered in 6.75.

> When author and title are not enough in an in-text citation: 6.15.

[6.31] Quoting and Paraphrasing Sources

How you integrate quotations and paraphrases into your prose and where you place in-text citations can help you distinguish the words and ideas of others from your own and maintain fidelity to the source. The rest of this chapter explains the mechanics of quoting and paraphrasing and gives guidance on where to place parenthetical citations so that they are clear and unobtrusive.

[6.32] Integrating Quotations into Prose

Construct a clear, grammatically correct sentence that allows you to introduce or incorporate a quotation accurately. When you quote, reproduce the source text exactly. Do not make changes in the spelling, capitalization, interior punctuation, italicization, or accents that appear in the source. Generally place citations at the end of your sentence or quotation.

> Placement of parenthetical citations: 6.43.
> Permissible alterations to quotations: 6.54–6.67.

[6.33] Prose works

[6.34] *Short quotations*

If a prose quotation runs no more than four lines in your paper and requires no special emphasis, place it in quotation marks and incorporate it into your prose.

> "It was the best of times, it was the worst of times," wrote Charles Dickens of the revolutionary moment during the eighteenth century.

You may quote just a word or phrase instead of a complete sentence.

> For Charles Dickens the revolutionary moment during the eighteenth century was both "the best" and "worst" of times.

You may put a quotation at the beginning, middle, or end of your sentence or, divide it by your own words, for the sake of variety, clarity, desired emphasis, or elegance.

Quotation at the end of your sentence

Joseph Conrad writes of the company manager in *Heart of Darkness*, "He was obeyed, yet he inspired neither love nor fear, nor even respect."

Quotation divided by your own words

"He was obeyed," writes Joseph Conrad of the company manager in *Heart of Darkness*, "yet he inspired neither love nor fear, nor even respect."

If a quotation ending a sentence requires a parenthetical citation, place the sentence period after the reference.

"He was obeyed," writes Joseph Conrad of the company manager in *Heart of Darkness*, "yet he inspired neither love nor fear, nor even respect" (87).

[6.35] *Long quotations (block quotations)*

A quotation that runs more than four lines in your prose should be set off from the text as a block indented half an inch from the left margin. Do not indent the first line an extra amount or add quotation marks not present in the source. Your prose introducing a quotation displayed in this way should end with a colon, except when the grammatical connection between your introductory wording and the quotation requires a different mark of punctuation or none at all. A parenthetical citation for a prose quotation set off from the text follows the last line of the quotation. The punctuation mark concluding the quotation comes before the parenthetical citation; no punctuation follows the citation.

Block quotation introduced with a colon

In *Moll Flanders*, Defoe follows the picaresque tradition by using a pseudoautobiographical narration:

> My true name is so well known in the records, or registers, at Newgate and in the Old Bailey, and there are some things of such consequence still depending there relating to my particular conduct, that it is not to be expected I should set my name or the account of my family to this work. . . .
>
> It is enough to tell you, that . . . some of my worst comrades, who are out of the way of doing me harm . . . know me by the name of Moll Flanders. . . . (1)

Block quotation integrated into the sentence structure of your prose

At the conclusion of *Lord of the Flies*, Ralph, realizing the horror of his actions, is overcome by emotion, and

> sobs shook him. He gave himself up to them now for the first time on the island; great, shuddering spasms of grief that seemed to wrench his whole body. His voice rose under the black smoke before the burning wreckage of the island; and infected by that emotion, the other little boys began to shake and sob too. (186)

After the concluding punctuation mark of the quotation, type a space and insert the parenthetical citation. Do not indent the prose that follows the quotation unless you intend a new paragraph to begin.

Block quotation followed by prose that continues your paragraph

Encouraged by technology, we have developed

> a notion of reading that structurally privileges locating information over deciphering and analyzing more-complex text. This structural bent becomes increasingly important in planning educational curricula as the number of online courses (along with online readings) skyrockets and as readers flock to e-books because they are nearly always less expensive than their print counterparts. We must not let pedagogical and economic pressures cause us to lose sight of the question of whether a new notion of reading is emerging, in which deep and sustained reading (for work or pleasure) runs second to information gathering and short-term distraction. (Baron 200)

What we do know, however, is that readers are not solely bent on extraction but also want to add to, complete, or even alter the text.

> Capitalization with quotations: 6.54–6.57.
> Ellipses in quotations: 6.58–6.62.

[6.36] Poetry

[6.37] *Short quotations*

If you quote part or all of a line of verse that does not require special emphasis, place it in quotation marks within your text, just as you would a line of prose. You may also incorporate two or three lines from the source in this way, using a forward slash with a space on each side (/) to indicate to your reader where the line breaks fall.

> In her poem, Bradstreet observes that life is ephemeral: "All things within this fading world hath end. . . ."

> Reflecting on the "incident" in Baltimore, Cullen concludes, "Of all the things that happened there / That's all that I remember."

If a stanza break occurs in the quotation, mark it with two forward slashes (//).

> The *Tao te ching*, in David Hinton's translation, says that the ancient masters were "so deep beyond knowing / we can only describe their appearance: // perfectly cautious, as if crossing winter streams. . . ."

For the placement of in-text citations for short quotations of poetry, follow the same guidelines as those for the placement of in-text citations for short prose quotations (see 6.34 and 6.43).

[6.38] *Long quotations (block quotations)*

A verse quotation of more than three lines in the source should be set off from your text as a block. Unless the quotation involves unusual spacing, indent it half an inch from the left margin. Do not add quotation marks not present in the source. The in-text citation for a verse quotation set off from the text in this way, if required, follows the last line of the quotation (as it does with prose quotations). If the citation will not fit on the same line as the end of the quotation, it should appear on a new line, flush with the right margin of the page.

Block verse quotation

> Making a couplement of proud compare
> With sun and moon, with earth and sea's rich gems,
> With April's first-born flowers, and all things rare,
> That heaven's air in this huge rondure hems.
>
> (Shakespeare, sonnet 21)

A line too long to fit within the right margin should be formatted with hanging indent, so that its continuation is indented more than the rest of the block.

Block verse quotation with hanging indent

In Walt Whitman's "When Lilacs Last in the Dooryard Bloom'd," the poet's gaze sweeps across the nation from east to west like the sun:

> Lo, body and soul—this land.
> My own Manhattan with spires, and the sparkling and hurrying
>   tides, and the ships.
> The varied and ample land, the South and the North in the light,
>   Ohio's shores and flashing Missouri,
> And ever the far-spreading prairies cover'd with grass and
>   corn. . . . (canto 12)

If the layout of the lines in the source text, including indent and spacing within and between the lines, is unusual, reproduce it as accurately as possible.

Block verse quotation reproducing indents and spacing in the source

E. E. Cummings concludes the poem with this vivid description of a carefree scene, reinforced by the carefree form of the lines themselves:

> it's
> spring
> and
>   the
>   goat-footed
> balloonMan   whistles
> far
> and
> wee (lines 16–24)

When a verse quotation begins in the middle of a line, the partial line should be positioned where it is in the source and not shifted to the left margin.

Block verse quotation reproducing a partial line shown in the source

In "I Sit and Sew," by Alice Dunbar-Nelson, the speaker laments that
social convention compels her to sit uselessly while her male compatriots
lie in need on the battlefield:

> My soul in pity flings
> Appealing cries, yearning only to go
> There in that holocaust of hell, those fields of woe—
> But—I must sit and sew.

[6.39] Dialogue

[6.40] *Drama*

In a play or screenplay, dialogue is typically preceded by a label identifying each speaker. Reproduce that label and set the quotation off from
the text when quoting an exchange between speakers. Begin each part of
the dialogue with the appropriate character's name, indented half an inch
from the left margin and written in all capital letters. Follow the name
with a period and then start the quotation. Indent all subsequent lines in
that character's speech an additional amount, as in a hanging indent. When
the dialogue shifts to another character, start a new line indented half an
inch, while reproducing any indents and spacing shown in the source. Maintain this pattern throughout the entire quotation. Follow the same guidelines for placement of the parenthetical citation as for prose and poetry block
quotations.

Block drama quotation

Marguerite Duras's screenplay for *Hiroshima mon amour* suggests at the
outset the profound difference between observation and experience:

> HE. You saw nothing in Hiroshima. Nothing. . . .
> SHE. I saw everything. Everything. . . . The hospital, for instance,
> I saw it. I'm sure I did. There is a hospital in Hiroshima. How
> could I help seeing it? . . .
> HE. You did not see the hospital in Hiroshima. You saw nothing in
> Hiroshima. (15–17)

Block drama quotation reproducing indents and spacing shown in the source

A short time later Lear loses the final symbol of his former power, the soldiers who make up his train:

> GONERIL.   Hear me, my lord.
>   What need you five-and-twenty, ten or five.
>   To follow in a house where twice so many
>   Have a command to tend you?
> REGAN.   What need one?
> LEAR. O, reason not the need! (2.4.254–58)

When a quotation of dialogue is very brief or partial, you may elect to integrate it into your prose instead of setting it as a block.

Drama quotation integrated into your prose

When Regan asks Lear, "What need one?," Lear responds in exasperation, "O, reason not the need!" (2.4.257–58).

The same guidelines apply when quoting from any source representing dialogue with speakers' names—for example, an online chat or interview transcript.

[6.41] *Prose*

When quoting dialogue from a nondramatic prose work, like a novel, set the quotation off from your text as a block if each character's speech starts on a new line. Indent the block half an inch from the left margin, as you would any block quotation. If your source begins each new speech indented, reproduce the indentation of dialogue as shown in the source. Use double quotation marks around the spoken words.

Block prose quotation with dialogue

Early in F. Scott Fitzgerald's *The Great Gatsby*, Miss Baker tells the narrator, Nick Carraway, that she knows someone from his town:

>   "You live in West Egg," she remarked contemptuously.
>   "I know somebody there."
>   "I don't know a single–"
>   "You must know Gatsby."
>   "Gatsby?" demanded Daisy. "What Gatsby?" (11)

[6.42] *Poetry*

When quoting dialogue from a poem in a block quotation, indent the block half an inch from the left margin and follow the line breaks of the poem.

> I was so out of things, I'd never heard
> of the Jehovah's Witnesses.
> "Are you a C.O.?" I asked a fellow jailbird.
> "No," he answered, "I'm a J.W." (lines 36–39)

You may also integrate the quotation into your prose, but be sure to designate any line breaks with a slash.

> In the poem "Memories of West Street and Lepke," Robert Lowell, a conscientious objector (or "C.O."), recounts meeting a Jehovah's Witness in prison: "'Are you a C.O.?' I asked a fellow jailbird. / 'No,' he answered, 'I'm a J.W.'" (lines 38–39).

[6.43] Placement of Parenthetical Citations

Parenthetical citations should be placed at the end of a sentence whenever doing so makes the reference clear.

> Others note that doctors have not yet adequately explained the effects climate change will have on human health (Lemery and Auerbach 4–5).

Sometimes clarity requires that you insert a citation before the end of your sentence. For example, when there are more quotations than page numbers, place the citation so that it clearly indicates the quotation it pairs with.

> In *The Limits of Critique*, Rita Felski argues that, instead of "digging down" or "standing back" (52), readers should be "forging links between things that were previously unconnected" to make "something new" (173, 174).

Even if the number of quotations matches the number of sources, when two parts of a sentence borrow from different sources, you can place the citation directly after the quotation to help your reader more immediately pair the quotation with the source.

> Canada's literary history has been described as "a fractured discourse" (Howells and Kröller 2), an idea echoed by a Jewish Canadian novelist who writes in French and feels she occupies a position "neither fully within nor fully without" (Robin 182).

You may consolidate citations to different sources in a single parenthetical citation at the end of the sentence if your prose makes it clear which citation applies to which quotation. Separate the citations with a semicolon.

> Coral Ann Howells and Eva-Marie Kröller suggest that Canada's literary history "has always been a fractured discourse" in which a writer may feel, in the words of the Jewish Canadian novelist Régine Robin, "neither fully within nor fully without" (2; 182).

When you are quoting from one source but paraphrasing from another, ensure that the source of the paraphrased idea is unambiguous—in the example below, placing the reference for the quotation mid-sentence achieves this goal.

> In addition to advocating "macroanalysis" (Jockers), some scholars have called for an approach to reading that involves describing texts and exploring the history of the book (Best and Marcus 17).

Also be sure to distinguish your own ideas from those of your source. In the example below, placing the citation at the end of the sentence would lead readers to believe that the assertion "other styles should be considered" was also Felski's idea, not the writer's.

> Despite the timeliness of "styles of suspicious reading that blend interpretation with moral judgment" (Felski 86), other styles should be considered.

[6.44] Consolidating citations

When you borrow from a source several times in succession, you can use one of the following techniques to make citations more concise, provided no ambiguity results.

[6.45] *References to a single source*

If you borrow more than once from the same source within a single paragraph and no other source intervenes, you may give a parenthetical citation at the end of each sentence that borrows from the source. In the second parenthetical citation below, the page number alone is sufficient because the reader can reasonably conclude that the same source is still being cited.

> Octavia Butler's works assert that "humans, as a species, won't behave more decently toward each other . . . until we have literally no other choice" (Canavan 150–51). Accordingly, readers will find "no manifestos or utopias" in Butler's writings (4).

Alternatively, you can place a single parenthetical citation after the last borrowing.

> Octavia Butler's works assert that "humans, as a species, won't behave more decently toward each other . . . until we have literally no other choice." Accordingly, readers will find "no manifestos or utopias" in Butler's writings (Canavan 150–51, 4).

Reintroduce the source in your prose or in the parenthetical citation whenever needed for clarity—for example, after adding your own ideas or citing another source.

> According to Gerry Canavan, Butler cynically imagines human beings as being unable to act "decently toward each other" if they have the option to avoid doing so (150). Readers will therefore find "no manifestos or utopias" in her writings (4). I contend, however, that in Butler's novel *Kindred* the ability to read and write is presented as optimism about the future. This is supported by Butler's own view of her writings as "her children" (Canavan 91).

[6.46] *References to multiple works citing the same idea*

When a single fact or paraphrased idea is attributable to more than one source, you should provide all the sources in the parenthetical citation, separating them with semicolons. The order of the sources (alphabetic, by importance, by date) is up to you.

While reading may be the core of literacy, literacy can be complete only when reading is accompanied by writing (Baron 194; Jacobs 55).

> Semicolons in parenthetical citations: 6.30.
> Using notes for a lengthy string of sources: 7.1.

[6.47] Omitting Citations for Repeated Quotations and Terms

When you provide an in-text citation for a quotation, you usually do not have to provide an in-text citation for a subsequent quotation of the same material as long as it is clear from your prose that you quoted the text earlier in your essay. This rule applies when the subsequent quotation appears directly after the first one.

> In *Romeo and Juliet,* Juliet asks, "What's in a name?" (2.2.43). By "name" she means Romeo's last name—Montague.

The rule also applies if the subsequent use of the quotation appears farther from the first use within an essay or a chapter in a longer work. (Typically, however, in multichapter works, like a thesis or dissertation, you should reintroduce a quotation and its source in each chapter unless it is frequently used and substantively engaged throughout your project.) A repeated quotation, like any quotation, must appear in your work exactly as given in the source.

First use of the quotation

In the beginning of David Lodge's novel *Changing Places,* the narrator remarks that "two professors of English Literature approached each other at a combined velocity of 1200 miles per hour" (7).

Second use of the quotation (incorrect)

Lest the reader wonder how two people could "approach" each other at such a fast speed, the narrator explains that the professors were on airplanes.

Second use of the quotation (correct)

Lest the reader wonder how two people could have "approached" each other at such a fast speed, the narrator explains that the professors were on airplanes.

Once terms and concepts have been introduced and attributed, they can be discussed without further citation or use of quotation marks.

The self-selecting and algorithmically generated narrowness of material individuals see on the Internet has been called a "filter bubble" (Pariser). Filter bubbles make it more difficult for Internet users to gain a complete and full understanding of important issues.

[6.48] Punctuation with Quotations

[6.49] Introducing quotations

Quoted material is usually preceded by a colon if the quotation is formally introduced and by a comma or no punctuation if the quotation is part of the sentence structure.

Quotation formally introduced

Shelley held a bold view: "Poets are the unacknowledged legislators of the World" (794).

Quotation integrated into the sentence structure of your prose

"Poets," according to Shelley, "are the unacknowledged legislators of the World" (794).

Shelley thought poets "the unacknowledged legislators of the World" (794).

A quotation introduced by a verb of saying (e.g., *writes, says, states, exclaims*) is introduced by a comma when integrated into your prose and by a colon if set as a block quotation.

Quotation integrated into your prose

In *Les Misérables*, Victor Hugo writes, "We have all had those moments of distress when everything falls apart inside us. We say the first thing that occurs to us, which is not exactly what should be said" (1246).

Block quotation

Explaining her decision to learn a trade, Hwang Sok-yong's narrator, Bari, says:

> I was well aware that most North Koreans in my position weren't
> paid for their work—they were grateful if they got so much as room
> and board. The police were not yet actively hunting down defectors,
> but they did show up if complaints were made. Regardless of the
> type of work they did, North Koreans earned no more than a third
> of what a documented Chinese resident might earn; but I was lucky,
> and earned half, and that was for doing mostly small errands as an
> apprentice. (87)

[6.50] Quotations within quotations

Use double quotation marks around short quotations integrated into your
prose—that is, those not set as block quotations. When quotation marks
appear in the source itself, convert them to single quotation marks so that
they are distinguished from your own.

> In the poem "Memories of West Street and Lepke," Robert Lowell, a
> conscientious objector (or "C.O."), recounts meeting a Jehovah's Witness in
> prison: "'Are you a C.O.?' I asked a fellow jailbird. / 'No,' he answered, 'I'm a
> J.W.'" (38–39).

> In *Bilingual*, François Grosjean explains that "in the sentence 'Look at the corns
> on that animal,' the meaning of the French word *cornes* (horns) has been
> added to that of the English word 'corn'" (70).

When your quotation consists entirely of material enclosed by quotation marks in the source work, usually one pair of double quotation marks
is sufficient, provided that the introductory wording makes clear the special character of the quoted material.

> Meeting a fellow prisoner, Lowell asks, "Are you a C.O.?" (38).

Since block quotations do not appear in quotation marks, quotation
marks that you reproduce from the source can be rendered as double quotation marks.

Block quotation (verse)

In the poem "Memories of West Street and Lepke," Robert Lowell, a conscientious objector (or "C.O."), recounts meeting a Jehovah's Witness in prison:

> I was so out of things, I'd never heard
> of the Jehovah's Witnesses.
> "Are you a C.O.?" I asked a fellow jailbird.
> "No," he answered, "I'm a J.W." (lines 36–39)

Block quotation (prose)

In *Bilingual*, François Grosjean notes:

> A more subtle type of lexical reference—the bête noire, so to speak, of bilinguals—is similar to a loanshift, where only the meaning of the word is brought in and added to an existing word. For example, in the sentence "Look at the *corns* on that animal," the meaning of the French word *cornes* (horns) has been added to that of the English word "corn." (70)

> When to use block quotations: 6.35, 6.38.

[6.51] Marking the end of a quotation

Whether you include the closing punctuation mark for a quotation depends on where the quoted material appears in your sentence, what type of punctuation mark it is, and whether it is followed by a parenthetical citation. For closing punctuation and parenthetical citations for block quotations, see 6.35 and 6.38.

[6.52] *Periods and commas*

Suppose that you want to quote the following sentence from Shawn Otto's *The War on Science*.

> Nuclear safety measures, supported by business interests, drove the abandonment of US cities.

If you conclude your sentence with this quotation and a parenthetical citation, omit the closing period inside quotation marks. A sentence-ending period should follow the parenthetical citation.

> In a study of anti-scientific thinking, Shawn Otto writes, "Nuclear safety measures, supported by business interests, drove the abandonment of US cities" (111).

If the quotation ends in the middle of your sentence, replace the period with a punctuation mark appropriate to the new context—in this case, a comma.

> "Nuclear safety measures, supported by business interests, drove the abandonment of US cities," writes Shawn Otto in a study of anti-scientific thinking (111).

By convention, commas and periods that directly follow quotations go inside the closing quotation marks, as shown above. If a quotation ends with both single and double quotation marks, the comma or period precedes both.

> "The song alludes to Rita Dove's 'Sightseeing,'" notes Anderson.

[6.53] *Other punctuation marks*

Any punctuation marks other than periods or commas that you use to construct your sentence—such as semicolons, colons, question marks, and exclamation points—go outside a closing quotation mark. For example, suppose you are quoting from the following line of Walt Whitman's "Song of Myself."

> I have no mockings or arguments, I witness and wait.

The punctuation—a colon in the first example, a question mark in the second—is placed outside the closing quotation mark.

> Whitman refers to "mockings or arguments": these concepts are central to the poem.

> Where does Whitman refer to "mockings or arguments"?

For quotations ending with a question mark or an exclamation point, however, retain the original punctuation. A sentence-ending period should follow the parenthetical citation.

> "How can I describe my emotions at this catastrophe, or how delineate the wretch whom with such infinite pains and care I had endeavoured to form?" wonders Victor Frankenstein in Mary Shelley's *Frankenstein* (42).

> Dorothea Brooke remarks to her sister, "What a wonderful little almanac you are, Celia!" (7).

If such a quotation ends your sentence and no parenthetical citation follows, the question mark or exclamation point is not replaced by or followed by a period.

> The first sentence of Jameson's *Political Unconscious* advises, "Always historicize!"

> Whitman asks, "Have you felt so proud to get at the meaning of poems?"

A question mark or an exclamation point is placed after the parenthetical citation for a paraphrase.

> Why did Karl Marx say that a commodity is a strange object (47)?

[6.54] Capitalization with Quotations

Whether to capitalize or lowercase the first letter of the first word of a quotation depends on how the quotation is integrated into your prose and what appears in the source.

[6.55] When to capitalize

After a verb of saying in your prose (e.g., *writes, says, states, exclaims*), capitalize the first word of a quotation, regardless of the case used in the source. Use square brackets to indicate when you have changed the case of your source.

Passage in source

Our possessions outlast us, surviving shocks that we cannot; we have to live up to them, as they will be our witnesses when we are gone.

Quoted in your work (short quotations)

In *The Mirror and the Light*, Hilary Mantel writes, "Our possessions outlast us."

Of our personal belongings, Hilary Mantel writes, "[T]hey will be our witnesses when we are gone."

Capitalize the first word of a block quotation introduced by a verb of saying, regardless of the case used in the source. Use square brackets to indicate a change in case.

Passage in source

The sun rose higher on its journey, guided, not by Phaethon, but by Apollo, competent, unswerving, divine. Its rays fell on the ladies whenever they advanced towards the bedroom windows; on Mr. Beebe down at Summer Street as he smiled over a letter from Miss Catharine Alan; on George Emerson cleaning his father's boots; and lastly, to complete the catalogue of memorable things, on the red book mentioned previously. The ladies move, Mr. Beebe moves, George moves, and movement may engender shadow. But this book lies motionless, to be caressed all the morning by the sun and to raise its covers slightly, as though acknowledging the caress.

Quoted in your work (block quotations)

In *A Room with a View* E. M. Forster writes:

> The sun rose higher on its journey, guided, not by Phaethon, but by Apollo, competent, unswerving, divine. Its rays fell on the ladies whenever they advanced towards the bedroom windows; on Mr. Beebe down at Summer Street as he smiled over a letter from Miss Catharine Alan; on George Emerson cleaning his father's boots; and lastly, to complete the catalogue of memorable things, on the red book mentioned previously. The ladies move, Mr. Beebe moves, George moves, and movement may engender shadow.

In *A Room with a View* E. M. Forster writes:

> [R]ays fell on the ladies whenever they advanced towards the bedroom
> windows; on Mr. Beebe down at Summer Street as he smiled over
> a letter from Miss Catharine Alan; on George Emerson cleaning his
> father's boots; and lastly, to complete the catalogue of memorable
> things, on the red book mentioned previously. The ladies move,
> Mr. Beebe moves, George moves, and movement may engender
> shadow. But this book lies motionless, to be caressed all the morning
> by the sun and to raise its covers slightly, as though acknowledging
> the caress.

When to use block quotations: 6.35, 6.38.
Punctuation to introduce quotations: 6.49.

[6.56] When to lowercase

When a quotation is integrated into the syntax of your sentence, lowercase
the first letter of the first word if it would normally be lowercase in your
prose, regardless of what appears in your source. Use square brackets to
indicate when you have made a change.

Passage in source

For months, the air in their flat was like cracked glass. Everyone tiptoed
around her mother, who had become a stranger, thin and knuckly and
severe.

Quoted in your work (short quotations)

In *Americanah*, Ifemelu's mother is described as "a stranger, thin and knuckly
and severe" (51).

Of the atmosphere at home, Ifemelu notes that "[e]veryone tiptoed around
her mother, who had become a stranger, thin and knuckly and severe" (51).

A block quotation also begins with a lowercase letter if it integrally
continues your introductory wording—that is, if it is not introduced by a
colon.

Passage in source

Ifemelu stood by the window while Aunty Uju sat at the table drinking orange juice and airing her grievances like jewels. It had become a routine of Ifemelu's visits: Aunty Uju collected all her dissatisfactions in a silk purse, nursing them, polishing them, and then on the Saturday of Ifemelu's visit, while Bartholomew was out and Dike upstairs, she would spill them out on the table, and turn each one this way and that, to catch the light.

Quoted in your work (block quotation)

Visiting her family, Ifemelu would find her aunt

> airing her grievances like jewels. It had become a routine of Ifemelu's visits: Aunty Uju collected all her dissatisfactions in a silk purse, nursing them, polishing them, and then on the Saturday of Ifemelu's visit, while Bartholomew was out and Dike upstairs, she would spill them out on the table, and turn each one this way and that, to catch the light. (224)

[6.57] When to follow the case of your source

A short quotation may be introduced with a colon when it is not integrated into the sentence structure of your prose. When a colon introduces such a quotation, the first letter of the quotation should follow the case of your source.

Passage in source

She did not want to leave Dike—the mere thought brought a sense of treasure already lost—and yet she wanted to leave Aunty Uju's apartment, and begin a life in which she alone determined the margins.

Quoted in your work

By the end of the summer, Ifemelu yearns for independence: "she wanted to leave Aunty Uju's apartment, and begin a life in which she alone determined the margins" (147).

Ifemelu mourns what she will lose when she leaves for school: "She did not want to leave Dike—the mere thought brought a sense of treasure already lost—and yet she wanted to leave Aunty Uju's apartment, and begin a life in which she alone determined the margins" (147).

[6.58] Using an Ellipsis to Mark Material Omitted from Quotations

Whenever you omit a word, a phrase, a sentence, or more from a quoted passage, you should be guided by two principles: fairness to the author quoted and the grammatical integrity of your writing. A quotation should never be presented in a way that could cause a reader to misunderstand the sense or meaning of the source. If it is not obvious that you omitted material from a sentence or series of sentences, mark the omission with ellipsis points, or three spaced periods (. . .). When you quote only a word or phrase, no ellipsis points are needed before or after the quotation, because it is obvious that you left out some of the original sentence.

> In his inaugural address, John F. Kennedy spoke of a "new frontier."

When your quotation reads like a complete sentence, however, an ellipsis is needed at the end of the quotation if the original sentence does not end there or in the middle of the quotation if material has been omitted there, as the examples below show. Whenever you omit words from a quotation, the resulting passage—your prose and the quotation integrated into it—should be grammatically complete and correct.

[6.59] Omission within a sentence

Identify an omission within a sentence by using an ellipsis.

Passage in source

Americans trained by Balanchine, for example, raised their hip in *arabesque* and engaged in all manner of distortions to achieve speed and a long, aerodynamic line.

Quotation with an ellipsis in the middle

According to Jennifer Homans's ballet history, *Apollo's Angels*, "Americans trained by Balanchine . . . engaged in all manner of distortions to achieve speed and a long, aerodynamic line" (xviii).

When the ellipsis coincides with the end of your sentence, place a period after the last word of the quotation and then add three periods with a space before each.

Quotation with an ellipsis at the end of your sentence

In *Apollo's Angels*, Jennifer Homans writes, "Americans trained by Balanchine, for example, raised their hip in *arabesque* and engaged in all manner of distortions. . . ." The purpose of these movements, as Homans notes, was to create a "long, aerodynamic line" (xviii).

If a parenthetical citation follows the ellipsis at the end of your sentence, use three periods with a space before each, and place the sentence period after the final parenthesis.

Quotation with an ellipsis at the end of your sentence followed by a parenthetical citation

Commenting on the techniques of different national schools of ballet, Homans remarks, "Americans trained by Balanchine, for example, raised their hip in *arabesque* and engaged in all manner of distortions . . ." (xviii).

[6.60] Omission in a quotation of one or more sentences

An ellipsis in the middle of a quotation can indicate the omission of any amount of text.

Passage in source

Presidential control reached its zenith under Andrew Jackson, the extent of whose attention to the press even before he became a candidate is suggested by the fact that he subscribed to twenty newspapers. Jackson was never content to have only one organ grinding out his tune. For a time, the *United States Telegraph* and the *Washington Globe* were almost equally favored as party organs, and there were fifty-seven journalists on the government payroll.

Quotation omitting a sentence

In discussing the historical relation between politics and the press, William L. Rivers notes:

> Presidential control reached its zenith under Andrew Jackson, the extent of whose attention to the press even before he became a candidate is suggested by the fact that he subscribed to twenty newspapers. . . . For a time, the *United States Telegraph* and the *Washington Globe* were almost equally favored as party organs, and there were fifty-seven journalists on the government payroll. (7)

Quotation with an omission from the middle of one sentence to the end of another

In discussing the historical relation between politics and the press, William L. Rivers notes, "Presidential control reached its zenith under Andrew Jackson. . . . For a time, the *United States Telegraph* and the *Washington Globe* were almost equally favored as party organs, and there were fifty-seven journalists on the government payroll" (7).

By convention, the period that marks the end of the sentence beginning "Presidential control" in the above example is placed before the ellipsis.

Quotation with an omission from the middle of one sentence to the middle of another

In discussing the historical relation between politics and the press, William L. Rivers notes that when presidential control "reached its zenith under Andrew Jackson, . . . there were fifty-seven journalists on the government payroll" (7).

[6.61] Omission in a quotation of poetry

Use three or four spaced periods in ellipses in quotations of poetry, as in quotations of prose. An ellipsis is needed at the end of the quotation below because without it readers would think that *people* was the last word of the original sentence.

Passage in source

In Worcester, Massachusetts,
I went with Aunt Consuelo
to keep her dentist's appointment
and sat and waited for her
in the dentist's waiting room.
It was winter. It got dark
early. The waiting room
was full of grown-up people,
arctics and overcoats,
lamps and magazines.

Quotation with an ellipsis at the end

Elizabeth Bishop's "In the Waiting Room" is rich in evocative detail:

> In Worcester, Massachusetts,
> I went with Aunt Consuelo
> to keep her dentist's appointment
> and sat and waited for her
> in the dentist's waiting room.
> It was winter. It got dark
> early. The waiting room
> was full of grown-up people . . .

The omission of a line or more in the middle of a poetry quotation that is set off from the text is indicated by a line of spaced periods approximately the length of a complete line of the quoted poem. No ellipsis is needed at the end of the quotation below because *early* is the last word of the original sentence.

Quotation omitting a line or more in the middle

Elizabeth Bishop's "In the Waiting Room" is rich in evocative detail:

> In Worcester, Massachusetts,
> I went with Aunt Consuelo
> to keep her dentist's appointment
>
> . . . .
> It was winter. It got dark
> early.

[6.62] An ellipsis in the source

If the author you are quoting uses ellipses, distinguish them from your ellipses by putting square brackets around the ones you add or by including an explanatory phrase in a parenthesis after the quotation.

Passage in source

"We live in California, my husband and I, Los Angeles. . . . This is beautiful country; I have never been here before."

Quotation with an added ellipsis

In N. Scott Momaday's *House Made of Dawn*, when Mrs. St. John arrives at the rectory, she tells Father Olguin, "We live in California, my husband and I, Los Angeles. . . . This is beautiful country [. . .]" (29).

Quotation with an added ellipsis and a parenthetical explanation

In N. Scott Momaday's *House Made of Dawn*, when Mrs. St. John arrives at the rectory, she tells Father Olguin, "We live in California, my husband and I, Los Angeles. . . . This is beautiful country . . ." (29; first ellipsis in source).

[6.63] Other Permissible Alterations of Quotations

[6.64] Emphasis

You may italicize words in quotations for emphasis; however, you need to explain to readers, in parentheses, that you have done so. Keep such alterations to a minimum.

> Lincoln specifically advocated a government "*for* the people" (emphasis added).

If a parenthetical citation is needed, the explanation follows the citation and is separated from it by a semicolon.

> Burlingame writes, "When drafting his speech, Lincoln *doubtless* recalled the language of Daniel Webster and Theodore Parker" (2: 570; my emphasis).

Italics in a quotation are assumed to be in the source unless otherwise indicated, so there is no need to indicate when emphasis is in the source.

[6.65] Errors in the source

When readers are likely to assume that an error in your source is an error you made in reproducing the quotation, add "sic" (an English word—so not italicized when used in your prose—from the Latin for *thus* or *so*) to preserve the accuracy of the quotation and indicate that the error appears in the source. Place "sic" in parentheses immediately following the quotation or in square brackets within the quotation.

Woods describes Andover House as a place where "graduates of colleges, seminaries, ministers of any creed or church, and other fit persons may come to study what has come to be known as the problem of the city—it's [sic] social, sanitary, economic, industrial, educational, moral, and religious aspects."

Do not use this device to call out other types of errors. If a quoted text has numerous or repeated errors, explain this fact in a note.

An alternative practice, sometimes used by publishers, is to silently correct obvious errors in quotations from printed material that do not change its meaning. This is done to avoid calling attention to an error that an author has made and may not wish to have reproduced, such as the misspelling of a well-known person's name.

[6.66] Clarification

If a quotation is likely to be unclear or confusing to your reader without explanation, you can use square brackets to provide contextual information necessary for understanding the quotation or to gloss the meaning of quoted words or phrases.

He claimed he could provide "hundreds of examples [of court decisions] to illustrate the historical tension between church and state."

Following Bartleby's refusal, the narrator sits at his desk in "deep study [contemplation]."

Similarly, if a pronoun in a quotation seems unclear, you may add an identification in square brackets.

In the first act Hamlet soliloquizes, "Why, she would hang on him [Hamlet's father] / As if increase of appetite had grown / By what it fed on. . . ."

The preferable method, however, is to ensure that the surrounding prose clarifies the pronouns in the quotation.

Hamlet, speaking of Gertrude's initial devotion to his father, soliloquizes, "Why, she would hang on him / As if increase of appetite had grown / By what it fed on. . . ."

[6.67] **Syntax**

You may use square brackets to change the tense of a verb so that a quotation fits grammatically into your sentence. But this technique should be used sparingly, and it is usually better to revise.

Brackets to show change in verb tense (acceptable)

If Charles Dickens were alive today, he would likely say, "It [is] the best of times, it [is] the worst of times."

Revision to avoid change in verb tense (preferred)

In 1859, Charles Dickens wrote in *A Tale of Two Cities*, "It was the best of times, it was the worst of times." If he were alive today, he would likely make a similar comment about our era.

Square brackets can also be used to indicate a pronoun change. An altered pronoun, however, often entails a tense change as well. Thus, when the integrated quotation is neither jarring nor unclear, it is preferable to maintain the quotation as shown in the source and allow disagreement between the pronoun and its antecedent noun.

Brackets to show change in pronoun (acceptable)

In a moment of self-reflection, Ourika observes that "[she] had no future."

Brackets to show change in pronoun and in verb tense (acceptable)

Ourika tells the marquise that "[she has] no friends. . . . [She has] protectors. And that's not the same thing at all."

Disagreement between pronoun and antecedent (preferred)

Ourika tells the marquise, "I have no friends. . . . I have protectors. And that's not the same thing at all."

In H. H. Munro's "The Bull," the character Laurence is boastful, repeating to his brother that the picture is "the best thing I've done yet."

Do not use empty square brackets to indicate the removal of letters from a verb. The best option is to paraphrase.

Passage in source

High, high above the North Pole, on the first day of 1969, two professors of English Literature approached each other at a combined velocity of 1200 miles per hour.

Quoted in your work (incorrect)

At the beginning of David Lodge's novel *Changing Places*, "two professors of English Literature approach[] each other at a combined velocity of 1200 miles per hour" (7).

Quoted in your work (correct)

As David Lodge's novel *Changing Places* opens, "two professors of English Literature" are coming toward each other "at a combined velocity of 1200 miles per hour" (7).

[6.68] What Not to Reproduce from Your Source

Do not reproduce your source's editorial apparatus—that is, note numbers or symbols, parenthetical citations, cross-references, figure references, and the like (**fig. 6.2**).

Passage in source

Smallpox was deployed as a weapon against Native Americans by the British in the eighteenth century.[10]

Quoted in your work

As Philip Bobbitt notes, "Smallpox was deployed as a weapon against Native Americans by the British in the eighteenth century" (692).

Except for italics (often used by writers to indicate emphasis), also do not reproduce most formatting (like bold type or small capitals) and design features (like shading and colors), unless they are directly pertinent to your discussion—as for analysis of a poem using these features.

> morale within the city walls. An outbreak of plague did ensue and Kaffa fell. Ships carrying refugees from Kaffa are thought to have begun the second plague pandemic in Europe.
>
> Smallpox was deployed as a weapon against Native Americans by the British in the eighteenth century.[10] During the French and Indian War, Sir Jeffrey Amherst proposed the use of this weapon in order to reduce the tribes hostile to the British. When smallpox broke out at Fort Pitt in 1763,

Fig. 6.2. A page from a book. An endnote number appearing in the source is not included in your quotation from the text.

[6.69] Languages Other Than Modern English

[6.70] Accents

Reproduce all accents exactly as they appear in the source, whether they appear over lowercase or capital letters (*año, brød, çimen, école, Éditions Gallimard, Fähre, pietà, tête*).

[6.71] Umlauts

The umlaut in German words should not be replaced with *e* (*ä, ö, ü* rather than *ae, oe, ue*), even for initial capitals (*Über*). But common usage must be observed for names: *Götz*, but *Goethe*.

Alphabetizing names with accented letters: 5.124.

[6.72] Ligatures

Some languages other than English use ligatures, which are two letters combined into one (e.g., *œ* and *Æ* in Danish, Norwegian, and Old English; *œ* and *Œ* in French; and *ß* in German). Students and most writers may either reproduce or omit the connection between letters (*ae, Ae, oe, Oe, ss*) as long as they do so consistently. Specialists writing for a specialist audience, however, should reproduce ligatures and other special characters. All writers should follow a dictionary for words adopted into English from other languages, omitting the connection between letters when a word has been naturalized into English (*aesthetic, oeuvre, schuss*).

[6.73] Letters in older languages

Some older languages use letters that are not used in modern English (e.g., the letters þ and ð in Old English). These letters should be reproduced from the source.

[6.74] Orthography (spelling)

In Latin quotations using *u* for *v* or *i* for *j*, regularize the spelling and use the consonants *v* and *j*. For example, change *ciuitas* to *civitas* and *iudicium* to *judicium*. In most other cases, quotations should follow the orthography in the source.

[6.75] Translations of quotations (bilingual quotations)

When writing in English and quoting material from other languages, you should generally provide a translation.

Translations may be unnecessary, however, when you are certain that each person reading your work knows the language being quoted or when your instructor specifically tells you not to include translations. Translations may also be unnecessary when the context makes the meaning clear or the phrase is close in spelling to its equivalent in English, as in the following example from Charlotte Brontë's *Jane Eyre*.

> "[H]e had once cherished what he called a 'grande passion.'"

Never supply your own translation—that is, a translation that is not from a published source—without also providing the original quotation you translate. Readers should be given the opportunity to assess the validity of your translation.

In general, the translation should immediately follow the quotation whether the two passages are incorporated into the text or set off in a block quotation. When you provide a translation for a quotation, whether published or supplied by you, give the source for both the quotation and the translation. If you choose to present the translation first, followed by the original quotation, follow the same pattern throughout your work and ensure that the order of citations corresponds to the order of quotations. If the quotation and the translation are incorporated into the text, distinguish them from each other by placing whichever comes second in double quotation marks and parentheses or in single quotation marks and not in parentheses. Separate elements in parentheses with semicolons.

Translation in double quotation marks, in parentheses

At the beginning of Dante's *Inferno*, the poet finds himself in "una selva oscura" ("a dark wood"; 1.2; Ciardi 28).

Translation in single quotation marks, not in parentheses

At the beginning of Dante's *Inferno*, the poet finds himself in "una selva oscura" 'a dark wood' (1.2; Ciardi 28).

The order of the citations is determined by the order of the quotation and translation: if the original-language quotation appears first in your prose, as in the examples above, put its citation first. Order quotations, translations, and their citations consistently as an aid to your reader.

If you created the translation, insert *my trans.* in place of a source in the parenthetical citation.

Translation in double quotation marks, in parentheses

Sévigné responds to praise of her much admired letters by acknowledging that "there is nothing stiff about them" ("pour figées, elles ne le sont pas"; my trans.; 489).

Translation in single quotation marks, not in parentheses

Sévigné responds to praise of her much admired letters by acknowledging that "there is nothing stiff about them" 'pour figées, elles ne le sont pas' (my trans.; 489).

Use an endnote to indicate when you repeatedly translate the same source, in which case you can omit the source of the translation from your in-text citations.

In your prose

At the beginning of Dante's *Inferno*, the poet finds himself in "una selva oscura" ("a dark wood"; 1.2).[1]

Note

1. All quotations and translations of Dante are from the Durling and Martinez edition unless otherwise noted.

Works cited

Dante Alighieri. *The Divine Comedy: Inferno*. Translated by Robert M. Durling, edited by Durling and Ronald L. Martinez, Oxford UP, 1996.

———. *The Inferno*. Translated by John Ciardi. 1965. Signet Classic, 2001.

As is the case for any quotation set as a block, do not place quotation marks around quotations and translations set off from the text.

> Dante's *Inferno* begins literally in the middle of things:
>
> Nel mezzo del cammin di nostra vita
> mi ritrovai per una selva oscura,
> che la diritta via era smarrita.
> Ahi quanto a dir qual era & cosa dura
> esta selva selvaggia e aspra e forte
> che nel pensier rinova la paura! (1.1–6)
>
> Midway in our life's journey, I went astray
> from the straight road and woke to find myself
> alone in a dark wood. How shall I say
> what wood that was! I never saw so drear,
> so rank, so arduous a wilderness!
> Its very memory gives a shape to fear. (Ciardi 28)

> Quotation marks to mark translations of words and phrases: 2.57. Translations of titles in prose: 2.125. When to use block quotations: 6.35, 6.38. Using bibliographic notes: 7.1.

[6.76] Quotations from languages in non-Latin alphabets

Quotations from works in a language not written in the Latin alphabet (e.g., Arabic, Chinese, Greek, Hebrew, Japanese, Russian) should be given consistently in the original writing system or in transliteration. Names of persons, places, and organizations, however, are usually transliterated.

> As Chekhov's *The Cherry Orchard* (Вишнёвый сад) opens, Lopakhin remembers being called a "little peasant" ("мужичок") when he was a boy (4; 117).

> Genesis 6.4 looks back to an earlier state of society: "הנפלים היו בארץ בימים ההם . . ." 'There were giants in the earth in those days . . .' (*Bible Hub*).

> Titles in languages using non-Latin alphabets: 2.98.

[6.77] Indirect Sources

Whenever you can, take material from the original and not a secondhand source. But if you quote an author's quotation of a source you did not personally consult, put the abbreviation *qtd. in* (for *quoted in*) before the indirect source you cite in your parenthetical citation. (Otherwise, you can clarify the relation between the original and secondhand sources in a note.)

Quoted in your work

Samuel Johnson admitted that Edmund Burke was an "extraordinary man" (qtd. in Boswell 289).

Work cited

Boswell, James. *Boswell's Life of Johnson.* Edited by Augustine Birrell, vol. 3, Times Book Club, 1912. *HathiTrust Digital Library*, hdl.handle.net/2027/uc1.b3123590.

The abbreviation *qtd. in* is not needed if your prose makes it clear that the source is secondhand.

Quoted in your work

In a speech urging listeners to reject physical destruction and to seek mutual understanding, Robert F. Kennedy quoted Aeschylus: "In our sleep, pain which cannot forget falls drop by drop upon the heart until, in our own despair, against our will, comes wisdom through the awful grace of God."

Work cited

Kennedy, Robert F. "Statement on Assassination of Martin Luther King, Jr.,
Indianapolis, Indiana, April 4, 1968." *John F. Kennedy Presidential Library
and Museum*, www.jfklibrary.org.

[6.78] Citations in Forms Other Than Print

Academic work can take many forms other than the research paper. Scholars produce presentations, videos, and interactive web projects.

The standards for source documentation in nonprint forms are certain to change as media themselves change, but the aims will remain the same: to provide information that enables you to give credit to those whose work influenced yours and that allows your audience to both understand and retrieve the sources that you discuss.

[6.79] Slides

In a slide-based presentation using software such as *PowerPoint* or *Keynote*, you might add brief citations on each slide that uses borrowed material, then put a works-cited list on a separate slide at the end. For an image, you might provide in a caption a brief citation that points to an entry on a works-cited-list slide, or, if you do not discuss the image elsewhere, you might provide complete publication details in the caption. You might also offer printed copies of your works-cited list to your audience, or you might post the list online.

[6.80] Videos

When you create a video, one option is to overlay text at the bottom of the screen to provide your viewers with brief information about what they are seeing (the producer and title of a borrowed video clip, for instance, or the name of a person being interviewed) and include full documentation in your closing credits.

[6.81] Web Projects

In web projects you can link from your citations to the online materials you cite, allowing readers to follow references of interest. A works-cited list remains desirable as an appendix to the project, since it gives readers an organized account of all your sources.

[6.82] Oral Presentations

When introducing a source for the first time in an oral presentation, provide enough information about the source for others to locate it and understand its context. Typically, the author, title, and date of the source are needed. Other publication information can be mentioned if relevant. Use clear and varied phrases to introduce a source that you quote or paraphrase. Conclude quotations clearly, by reestablishing yourself as the speaker (e.g., "In this quotation we see . . ."; "As we can discern from Katzmann's statement . . ."; "Jefferson's words are especially apt because . . .").

7. Notes

Although the MLA's system of documentation relies on in-text references in order to keep the reader's focus on the text, sometimes a note is needed to provide commentary or additional information. Notes are compatible with MLA style.

[7.1] Bibliographic Notes

Bibliographic notes can help writers avoid cluttering the text or digressing from the paper's argument. Below are examples of common uses of notes. Like sources cited parenthetically in the text, sources cited in bibliographic notes must correspond to entries in the list of works cited.

To cite a lengthy string of sources

[1] See Piketty, *Capital* 291 and "On the Long-Run Evolution" 1072; Acemoglu and Robinson; Stiglitz, *Price* and *Globalization*, esp. ch. 7; Atkinson et al.; Dell, "Top Incomes" 415.

[2] For a sampling of materials that reflect the range of experiences related to recent technological changes, see Taylor A1; Moulthrop, pars. 39–53; Armstrong et al. 80–82; Craner 308–11; Fukuyama 42.

To explain an unusual documentation practice

[3] Citations of the Latin marginalia refer to Macaulay's edition of the poem and are cited by page number. References to the Middle English poem cite Peck's edition by line number.

To flag editions and translations used

[4] Citations of *Othello* refer to Bevington's *Complete Works* unless otherwise noted.

[5] Translations are mine unless otherwise noted.

Editions and translations generally require a note only when more than one edition or translation of the same work is cited; the clearest method is often to place the note in the text where the work is first quoted. An alternative is to create an initial, unnumbered note.

Notes

In this essay, the translations of *Usos amorosos* are by Margaret E. W. Jones. All other translations are mine.

[1] Labanyi's "Resemanticizing Feminine Surrender" could also be assigned.

[2] *Topolino* can also be translated as "scamp."

> Bilingual quotations: 6.75.

[7.2] Content Notes

Content notes offer the reader commentary or information that the main text cannot accommodate. Use them in the following ways.

To amplify

[1] Often the heroine and her eventual husband are kept apart by misunderstanding, by the hero's misguided attraction to another, by financial obstacles, or by family objections.

[2] Green considers *Mansfield Park* a courtship novel, including it in a list of such novels in the period 1740–1820 (163–64).

[3] Blackstone makes this point explicit: "literary Composition, as it lies in the Author's Mind, before it is substantiated by reducing it to Writing, has the essential Requisites to make it the subject of property" (322).

To explain word choice

[4] She refers here to a form of theoretical knowledge.

[5] I chose to translate the verb (rendered by Tan as "to see") as "to discern" in order to focus on the role of cognition.

To justify the scope of your study

[6] The charter school debate is beyond the scope of this essay, but I point readers to Ravitch's discussion.

[7] Whether the *Gawain* poet might have written *Saint Erkenwald* is not pertinent to my argument.

To provide more examples

[8] The same point applies to Irish writers, as David Lloyd's *Nationalism and Minor Literature* attests (160).

[9] Readers will call to mind, for instance, that Othello's jealousy focuses on the handkerchief.

To provide counterexamples

[10] Alvarez (102–32) advances an alternative thesis.

To identify or comment on allusions

[11] The references to Mordor and Gollum in Led Zeppelin's lyrics recall J. R. R. Tolkien's *Lord of the Rings*.

To point to an area of future research

[12] Important scholarship remains to be done on this topic.

To identify authors whose names appear as *et al.* in documentation

[13] The editors of *Cross-Language Relations in Composition* are Bruce Horner, Min-Zhan Lu, and Paul Kei Matsuda.

To acknowledge

[14] Meghan Dutra, from our astrophysics department, brought *The Demolished Man* to my attention.

[7.3] **Styling of Notes**

Notes may be styled either as footnotes or as endnotes. (In its publications, the MLA uses endnotes. Your instructor may specify the use of one or the other.) Select arabic numerals (*1, 2, 3*) for the number format in your word processing program. Do not use the abbreviation *ibid.* in a note to refer the reader to the information contained in the note above. Your word processing program will, by default, likely style note numbers in the text and notes section in superscript.

A notes section appearing at the end can be titled Notes or Endnotes. In notes, use parentheses around page numbers when page numbers interrupt a sentence or when they are given at the end of a sentence. Like parenthetical citations in the text, citations in notes are generally placed at the end of a sentence, but they may be placed mid-sentence, as in the first example below.

[1] As Baron (194) and Jacobs (55) argue, while reading may be the core of literacy, literacy can be complete only when reading is accompanied by writing.

[2] Baron considers the relation between literacy, reading, and writing (194).

Omit parentheses around page numbers when the note simply points the reader to the location of the information in the source.

[3] See Baron 194.

Placement of parenthetical citations: 6.43.

[7.4] Placement of Notes in the Text

Note numbers in the text are generally placed after a mark of punctuation. Whenever possible, place them at the end of sentences.

> Critics are divided on whether the interplay of genres is successful in the film.[1]
>
> Young wizards at Hogwarts learn how to throw flames by incanting "incendio."[2]
>
> Las Casas asserts that preachers who spread the gospel in the context of war are "unworthy to have their words believed" (173).[3]

An exception is the dash, which is placed after, not before, a note number.

> Positioned in the margins of each scene, the servant[4]—immobilized, silent, cast in shadow—uncannily substantiates Rodriguez's claim.

If clarity demands that the note be placed somewhere other than at the end of the sentence or if the sentence requires more than one note, find the least distracting unambiguous spot.

Placement of note mid-sentence, for clarity of citations

Despite Fredric Jameson's influential imperative to historicize,[5] Chakrabarty has criticized the "continuous, homogenous" characteristics of this understanding of history (111).

Placement of more than one note in a sentence

Huck's reverence for the circus—like his admiration for the Shakespeare rehearsal (which he says "knocked the spots out of any acting ever / see before" [Twain 125][6])—is so intense that it ultimately parodies itself.[7]

Appendix 1

Abbreviations

Abbreviations are often used in the list of works cited and in parenthetical citations but rarely in academic prose. If you use abbreviations in your prose, always choose accepted forms, often found in the dictionary. While economy of space is important, clarity is more so. Spell out a term if the abbreviation may puzzle your readers.

Punctuation

Use neither periods after letters nor spaces between letters for abbreviations made up predominantly of capital letters.

AD	BCE	DVD	PhD
BC	CE	NJ	US

The chief exception is the initials used in the names of persons: a period and a space follow each initial unless the name is entirely reduced to initials.

JFK   J. R. R. Tolkien

Most abbreviations that end in lowercase letters are followed by periods.

ed.   pp.   vol.

In most abbreviations made up of lowercase letters that each represent a word, a period follows each letter, but no space intervenes between letters.

a.m.   p.m.   e.g.   i.e.

Common Academic Abbreviations

The following abbreviations should generally be used in the works-cited list and parenthetical citations. Spell out the words, however, if confusion may result. Unless indicated below, the plurals of the noun abbreviations given here are formed through the addition of *s* (e.g., *chs.*).

app.	appendix
bk.	book
ch.	chapter
col.	column
def.	definition
dept.	department
ed.	edition
	(but spell out *editor, edited by*)
e.g.	for example
	(from the Latin *exempli gratia*; set off by commas, unless preceded by a different punctuation mark)
et al.	and others
	(from the Latin *et alii, et aliae, et alia*)
etc.	and so forth
	(from the Latin *et cetera*; like most abbreviations, not appropriate in text)
fig.	figure
i.e.	that is
	(from the Latin *id est*; set off by commas, unless preceded by a different punctuation mark)
MS, MSS	manuscript, manuscripts
n, nn	note, notes
no.	number
p., pp.	page, pages
par.	paragraph
qtd.	quoted
	(chiefly used with *qtd. in*: see 6.77)
r.	recto
rev.	revised
sec.	section
st.	stanza

supp.	supplement
trans.	translation
	(but spell out *translator, translated by*)
U	University
	(also French *Université*, German *Universität*, Italian *Università*, Spanish *Universidad*, etc.; used in documentation—e.g., U of Tennessee, Knoxville)
un	unnumbered note
UP	University Press
	(used in documentation—e.g., Columbia UP)
vers.	version
v.	verso, versus
vol.	volume

Months

The names of months that are longer than four letters are abbreviated in the works-cited list.

Jan.	Mar.	Aug.	Oct.	Dec.
Feb.	Apr.	Sept.	Nov.	

Titles of Works

Abbreviations of titles of works can be used in some research projects as an alternative method of referring to works in parenthetical citations. See 6.13 for guidance on when and how to use this method.

Bible

Hebrew Bible or Old Testament (OT)

Amos	Amos
Cant. of Cant.	Canticle of Canticles (also called Song of Solomon and Song of Songs)
1 Chron.	1 Chronicles
2 Chron.	2 Chronicles
Dan.	Daniel
Deut.	Deuteronomy

Eccles.	Ecclesiastes (also called Qoheleth)
Esth.	Esther
Exod.	Exodus
Ezek.	Ezekiel
Ezra	Ezra
Gen.	Genesis
Hab.	Habakkuk
Hag.	Haggai
Hos.	Hosea
Isa.	Isaiah
Jer.	Jeremiah
Job	Job
Joel	Joel
Jon.	Jonah
Josh.	Joshua
Judg.	Judges
1 Kings	1 Kings
2 Kings	2 Kings
Lam.	Lamentations
Lev.	Leviticus
Mal.	Malachi
Mic.	Micah
Nah.	Nahum
Neh.	Nehemiah
Num.	Numbers
Obad.	Obadiah
Prov.	Proverbs
Ps.	Psalms
Qoh.	Qoheleth (also called Ecclesiastes)
Ruth	Ruth
1 Sam.	1 Samuel
2 Sam.	2 Samuel
Song of Sg.	Song of Songs (also called Canticle of Canticles and Song of Solomon)
Song of Sol.	Song of Solomon (also called Canticle of Canticles and Song of Songs)
Zech.	Zechariah
Zeph.	Zephaniah

New Testament (NT)

Acts	Acts
Apoc.	Apocalypse (also called Revelation)
Col.	Colossians
1 Cor.	1 Corinthians
2 Cor.	2 Corinthians
Eph.	Ephesians
Gal.	Galatians
Heb.	Hebrews
Jas.	James
John	John
1 John	1 John
2 John	2 John
3 John	3 John
Jude	Jude
Luke	Luke
Mark	Mark
Matt.	Matthew
1 Pet.	1 Peter
2 Pet.	2 Peter
Phil.	Philippians
Philem.	Philemon
Rev.	Revelation (also called Apocalypse)
Rom.	Romans
1 Thess.	1 Thessalonians
2 Thess.	2 Thessalonians
1 Tim.	1 Timothy
2 Tim.	2 Timothy
Tit.	Titus

Selected Apocrypha

Bar.	Baruch
Bel and Dr.	Bel and the Dragon
Ecclus.	Ecclesiasticus (also called Sirach)
1 Esd.	1 Esdras
2 Esd.	2 Esdras
Esth. (Apocr.)	Esther (Apocrypha)

Jth.	Judith
1 Macc.	1 Maccabees
2 Macc.	2 Maccabees
Pr. of Man.	Prayer of Manasseh
Sg. of 3 Childr.	Song of Three Children
Sir.	Sirach (also called Ecclesiasticus)
Sus.	Susanna
Tob.	Tobit
Wisd.	Wisdom (also called Wisdom of Solomon)
Wisd. of Sol.	Wisdom of Solomon (also called Wisdom)

Works by Chaucer

BD	*The Book of the Duchess*
CkT	The Cook's Tale
ClT	The Clerk's Tale
CT	*The Canterbury Tales*
CYT	The Canon's Yeoman's Tale
FranT	The Franklin's Tale
FrT	The Friar's Tale
GP	The General Prologue
HF	*The House of Fame*
KnT	The Knight's Tale
LGW	*The Legend of Good Women*
ManT	The Manciple's Tale
Mel	The Tale of Melibee
MerT	The Merchant's Tale
MilT	The Miller's Tale
MkT	The Monk's Tale
MLT	The Man of Law's Tale
NPT	The Nun's Priest's Tale
PardT	The Pardoner's Tale
ParsT	The Parson's Tale
PF	*The Parliament of Fowls*
PhyT	The Physician's Tale
PrT	The Prioress's Tale
Ret	Chaucer's Retraction

RvT	The Reeve's Tale
ShT	The Shipman's Tale
SNT	The Second Nun's Tale
SqT	The Squire's Tale
SumT	The Summoner's Tale
TC	*Troilus and Criseyde*
Th	The Tale of Sir Thopas
WBT	The Wife of Bath's Tale

Works by Shakespeare

Ado	*Much Ado about Nothing*
Ant.	*Antony and Cleopatra*
AWW	*All's Well That Ends Well*
AYL	*As You Like It*
Cor.	*Coriolanus*
Cym.	*Cymbeline*
Err.	*The Comedy of Errors*
F1	First Folio edition (1623)
F2	Second Folio edition (1632)
Ham.	*Hamlet*
1H4	*Henry IV, Part 1*
2H4	*Henry IV, Part 2*
H5	*Henry V*
1H6	*Henry VI, Part 1*
2H6	*Henry VI, Part 2*
3H6	*Henry VI, Part 3*
H8	*Henry VIII*
JC	*Julius Caesar*
Jn.	*King John*
LC	*A Lover's Complaint*
LLL	*Love's Labour's Lost*
Lr.	*King Lear*
Luc.	*The Rape of Lucrece*
Mac.	*Macbeth*
MM	*Measure for Measure*
MND	*A Midsummer Night's Dream*

MV	*The Merchant of Venice*
Oth.	*Othello*
Per.	*Pericles*
PhT	*The Phoenix and the Turtle*
PP	*The Passionate Pilgrim*
Q	Quarto edition
R2	*Richard II*
R3	*Richard III*
Rom.	*Romeo and Juliet*
Shr.	*The Taming of the Shrew*
Son.	*Sonnets*
TGV	*The Two Gentlemen of Verona*
Tim.	*Timon of Athens*
Tit.	*Titus Andronicus*
Tmp.	*The Tempest*
TN	*Twelfth Night*
TNK	*The Two Noble Kinsmen*
Tro.	*Troilus and Cressida*
Ven.	*Venus and Adonis*
Wiv.	*The Merry Wives of Windsor*
WT	*The Winter's Tale*

Guidelines and Examples for Abbreviating the Title of Any Work

Aen.	Virgil, *Aeneid* *(Some works have conventional abbreviations. Use them if known.)*
Be.	Morrison, *Beloved* *(Generally use the first syllable for single-word titles.)*
CO	Chekhov, *The Cherry Orchard* *(Use the first letter of each capitalized word for most multiword titles, omitting punctuation and initial articles.)*
DQ	Cervantes, *Don Quixote*
Fledg.	Butler, *Fledgling*
GGG	Erpenbeck, *Gehen, ging, gegangen* *(Capitalize the first letters of lowercase words when abbreviating foreign language titles.)*

HUG	Thomas, *The Hate U Give*
Il.	Homer, *Iliad*
Inf.	Dante, *Inferno*
Kin.	Butler, *Kindred*
LTV	Christine de Pizan, *Le livre des trois vertus*
LW	King, *The Long Walk*
MD	Melville, *Moby-Dick*
	(Ignore punctuation.)
Mis.	Molière, *Le misanthrope*
Od.	Homer, *Odyssey*
QL	Oe, *A Quiet Life*
Per.	Austen, *Persuasion*
PP	Austen, *Pride and Prejudice*
Re.	Beatles, *Revolver*
RJ	*Return of the Jedi*
SGGK	*Sir Gawain and the Green Knight*
SLL	Bâ, *So Long a Letter*
SP	Beatles, *Sgt. Pepper's Lonely Hearts Club Band*
	(Shorten when useful.)
SS	Morrison, *Song of Solomon*
ST2	*Star Trek II*
	(Emend roman numerals to arabic for readability.)
ST3	*Star Trek III*
SW	*Star Wars*
Sym.	Nguyen, *The Sympathizer*
TL	Silko, *The Turquoise Ledge*
VRW	Wollstonecraft, *A Vindication of the Rights of Woman*
Upan.	Upanishads
	(Use two syllables when a one-syllable abbreviation is too short to be practical.)

Appendix 2

Works-Cited-List Entries by Publication Format

Many source types are illustrated in the following examples of works-cited-list entries, but the list is not exhaustive. The elements you use will depend on the version of a work you consult and the information it provides. Works-cited-list entries, even for the same work, can thus vary (see 5.104).

Books

By One Author

Davis, Angela Y. *Blues Legacies and Black Feminism: Gertrude "Ma" Rainey, Bessie Smith, and Billie Holiday*. Pantheon, 1998.

Shen Fu. *Six Records of a Life Adrift*. Translated by Graham Sanders, Hackett Publishing, 2011.

By Two Authors

Dorris, Michael, and Louise Erdrich. *The Crown of Columbus*. HarperCollins Publishers, 1999.

By More Than Two Authors

Charon, Rita, et al. *The Principles and Practice of Narrative Medicine*. Oxford UP, 2017.

By an Unknown Author (Anonymous)

Beowulf. Translated by Alan Sullivan and Timothy Murphy, edited by Sarah Anderson, Pearson, 2004.

Lazarillo de Tormes. Medina del Campo, 1554.

By an Organization (Corporate Author), Published by a Different Entity

United Nations. *Consequences of Rapid Population Growth in Developing Countries*. Taylor and Francis, 1991.

By an Organization That Wrote and Published the Work

The Adirondack Park in the Twenty-First Century. New York State, Commission on
the Adirondacks in the Twenty-First Century, 1990.

Edited

Baron, Sabrina Alcorn, et al., editors. *Agent of Change: Print Culture Studies after
Elizabeth L. Eisenstein.* U of Massachusetts P / Library of Congress, Center
for the Book, 2007.

Dunbar, William. *The Complete Works.* Edited by John Conlee, Medieval
Institute Publications, 2004. *TEAMS Middle English Texts,* U of Rochester,
d.lib.rochester.edu/teams/publication/conlee-dunbar-complete-works.

Milton, John. *The Riverside Milton.* Edited by Roy Flannagan, Houghton Mifflin,
1998.

Sánchez Prado, Ignacio M., editor. *Mexican Literature in Theory.* Bloomsbury
Academic, 2018.

Translated

Pevear, Richard, and Larissa Volokhonsky, translators. *Crime and Punishment.* By
Fyodor Dostoevsky, e-book ed., Vintage Books, 1993.

Stendhal. *The Red and the Black.* Translated by Roger Gard, Penguin Books, 2002.

Edited and Translated by the Same Person

Freud, Sigmund. *Civilization and Its Discontents.* Edited and translated by James
Strachey, W. W. Norton, 2005.

In a Language Other Than English

Chreiteh, Alexandra [Shuraytiḥ, Aliksandrā]. عليّ و أمّه الرُّوسيّة [*'Alī wa-ummuhu al-
Rūsīyah; Ali and His Russian Mother*]. Al-Dār al-'Arabīyah lil-'Ulūm
Nāshirūn, 2009.

Fallani, Giovanni. *Dante e la cultura figurativa medievale.* Minerva Italica, 1971.

With Illustrations

Carroll, Lewis. Alice's Adventures in Wonderland and Through the Looking-Glass. Illustrated by John Tenniel, Bantam Books, 2006.

Published in a Numbered or Named Edition

Milkis, Sidney M., and Michael Nelson. *The American Presidency: Origins and Development, 1776–1993*. 2nd ed., CQ Press, 1994.

Wollstonecraft, Mary. *A Vindication of the Rights of Woman*. Edited by Deidre Shauna Lynch, Norton Critical Edition, 3rd ed., W. W. Norton, 2009.

In a Named Series

Neruda, Pablo. *Canto general*. Translated by Jack Schmitt, U of California P, 1991. Latin American Literature and Culture 7.

With More Than One Publisher

Tomlinson, Janis A., editor. *Goya: Images of Women*. National Gallery of Art / Yale UP, 2002.

Self-Published

Hocking, Amanda. *Fate*. 2010.

Published before 1900

Goethe, Johann Wolfgang von. *Conversations of Goethe with Eckermann and Soret*. Translated by John Oxenford, new ed., London, 1875.

Republished, with Original Publication Date Given in Middle Supplemental Element

London, Jack. *Call of the Wild*. 1903. Dover, 1990.

Comic Book or Graphic Narrative

Clowes, Daniel. *David Boring. Eightball*, no. 19, Fantagraphics, 1998.

Superman: Birthright. By Marc Waid, illustrated by Leinil Francis Yu, inked by Gerry Alanguilan, colored by Dave McCaig, DC Comics, 2005.

In a Multivolume Set

Individually titled volume in an ongoing series

Caro, Robert A. *The Passage of Power.* Vintage Books, 2012. Vol. 4 of *The Years of Lyndon Johnson.*

Individually titled and edited volume

Howells, W. D. *Their Wedding Journey.* Edited by John K. Reeves, 1968. *A Selected Edition of W. D. Howells,* Edwin H. Cady, general editor, vol. 5, Indiana UP, 1968–83.

All volumes of the multivolume set

Rampersad, Arnold. *The Life of Langston Hughes.* 2nd ed., Oxford UP, 2002. 2 vols.

One volume without an individual title

Wellek, René. *A History of Modern Criticism, 1750–1950.* Vol. 8, Yale UP, 1992.

From Conference Proceedings

Chang, Steve S., et al., editors. *Proceedings of the Twenty-Fifth Annual Meeting of the Berkeley Linguistics Society, February 12–15, 1999: General Session and Parasession on Loan Word Phenomena.* Berkeley Linguistics Society, 2000.

Published in an E-Book Version

MLA Handbook. 9th ed., e-book ed., Modern Language Association of America, 2021.

O'Connor, Patricia. *Woe Is I: The Grammarphobe's Guide to Better English in Plain English.* E-book ed., Riverhead Books, 2009.

Published on a Website

Gikandi, Simon. *Ngugi wa Thiong'o.* Cambridge UP, 2000. *ACLS Humanities E-Book,* hdl.handle.net/2027/heb.07588.0001.001.

Miller, Daniel, et al. *How the World Changed Social Media.* UCL Press, 2016, https://doi.org/10.2307/j.ctt1g69z35.

Published in an App

The Bible. King James Version. *Bible Gateway*, version 42, Bible Gateway / Zondervan, 2016. App.

Published in Audiobook Format

Lee, Harper. *To Kill a Mockingbird*. Narrated by Sissy Spacek, audiobook ed., unabridged ed., HarperAudio, 2014.

Contributions to Books

Play

Euripides. *The Trojan Women*. *Ten Plays*, translated by Paul Roche, New American Library, 1998, pp. 457–512.

Translation

Fagih, Ahmed Ibrahim al-. *The Singing of the Stars*. Translated by Leila El Khalidi and Christopher Tingley. *Short Arabic Plays: An Anthology*, edited by Salma Khadra Jayyusi, Interlink Books, 2003, pp. 140–57.

Poem

Marvell, Andrew. "The Mower's Song." *The Norton Anthology of English Literature*, M. H. Abrams, general editor, 4th ed., vol. 1, W. W. Norton, 1979, p. 1368.

Short Story

Poe, Edgar Allan. "The Masque of the Red Death." *The Complete Works of Edgar Allan Poe*, edited by James A. Harrison, vol. 4, Thomas Y. Crowell, 1902, pp. 250–58.

"A Witchcraft Story." *The Hopi Way: Tales from a Vanishing Culture*, compiled by Mando Sevillano, Northland, 1986, pp. 33–42.

Introduction, Preface, Foreword, or Afterword

With a generic label and no unique title

Felstiner, John. Preface. *Selected Poems and Prose of Paul Celan*, translated by
    Felstiner, W. W. Norton, 2001, pp. xix–xxxvi.

Gere, Anne Ruggles. Foreword. *Improving Outcomes: Disciplinary Writing,
    Local Assessment, and the Aim of Fairness*, edited by Diane Kelly-Riley
    and Norbert Elliot, Modern Language Association of America, 2021,
    pp. vii–viii.

With a unique title

Seyhan, Azade. "Novel Moves." *Tales of Crossed Destinies: The Modern Turkish
    Novel in a Comparative Context*, by Seyhan, Modern Language Association
    of America, 2008, pp. 1–22.

*With a unique title and a generic label given as a supplemental
element*

Wallach, Rick. "Cormac McCarthy's Canon as Accidental Artifact." Introduction.
    Myth, Legend, Dust: Critical Responses to Cormac McCarthy, edited by
    Wallach, Manchester UP, 2000, pp. xiv–xvi.

Essay

Dewar, James A., and Peng Hwa Ang. "The Cultural Consequences of Printing
    and the Internet." *Agent of Change: Print Culture Studies after Elizabeth L.
    Eisenstein*, edited by Sabrina Alcorn Baron et al., U of Massachusetts P /
    Library of Congress, Center for the Book, 2007, pp. 365–77.

Republished Essay, with Original Publication Information

Johnson, Barbara. "My Monster / My Self." *The Barbara Johnson Reader: The
    Surprise of Otherness*, edited by Melissa Feuerstein et al., Duke UP, 2014,
    pp. 179–90. Originally published in *Diacritics*, 1982.

Republished Work, with Original Publication Date

Franklin, Benjamin. "Emigration to America." 1782. *The Faber Book of America*, edited by Christopher Ricks and William L. Vance, Faber and Faber, 1992, pp. 24–26.

Contributions to Scholarly Journals

With a Volume Number and Issue Number

Boggs, Colleen Glenney. "Public Reading and the Civil War Draft Lottery." *American Periodicals*, vol. 26, no. 2, 2016, pp. 149–66.

With an Issue Number

Kafka, Ben. "The Demon of Writing: Paperwork, Public Safety, and the Reign of Terror." *Representations*, no. 98, 2007, pp. 1–24.

With a Season

Belton, John. "Painting by the Numbers: The Digital Intermediate." *Film Quarterly*, vol. 61, no. 3, spring 2008, pp. 58–65.

By an Organization (Corporate Author)

MLA Ad Hoc Committee on Foreign Languages. "Foreign Languages and Higher Education: New Structures for a Changed World." *Profession*, 2007, pp. 234–45.

With a Translator

Tibullus. "How to Be Tibullus." Translated by David Wray. *Chicago Review*, vol. 48, no. 4, 2002–03, pp. 102–06.

In a Language Other Than English

Litvak, Lily. "La buena nueva: Cultura y prensa anarquista (1880–1913)." *Revista de occidente*, vol. 304, 2006, pp. 5–18.

In a Journal with More Than One Series

Helmling, Steven. "A Martyr to Happiness: Why Adorno Matters." *Kenyon Review*, new series, vol. 28, no. 4, 2006, pp. 156–72.

In a Special Issue of a Journal

Charney, Michael W. "Literary Culture on the Burma-Manipur Frontier in the Eighteenth and Nineteenth Centuries." *Literary Cultures at the Frontiers: Literature and Identity in the Early Modern World*, special issue of *The Medieval History Journal*, edited by Sumit Guha, vol. 14, no. 2, 2011, pp. 159–81.

In a Database, with a DOI

Bockelman, Brian. "Buenos Aires *Bohème*: Argentina and the Transatlantic Bohemian Renaissance, 1890–1910." *Modernism/Modernity*, vol. 23, no. 1, Jan. 2016, pp. 37–63. *Project Muse*, https://doi.org/10.1353/mod.2016.0011.

In a Database, with a Permalink

Goldman, Anne. "Questions of Transport: Reading Primo Levi Reading Dante." *The Georgia Review*, vol. 64, no. 1, spring 2010, pp. 69–88. *JSTOR*, www.jstor.org/stable/41403188.

From an Online Journal

Alpert-Abrams, Hannah. "Machine Reading the *Primeros Libros*." *Digital Humanities Quarterly*, vol. 10, no. 4, 2016, www.digitalhumanities.org/dhq/vol/10/4/000268/000268.html.

PDF of an Online Journal Article

Fisher, Margaret. "The Music of Ezra Pound." *Yale University Library Gazette*, vol. 80, nos. 3–4, Apr. 2006, pp. 139–60. *JSTOR*, www.jstor.org/stable/40859548. PDF download.

Supplementary Data for an Online Journal Article

Moskowitz, Daniel J. "Local News, Information, and the Nationalization of U.S. Elections." *American Political Science Review*, vol. 115, no. 1, Feb. 2021, pp. 114–29. *Cambridge Core*, https://doi:10.1017/S0003055420000829. Moskowitz supplementary material.

Published Online ahead of Print

Erhardt, Julian, et al. "National Identity between Democracy and Autocracy: A Comparative Analysis of Twenty-Four Countries." *European Political Science Review*, 2020. *Cambridge Core*, https://doi.10.1017/S1755773920000351.

Entire Special Issues of Journals

Appiah, Kwame Anthony, and Henry Louis Gates, Jr., editors. *Identities*, special issue of *Critical Inquiry*, vol. 18, no. 4, 1992.

Contributions to News Publications

Opinion or Editorial

Editorial Board. "How to Tell Truth from Fiction in the Age of Fake News." *Chicago Tribune*, 21 Nov. 2016, www.chicagotribune.com/news/opinion/editorials/ct-fake-news-facebook-edit-1120-md-20161118-story.html.

Gergen, David. "A Question of Values." *US News and World Report*, 11 Feb. 2002, p. 72. Op-ed.

Reported by a News Service

"Evacuation Order Lifted at Nice Airport." *The Boston Globe*, 15 July 2016, www.bostonglobe.com/news/world/2016/07/15/evacuation-progress-nice-airport/KO4BytWK4wFUOxjEkSpKTN/story.html.

One-Page Article

Magra, Iliana, and Andrea Zaratemay. "Hikers' Love of a Rarity in the Andes Takes a Toll." *The New York Times*, 3 May 2018, p. A7.

Perrier, Jean-Louis. "La vie artistique de Budapest perturbée par la loi du marché." *Le monde*, 26 Feb. 1997, p. 28.

Soloski, Alexis. "The Time Has Come to Play Othello." *The New York Times*, 20 Nov. 2016, Arts and Leisure sec., p. 5.

Consecutively Paginated Article

Sharpe, Rochelle. "Those Hidden Fees." *The New York Times Education Life*, 6 Nov. 2016, pp. 18–19.

Nonconsecutively Paginated Article

Haughney, Christine. "Women Unafraid of Condo Commitment." *The New York Times*, late ed., 10 Dec. 2006, sec. 11, pp. 1+.

Published Online, without Page Numbers

Parker-Pope, Tara. "How to Age Well." *The New York Times*, 2 Nov. 2017, www .nytimes.com/guides/well/how-to-age-well.

Tribble, Ivan. "Bloggers Need Not Apply." *The Chronicle of Higher Education*, 8 July 2005, chronicle.com/article/Bloggers-Need-Not-Apply/45022.

With City of Publication Given

Alaton, Salem. "So, Did They Live Happily Ever After?" *The Globe and Mail* [Toronto], 27 Dec. 1997, pp. D1+.

In a Series

Glatter, Hayley, et al. "Reimagining the Modern Classroom." *The Atlantic*, 2 Sept. 2016, www.theatlantic.com/education/archive/2016/09/reimagining-the -modern-classroom/498224/. Educational Eden: Imagining the Ideal School System.

Contributions to Magazines

With No Season, Volume Number, or Issue Number

Deresiewicz, William. "The Death of the Artist—and the Birth of the Creative Entrepreneur." *The Atlantic*, Jan.-Feb. 2015, pp. 92–97.

"Giant of France: The Frenchman Who Changed Literature." *The Economist*, 19 Jan. 2017, www.economist.com/news/books-and-arts/21714971 -frenchman-who-changed-literature-giant-france.

With Season, Volume Number, and Issue Number

Riis, Jacob. "Huddled Masses." 1890. *Lapham's Quarterly*, vol. 10, no. 1, winter 2017, www.laphamsquarterly.org/home/huddled-masses.

Reviews

Titled and Signed (by an Author)

Tommasini, Anthony. "A Feminist Look at Sophocles." *The New York Times*, late ed., 11 June 1998, p. E5.

Untitled and Signed (by an Author)

Rohrbaugh, Lisa. Review of *Zero Zone*, by Scott O'Connor. *Library Journal*, 1 July 2020, www.libraryjournal.com/?reviewDetail=zero-zone.

Titled and Unsigned (Anonymous)

"Racial Stereotype Busters: Black Scientists Who Made a Difference." *Journal of Blacks in Higher Education*, vol. 25, 1999, pp. 133–34.

Untitled and Unsigned (Anonymous)

Review of *You Will Know Me*, by Megan Abbott. *Kirkus Reviews*, 5 May 2016, www .kirkusreviews.com/book-reviews/megan-abbott/you-will-know-me/.

Websites

Digital Monograph with Author and Publisher

Bauch, Nicholas. *Enchanting the Desert: A Pattern Language for the Production of Space*. Stanford UP, 2016, www.enchantingthedesert.com/home/.

Site with Editors and No Publisher

Eaves, Morris, et al., editors. *The William Blake Archive*. 1996–2014, www .blakearchive.org.

Visualizing Emancipation. Directed by Scott Nesbit and Edward L. Ayers, dsl.richmond.edu/emancipation/.

Site with Editors and a Publisher

Piers Plowman *Electronic Archive*. Edited by Robert Adams et al., Society for Early English and Norse Electronic Texts, 7 June 2018, piers.chass.ncsu.edu/.

Site Written and Published by an Organization

Folgerpedia. Folger Shakespeare Library, 17 July 2018, folgerpedia.folger.edu/ Main_Page.

Jointly Published Site

Manifold Greatness: The Creation and Afterlife of the King James Bible. U of Texas, Austin, Harry Ransom Center / U of Oxford, Bodleian Libraries / Folger Shakespeare Library, 2016, manifoldgreatness.org.

Works Contained on a Website

From a Book

Poe, Edgar Allan. "The Masque of the Red Death." *The Complete Works of Edgar Allan Poe*, edited by James A. Harrison, vol. 4, Thomas Y. Crowell, 1902, pp. 250–58. *HathiTrust Digital Library*, hdl.handle.net/2027/ coo.31924079574368.

From a Book, Contained in a Database

Toorn, Penny van, and Daniel Justice. "Aboriginal Writing." *The Cambridge Companion to Canadian Literature*, edited by Eva-Marie Kröller, Cambridge UP, 2017, pp. 26–58. *Cambridge Core*, https://doi.org/ 10.1017/9781316671764.004.

From a Scholarly Journal, Published Online

Fişek, Emine. "Palimpsests of Violence: Urban Dispossession and Political Theatre in Istanbul." *Comparative Drama*, vol. 52, no. 3, scholarworks .wmich.edu/compdr/vol52/iss3/7.

From a Scholarly Journal, Published in a Database

Originally published online

Chan, Evans. "Postmodernism and Hong Kong Cinema." *Postmodern Culture*, vol. 10, no. 3, May 2000. *Project Muse*, https://doi.org/10.1353/pmc .2000.0021.

Originally published in print

Goldman, Anne. "Questions of Transport: Reading Primo Levi Reading Dante." *The Georgia Review*, vol. 64, no. 1, spring 2010, pp. 69–88. *JSTOR*, www.jstor.org/stable/41403188.

With Supplementary Material or Data Set

Published separately

"Replication Data for: 'The Non-Democratic Roots of Mass Education: Evidence from 200 Years.'" *Harvard Dataverse*, https://doi.org/10.7910/DVN/ X2VJJX.

Published alongside the work

Moskowitz, Daniel J. "Local News, Information, and the Nationalization of U.S. Elections." *American Political Science Review*, vol. 115, no. 1, Feb. 2021, pp. 114–29. *Cambridge Core*, https://doi:10.1017/S0003055420000829. Moskowitz supplementary material.

From a News Publication

Parker-Pope, Tara. "How to Age Well." *The New York Times*, 2 Nov. 2017, www
.nytimes.com/guides/well/how-to-age-well.

From a Magazine

Chou, Elaine Hsieh. "Carrot Legs." *Guernica*, 12 Sept. 2019, www.guernicamag
.com/carrot-legs/.

From a Blog

Hayes, Terrence. "The Wicked Candor of Wanda Coleman." *The Paris Review*,
12 June 2020, www.theparisreview.org/blog/2020/06/12/the-wicked
-candor-of-wanda-coleman/. The Daily.

From the Comment Section

Max the Pen. Comment on "Why They're Wrong." *The Economist*, 29 Sept. 2016,
6:06 p.m., www.economist.com/node/21707926/comments.

From a Discussion List

Grooms, Russell W. Comment on "FW: Chicago Style Citation Question" thread.
Infolit, 6 Sept. 2016, 20:02:16, lists.ala.org/sympa/arc/infolit/2016-09/
msg00005.html.

On Social Media

Chaucer Doth Tweet [@LeVostreGC]. "A daye wythout anachronism ys
lyke Emily Dickinson wythout her lightsaber." *Twitter*, 7 Apr. 2018,
twitter.com/LeVostreGC/status/982829987286827009.

Lilly [@uvisaa]. "[I]f u like dark academia there's a good chance you've seen
my tumblr #darkacademia." *TikTok*, 2020, www.tiktok.com/@uvisaa/
video/6815708894900391173.

MacLeod, Michael. Cover of *Space Cat and the Kittens*, by Ruthven Todd. *Pinterest*,
2020, www.pinterest.com/pin/565412928193207246/.

Modern Language Association. "Business leaders say college graduates are not effectively prepared with either soft or technical skills for today's workforce. . . . " *LinkedIn*, 2020, www.linkedin.com/posts/modern -language-association_are-colleges-finally-going-to-start-training -activity-6683424396222193664-y29x.

Ng, Celeste [@pronounced_ing]. Photo of a letter from Shirley Jackson. *Twitter*, 22 Jan. 2018, twitter.com/pronounced_ing/status/955528799357231104.

Thomas, Angie. Photo of *The Hate U Give* cover. *Instagram*, 4 Dec. 2018, www.instagram.com/p/Bq_PaXKgqPw/.

World Wildlife Fund. "Five Things to Know on Shark Awareness Day." *Facebook*, 14 July 2020, www.facebook.com/worldwildlifefund/ videos/745925785979440/.

On a Repository or Preprint Server

Wang, Lijing, et al. "Using Mobility Data to Understand and Forecast COVID19 Dynamics." *MedRxiv: The Preprint Server for Health Sciences*, 15 Dec. 2020, https://doi.org/10.1101/2020.12.13.20248129. Preprint.

Werner, Sarah. "When Is a Source Not a Source?" Stanford Primary Source Symposium: The Phenomenology of the Source, 14 Nov. 2015, Stanford U. *CORE*, https://doi.org/10.17613/M6PG6F.

Work with No Publication Date

Beaton, Kate. "The Secret Garden." *Hark! A Vagrant*, www.harkavagrant.com/ index.php?id=350. Accessed 17 Jan. 2017.

Entries in Reference Works

Unsigned (Anonymous)

"Patanjali." *Benét's Reader's Encyclopedia*, edited by Bruce Murphy, 4th ed., HarperCollins Publishers, 1996, p. 782.

Signed (by an Author)

Botterill, Steven N. "Angela Da Foligno, Saint." *Medieval Italy: An Encyclopedia*, edited by Christopher Kleinhenz et al., vol. 1, Routledge, 2004, pp. 35–36. *Google Books*, books.google.com.

From a Dictionary

"Content, *N*. (1)." *Merriam-Webster*, 2020, www.merriam-webster.com/dictionary/content.

"Content, *N*. (4)." *Merriam-Webster's Collegiate Dictionary*, 11th ed., Merriam-Webster, 2003, p. 269.

"Emoticon, *N*." *Merriam-Webster's Collegiate Dictionary*, 11th ed., Merriam-Webster, 2003, p. 408.

"Emoticon, *N*." *Oxford English Dictionary*, Oxford UP, 2018, www.oed.com/view/Entry/249618.

"Heavy, *Adj*. (1) and *N*." *Oxford English Dictionary*, Oxford UP, 2018, www.oed.com/view/Entry/85246.

Films and Videos

With One Publisher

Opening Night. Directed by John Cassavetes, Faces Distribution, 1977.

With Copublishers

Sairat. Directed by Nagraj Manjule, Zee Studios / Aatpat Production, 2016.

Foreign Language Film with Original Title Given Optionally

Like Water for Chocolate [*Como agua para chocolate*]. Directed by Alfonso Arau, screenplay by Laura Esquivel, Miramax, 1993.

With Original Release Date Given as Supplemental Element

Blade Runner. 1982. Directed by Ridley Scott, director's cut, Warner Bros., 1992.

Viewed through an App

E.T. the Extra-Terrestial. Universal Studios, 1982. *Netflix* app.

Uploaded to a Sharing Site

"What Is the MLA International Bibliography?" *Vimeo,* uploaded by MLA International Bibliography, 14 Oct. 2016, vimeo.com/187399565.

Television Episodes

Viewed as a Television Broadcast

"Hush." *Buffy the Vampire Slayer,* created by Joss Whedon, season 4, episode 10, Mutant Enemy / WB Television Network, 14 Dec. 1999.

Viewed on a Website

"I, Borg." *Star Trek: The Next Generation,* season 5, episode 23, Paramount Pictures, 1992. *Netflix,* www.netflix.com.

Viewed on Physical Media

"Hush." 1999. *Buffy the Vampire Slayer: The Complete Fourth Season,* created by Joss Whedon, episode 10, Mutant Enemy / Twentieth Century Fox, 2003, disc 3. DVD.

Viewed through an App

"New Normal." Directed by Dan Attias. *Homeland,* season 5, episode 10, Showtime, 24 July 2016. *Amazon Prime Video* app.

Without an Episode Title

Fleabag. Created by Phoebe Waller-Bridge, season 2, episode 3, BBC, 18 Mar. 2019.

Jeopardy! ABC, 7 Nov. 2019.

Saturday Night Live. Hosted by Sandra Oh, season 44, episode 16, NBC, 30 Mar. 2019.

Audiovisual Works

Audiobook

Lee, Harper. *To Kill a Mockingbird.* Narrated by Sissy Spacek, audiobook ed., unabridged ed., HarperAudio, 8 July 2014.

Musical Recording

Album

Beatles. *The Beatles.* EMI Records, 1968.

Song

Beyoncé. "Pretty Hurts." *Beyoncé,* Parkwood Entertainment, 2013, www.beyonce.com/album/beyonce/?media_view=songs.

Lopez, Jennifer. "Vivir mi vida." Sony Music Latin, 2017. *Spotify* app.

With medium of publication given in final supplemental element

Schubert, Franz. *Piano Trio in E-flat Major D 929.* Performance by Wiener Mozart-Trio, unabridged version, Preiser Records, 2011. Vinyl LP.

With original recording date given in middle supplemental element

Beethoven, Ludwig van. *Symphony No. 9 in D Minor "Choral."* Recorded 29 July 1951. Conducted by Wilhelm Furtwängler, EMI, 1998.

Literary Reading, Spoken-Word Recording, or Podcast

With the same author and narrator

Li, Yiyun. "On the Street Where You Live." Narrated by Li. *The Writer's Voice: Fiction from the Magazine,* hosted by Deborah Treisman, 3 Jan. 2017. *The New Yorker,* www.newyorker.com/podcast/the-authors-voice/ yiyun-li-reads-on-the-street-where-you-live.

With a different author and narrator

Chaucer, Geoffrey. "The Former Age." Narrated by Susan Yager. *Baragona's Literary Resources,* alanbaragona.wordpress.com/the-criyng-and-the -soun/the-former-age/. Accessed 8 Mar. 2017, MP3 format.

With podcast specified as the version

"Yiyun Li Reads 'On the Street Where You Live.'" *The Writer's Voice: New Fiction from* The New Yorker, hosted by Deborah Treisman, podcast ed., *The New Yorker /* WNYC, 3 Jan. 2017. *iTunes* app.

Live Radio Broadcast

"The Music of Edgar Allan Poe–Inspired Films on his 197th Birthday." *Morricone Island,* hosted by Devon E. Levins, WFMU, 19 Jan. 2016.

Art Exhibition

Cave, Nick. *Until.* 15 Oct. 2016–4 Sept. 2017, Mass MOCA, North Adams.

Unbound: Narrative Art of the Plains. 12 Mar.–4 Dec. 2016, National Museum of the American Indian, New York City.

Sculpture or Other Object

With format given in final supplemental element

Rodin, Auguste. *Christ and Mary Magdalene.* 1908, J. Paul Getty Museum, Los Angeles. Marble sculpture.

Untitled

Jar with feathered serpent design. National Museum of the American Indian, New York City.

Mackintosh, Charles Rennie. Chair of stained oak. 1897–1900, Victoria and Albert Museum, London.

Painting

Viewed firsthand

Bearden, Romare. *The Train.* 1975, Museum of Modern Art, New York City.

Viewed online

Bearden, Romare. *The Train.* 1975. *MOMA,* www.moma.org/collection/works/65232?locale=en.

Viewed in a book

Velázquez, Diego. *An Old Woman Cooking Eggs.* Circa 1618, Scottish National Gallery. *The Vanishing Velázquez: A Nineteenth-Century Bookseller's Obsession with a Lost Masterpiece,* by Laura Cumming, Scribner, 2016, p. 27.

Photograph

Viewed firsthand

Cameron, Julia Margaret. *Alfred, Lord Tennyson.* 1866, Metropolitan Museum of Art, New York City.

Viewed online

Sheldon, Natasha. Photograph of *The Muleteer.* "Human Remains in Pompeii: The Body Casts," by Sheldon, 23 Mar. 2014. *Decoded Past,* decodedpast.com/human-remains-pompeii-body-casts/7532/.

Silver, Walter. *Factory.* 1986. *New York Public Library Digital Collections,* digitalcollections.nypl.org/items/51fd9310-ea71-0131-8221-58d385a7bbd0.

Illustrated Work or Cartoon

Beaton, Kate. "The Secret Garden." *Hark! A Vagrant*, www.harkavagrant.com/index.php?id=350. Accessed 17 Jan. 2017.

Karasik, Paul. Cartoon. *The New Yorker*, 14 Apr. 2008, p. 49.

Trudeau, Garry. "Doonesbury." *The Star-Ledger* [Newark], 4 May 2002, p. 26.

Slides

Benton, Thomas Hart. *Instruments of Power* from *America Today*. 1930–31. *The Met*, 2012, Metropolitan Museum of Art, www.metmuseum.org/blogs/now-at-the-met/from-the-director/2012/benton/slideshow. Slide 1.

Monet, Claude. *Bridge over a Pond of Water Lilies*. 1899. Introduction to the History of Art, taught by Jane Ford, 4 Apr. 2016, Bates College. Slide 2.

Slide of Linus, Lucy, and Snoopy. English 204: Animals in Graphic Art, 4 Apr. 2016, Evergreen State College. Slide 2.

Text Accompanying Audio and Visual Works

Text Accompanying Audio Works (Including Liner Notes)

Beyoncé. "Pretty Hurts." *Beyoncé*, Parkwood Entertainment, 2013, www.beyonce.com/album/beyonce/?media_view=songs. Transcript of lyrics.

Titled, with format given in final supplemental element

Clapton, Eric. "Discovering Robert Johnson." *Robert Johnson: The Complete Recordings*, Columbia, 1990, pp. 22–23. Booklet accompanying CD.

Untitled

Race, Steve. Liner notes. *Time Out*, by Dave Brubeck Quartet, Columbia Records, 1959.

Undated

Lewiston, David. Liner notes. *The Balinese Gamelan: Music from the Morning of the World*, Nonesuch.

Unsigned (anonymous)

"Appendix C: Resuscitation from Apparent Death by Electric Shock." *At Action Park*, by Shellac, Touch and Go Records, 1994.

Museum Wall Text

Wall text for *A Warrior's Story, Honoring Grandpa Blue Bird*, by Lauren Good Day Giago. *Unbound: Narrative Art of the Plains*, 12 Mar.–4 Dec. 2016, National Museum of the American Indian, New York City.

Wall text for jar with feathered serpent design. National Museum of the American Indian, New York City.

Librettos and Musical Scores

Clyne, Anna. *Night Ferry*. Boosey and Hawkes, 2012.

Oakes, Meredith, librettist. *The Tempest: An Opera in Three Acts*. Composed by Thomas Adès, Faber Music, 2004.

Performances

Play

Shaw, George Bernard. *Heartbreak House*. Directed by Robin Lefevre, Roundabout Theatre Company, 11 Oct. 2006, American Airlines Theatre, New York City.

Concert

Beyoncé. *The Formation World Tour*. 14 May 2016, Rose Bowl, Los Angeles.

Lynn, Loretta. Concert. South by Southwest, 17 Mar. 2016, Stubb's, Austin.

Sing Me the Universal: A Walt Whitman Bicentennial. Conducted by Mark Shapiro, performed by Cecilia Chorus of New York, 2 Mar. 2019, Church of Saint Francis Xavier, New York City.

Dance

Brown, Trisha. *Foray Forêt.* Performance by Trisha Brown Dance Company, 28 Sept. 2019, Fairmount Park, Philadelphia.

Performance Art

Alÿs, Francis. *Cuando la fe mueve montañas.* 11 Apr. 2002, Lima, Peru.

Live Presentations (Lectures, Talks, Conference Presentations, and Speeches)

Atwood, Margaret. "Silencing the Scream." Boundaries of the Imagination Forum. MLA Annual Convention, 29 Dec. 1993, Royal York Hotel, Toronto.

Ford, Jane. Lecture. Introduction to the History of Art, 4 Apr. 2016, Bates College.

Video Recording of Live Presentation

Allende, Isabel. "Tales of Passion." *TED*, Mar. 2007, www.ted.com/talks/isabel_allende_tells_tales_of_passion?language=en.

Transcript or Captioning of Live Presentation Accompanying Video Recording

Allende, Isabel. "Tales of Passion." *TED*, Mar. 2007, www.ted.com/talks/isabel_allende_tells_tales_of_passion/transcript?language=en. Transcript.

Transcript of Live Presentation Published without Accompanying Audio or Video

Scholes, Robert. "Presidential Address 2004: The Humanities in a Posthumanist World." *PMLA*, vol. 120, no. 3, May 2005, pp. 724–33.

Interviews

Interviewer's Name Not Given

Nguyen, Viet Thanh. "Viet Thanh Nguyen: By the Book." *The New York Times*,
30 Jan. 2017, www.nytimes.com/2017/01/30/books/review/viet-thanh
-nguyen-by-the-book.html. Interview.

Interviewer's Name Given

Bacon, Francis. *Interviews with Francis Bacon*. Conducted by David Sylvester,
Thames and Hudson, 2016.

Saro-Wiwa, Ken. "English Is the Hero." Interview by Diri I. Teilanyo. *No Condition
Is Permanent: Nigerian Writing and the Struggle for Democracy*, edited
by Holger Ehling and Claus-Peter Holste-von Mutius, Rodopi, 2001,
pp. 13–19.

Unpublished

Salter, Margaret. Interview. Conducted by Susan Lang, 22 Oct. 2002.

Wexler, Jojo. Telephone interview with the author. 3 Nov. 2019.

Personal Communications

Santiago, Robert. Personal communication with author. 11 Feb. 2017.

Letters

Published

In a book

Woolf, Virginia. "To T. S. Eliot." 28 July 1920. *The Letters of Virginia Woolf*, edited
by Nigel Nicolson and Joanne Trautmann, vol. 2, Harvest Books /
Harcourt Brace Jovanovich, 1976, pp. 437–38.

To the editor, published in a news publication

Malone, Ruth. "Bonds That Bind." *East Bay Express*, 24 Apr. 2013, www
    .eastbayexpress.com/oakland/letters-for-the-week-of-april-24-30
    -2012/Content?oid=3530171.

Schlesinger, Arthur, Jr. Letter. *The New York Review of Books*, 8 Apr. 2004, p. 84.

Unpublished

In a personal collection

Apfelbaum, D. S. Letter to Vincent Marist. 11 Mar. 1946. Manuscript.

Murrow, Irena. Letter to the author. 5 Apr. 2016. Typescript.

In an archive

Benton, Thomas Hart. Letter to Charles Fremont. 22 June 1847. John Charles
    Fremont Papers, Southwest Museum Library, Los Angeles. Manuscript.

E-mails and Text Messages

Elahi, Nareen. E-mail to Standards Committee. 15 Jan. 2019.

Lemuelson, Erik. Text message to the author. 3 May 2018.

Pierson, Collette. E-mail to the author. 1 June 2019.

Zamora, Estelle. E-mail to Penny Kinkaid. 3 May 2018.

E-mail Newsletters

"Member Success Stories." *The MLA Commons Newsletter*, Modern Language
    Association of America, 7 Sept. 2016. E-mail.

Press Releases

"SPLC Joins National Day of Mourning." *SPLC: Southern Poverty Law Center*, 4 June
    2020, www.splcenter.org/presscenter/splc-joins-national-day-mourning.
    Press release.

Advertisements

Filmed Commercial

"Air Canada: We're in the Business of You." *YouTube*, uploaded by Air Canada, 8 Apr. 2019, www.youtube.com/watch?v=GE9AFpsg7H8.

Print Advertisement

Advertisement for Upton Tea Imports. *Smithsonian*, Oct. 2018, p. 84.

Billboard

Advertisement for *School of Rock: The Musical*. 29 Jan. 2017, Times Square, New York City. Billboard.

Digital Advertisement

"Get the Best of *The New Yorker*." *The New Yorker*, 10 Jan. 2017, www.newyorker .com. Pop-up advertisement.

Reports

Written and Published by the Same Organization

Reading at Risk: A Survey of Literary Reading in America. National Endowment for the Arts, June 2004.

With a Different Author and Publisher

Powell, Catherine, and Ann Mei Chang. *Women in Tech as a Driver for Growth in Emerging Economies*. Council on Foreign Relations Press, July 2016, cdn.cfr .org/sites/default/files/pdf/2016/06/Discussion_Paper_Powell_Chang_ Women_ICT_OR.pdf.

Executive Summary

Executive summary. *Report of the Task Force on Doctoral Study in Modern Language and Literature,* Modern Language Association of America, 2014, www.mla.org/content/download/25438/1164362/ execsumtaskforcedocstudy.pdf.

Scripture

With a General Editor

The New Jerusalem Bible. Henry Wansbrough, general editor, Doubleday, 1985.

With a Translator Specified

The Qu'ran. Translated by M. A. S. Abdel Haleem, Oxford UP, 2015.

In a Named Version

The Bible. Authorized King James Version, Oxford UP, 1998.

The Bible. Douay-Rheims American ed., 1899. *Bible Gateway,* www.biblegateway .com. Accessed 13 Jan. 2017.

Published in an App

The Bible. King James Version. *Tecarta Bible,* app version 7.10, Tecarta, 6 Sept. 2016.

Dissertations and Theses

Njus, Jesse. *Performing the Passion: A Study on the Nature of Medieval Acting.* 2010. Northwestern U, PhD dissertation.

Njus, Jesse. *Performing the Passion: A Study on the Nature of Medieval Acting.* 2010. Northwestern U, PhD dissertation. *ProQuest,* search.proquest.com/ docview/305212264.

Brochures and Pamphlets

Language Study in the Age of Globalization: The College-Level Experience. Modern
Language Association of America. Pamphlet.

Washington, DC. Trip Builder, 2000. Brochure.

Maps, Charts, and Tables

Japanese Fundamentals. Barron, 1992. Chart.

Michigan. Rand, 2000. Map.

"Table 311.80: Number and Percentage Distribution of Course Enrollments
in Languages Other Than English at Degree-Granting Postsecondary
Institutions, by Language and Enrollment Level: Selected Years, 2002
through 2013." *Digest of Education Statistics*, National Center for Education
Statistics, 2015, nces.ed.gov/programs/digest/d15/tables/dt15_311.80
.asp.

"Western Boundaries of Brazil, 1600, 1780, and the Present." *Brazilian Narrative
Traditions in a Comparative Context*, by Earl E. Fitz, Modern Language
Association of America, 2005, p. 43.

Unpublished Works

Letter, Memo, or Other Written Communication

Benton, Thomas Hart. Letter to Charles Fremont. 22 June 1847. John Charles
Fremont Papers, Southwest Museum Library, Los Angeles. Manuscript.

Cahill, Daniel J. Memo to English department faculty. Brooklyn Technical High
School, New York City, 1 June 2000. PDF.

Murrow, Irena. Letter to the author. 5 Apr. 2016. Typescript.

Interview

Sternberg, Rachel. E-mail interview with the author, 7 Jan. 2021.

Forthcoming Work

Jespersen, T. Christine, and David J. Plante. "Critical Globalization and Political Economy in *Tropic of Orange*." *Approaches to Teaching the Works of Karen Tei Yamashita*, edited by Ruth Y. Hsu and Pamela Thoma, Modern Language Association of America, forthcoming.

Essay Manuscript

Moskowitz, Julie. "Service Learning and Online Courses." 20 Feb. 2017.

Book Manuscript

Jones, Celia. "Shakespeare's Dark Lady Illuminated." 1988.

Manuscript in an Archive

Auden, W. H., and Klaus Mann. Prospectus. *Decision* magazine papers, Yale U Library, Manuscripts and Archives, MS 176, box 1, folder 20.

Benton, Thomas Hart. Letter to Charles Fremont. 22 June 1847. John Charles Fremont Papers, Southwest Museum Library, Los Angeles. Manuscript.

Dickinson, Emily. "Distance Is Not the Realm of Fox." 1870?, Pierpont Morgan Library, New York City. Manuscript.

Classroom Materials

Syllabus

Syllabus for Social Networking in the Scriptorium. Taught by Alex Mueller, spring 2014, U of Massachusetts, Boston.

On a learning management system

"Slides 040720." Introduction to Digital Media Theory, taught by Kathleen Fitzpatrick. *D2L*, Michigan State U, 7 Apr. 2020, d2l.msu.edu/d2l/le/content/909183/viewContent/8746820/View.

In a printed course pack

Jackson, Shirley. "The Lottery." Course pack for English 285: American Short Story Writers, compiled by Anne Smith, spring 2015, Iowa State U.

Works Published Informally in a Repository or Preprint Server

Glass, Erin Rose, and Micah Vandegrift. "Public Scholarship in Practice and Philosophy." *CORE*, 2018, https://doi.org/10.17613/g64d-gd16. PDF download, draft of working paper.

Lawson, Stuart. "Public Libraries and Knowledge Politics." *E-LIS*, 8 Feb. 2018, eprints.rclis.org/32361/.

Wang, Lijing, et al. "Using Mobility Data to Understand and Forecast COVID19 Dynamics." *MedRxiv: The Preprint Server for Health Sciences*, 15 Dec. 2020, https://doi.org/10.1101/2020.12.13.20248129. Preprint.

Digital Media

Video Game

Angry Birds. Version 7.0.0, Rovio Entertainment, 10 Dec. 2016.

Virtual Reality Experience

VidaSystems. *Aurora Borealis. Google Expeditions* app. Accessed 3 Jan. 2020.

Works Missing Publication Information

Without an Author

Beowulf. Translated by Alan Sullivan and Timothy Murphy, edited by Sarah Anderson, Pearson, 2004.

Untitled

Description in Title of Source element

Boyd, Malcolm. Booklet. *The Bach Album*, Deutsche Grammophon, 1992.

Review of *You Will Know Me*, by Megan Abbott. *Kirkus Reviews*, 5 May 2016, www .kirkusreviews.com/book-reviews/megan-abbott/you-will-know-me/.

Poem with first line used as title

Dickinson, Emily. "I heard a Fly buzz—when I died—." *The Poems of Emily Dickinson*, edited by R. W. Franklin, Harvard UP, 1999, pp. 265–66.

Without a Publisher

Hocking, Amanda. *Fate*. 2010.

Without a Date of Publication

Bauer, Johann. *Kafka und Prag*. Belser.

Bauer, Johann. *Kafka und Prag*. Belser, [1971?].

Language Study in the Age of Globalization: The College-Level Experience. Modern Language Association of America. Pamphlet.

Without Page Numbers

United Nations, General Assembly. Universal Declaration of Human Rights. Resolution 217 A, 10 Dec. 1948. *United Nations*, www.un.org/en/universal-declaration-human-rights/. PDF download.

Government Publications

With Government Name as It Appears on Source

Australia's Welfare, 2017. Australian Institute of Health and Welfare, 2017.

Great Britain, Ministry of Agriculture, Fisheries, and Food. *Our Countryside, the Future: A Fair Deal for Rural England*. Her Majesty's Stationery Office, 2000.

New York State, Committee on State Prisons. *Investigation of the New York State Prisons*. 1883. Arno Press, 1974.

United Nations. *Consequences of Rapid Population Growth in Developing Countries*. Taylor and Francis, 1991.

U.S. Department of Labor. *Occupational Outlook Handbook, 2014–2015*. Skyhorse Publishing, 2014.

With Government Name Standardized to Consolidate Entries

United States, Congress, House. Improving Broadband Access for Veterans Act of 2016. *Congress.gov*, www.congress.gov/bill/114th-congress/house -bill/6394/text. 114th Congress, 2nd session, House Resolution 6394, passed 6 Dec. 2016.

——, ——, ——, Permanent Select Committee on Intelligence. *Al-Qaeda: The Many Faces of an Islamist Extremist Threat*. Government Printing Office, 2006. 109th Congress, 2nd session, House Report 615.

Legal Works

United States Supreme Court

Decisions

United States, Supreme Court. *Brown v. Board of Education*. 17 May 1954. *Legal Information Institute*, Cornell Law School, www.law.cornell.edu/ supremecourt/text/347/483.

United States, Supreme Court. *Brown v. Board of Education*. *United States Reports*, vol. 347, 17 May 1954, pp. 483–97. *Library of Congress*, tile.loc.gov/storage -services/service/ll/usrep/usrep347/usrep347483/usrep347483.pdf.

Dissenting opinions

Ginsburg, Ruth Bader. Dissenting opinion. *Lilly Ledbetter v. Goodyear Tire and Rubber Co. United States Reports*, vol. 550, 29 May 2007, pp. 643–61. *Supreme Court of the United States*, www.supremecourt.gov/opinions/ boundvolumes/550bv.pdf.

Federal Statutes (United States Code)

United States, Congress, House. United States Code. Office of the Law Revision Counsel, 14 Jan. 2017, uscode.house.gov.

United States, Congress, House. United States Code. Title 17, section 304, Office of the Law Revision Counsel, 14 Jan. 2017, uscode.house.gov.

United States Code. *Legal Information Institute*, Cornell Law School, www.law
.cornell.edu/uscode/text.

United States Code. Title 17, U.S. Government Publishing Office, 2011,
www.gpo.gov/fdsys/pkg/USCODE-2011-title17/html/USCODE-2011
-title17.htm.

Public Laws

United States, Congress. Public Law 111–122. *United States Statutes at Large*,
vol. 123, 2009, pp. 3480–82. *U.S. Government Publishing Office*, www
.gpo.gov/fdsys/pkg/STATUTE-123/pdf/STATUTE-123.pdf.

Federal Appeals Court Decisions

United States, Court of Appeals for the Second Circuit. *Moss v. Colvin*. Docket
no. 15–2272, 9 Jan. 2017. *United States Court of Appeals for the Second
Circuit*, www.ca2.uscourts.gov/decisions.html. PDF download.

Federal Bills

United States, Congress, House. Improving Broadband Access for Veterans Act
of 2016. *Congress.gov*, www.congress.gov/bill/114th-congress/house
-bill/6394/text. 114th Congress, 2nd session, House Resolution 6394,
passed 6 Dec. 2016.

Hearings

United States, Congress, House, Committee on Education and Labor. *The
Future of Learning: How Technology Is Transforming Public Schools*. U.S.
Government Publishing Office, 16 June 2009, www.gpo.gov/fdsys/pkg/
CHRG-111hhrg50208/html/CHRG-111hhrg50208.htm. Text transcription
of hearing.

Executive Orders

United States, Executive Office of the President [Barack Obama]. Executive Order
13717: Establishing a Federal Earthquake Risk Management Standard.
2 Feb. 2016. *Federal Register*, vol. 81, no. 24, 5 Feb. 2016, pp. 6405–10,
www.gpo.gov/fdsys/pkg/FR-2016-02-05/pdf/2016-02475.pdf.

State Court of Appeals, Unpublished Decisions

Minnesota State, Court of Appeals. *Minnesota v. McArthur.* 28 Sept. 1999,
mn.gov/law-library-stat/archive//ctapun/9909/502.htm. Unpublished
decision.

State Senate Bills

Wisconsin State, Legislature. Senate Bill 5. *Wisconsin State Legislature*, 20 Jan. 2017,
docs.legis.wisconsin.gov/2017/related/proposals/sb5.

Constitutions

The Constitution of the United States: A Transcription. National Archives, U.S. National
Archives and Records Administration, 28 Feb. 2017, www.archives.gov/
founding-docs/constitution-transcript.

The Constitution of the United States, with Case Summaries. Edited by Edward
Conrad Smith, 9th ed., Barnes and Noble Books, 1972.

Treaties

Kyoto Protocol to the United Nations Framework Convention on Climate
Change. United Nations, 1998, unfccc.int/resource/docs/convkp/kpeng
.pdf. Multilateral treaty.

United States, Senate. Beijing Treaty on Audiovisual Performances. *Congress.gov*,
www.congress.gov/114/cdoc/tdoc8/CDOC-114tdoc8.pdf. Treaty
between the United States and the People's Republic of China.

Resolutions of International Governing Bodies

United Nations, General Assembly. Universal Declaration of Human Rights.
Resolution 217 A, 10 Dec. 1948. *United Nations*, www.un.org/en/
universal-declaration-human-rights/. PDF download.

Index

colons
    overview, 2.27
    for introducing quotations, 6.35, 6.49,
        6.57
    with lists, 1.9, 1.11, 2.27
    quotation marks with, 6.53
    for scope of multivolume works, 2.104
    for subtitles, *fig. 2.4, fig. 2.10*, 2.89,
        2.101
    for volume numbers, 6.27
column titles, 2.110
comic books. *See* graphic narratives
commas, 2.5–2.25
    in alphabetization, 5.124
    with appositives, 2.14
    after author's surname, in works-cited
        list, 5.6, 5.7, 5.8, 5.10
    in captions, 1.7
    with contrasting phrases, 2.11
    with contributor labels, 5.44
    with coordinate adjectives, 2.8
    with coordinating conjunctions, 2.7,
        2.25
    for dates and locations, 2.13, 2.138
    incorrect usages, 2.15–2.21
    with independent clauses, 2.7, 2.24, 2.25
    for introducing quotations, 6.49, 6.52
    with introductory elements, 2.10, 2.23,
        2.105
    with location markers, 6.30
    between multiple items in elements of
        works-cited list, 5.121
    with nonrestrictive modifiers, 2.14
    in Number element, 5.53
    in numbers, 2.137
    optional usage, 2.22–2.25
    other punctuation with, 5.26, 6.52
    in parenthetical citations, 6.30
    with parenthetical comments in prose,
        2.9
    serial (Oxford), *figs. 2.7–2.8*, 2.12, 2.100,
        6.30
    for series, 2.12, 2.26, 2.105
    with specific words and phrases, 2.24
    with suffixes of personal names, 2.84
    after title of container, 5.37

commas (*cont.*)
    in titles of works, 2.100, 2.102, 2.103,
        2.104
    with titles of works, in prose, 2.105
common knowledge, 4.13
commonly cited works, location markers
    for, 6.21–6.25, 6.30
comparatives, 2.41
compound adjectives, hyphenation for,
    2.33–2.44
    with adverbs, 2.35, 2.40
    clarity and, 2.38
    comparatives and superlatives, 2.41
    familiar terms, 2.42
    foreign language, 2.43
    with numbers, 2.36
    with prepositional phrases, 2.37
    with proper nouns, 2.44
compound objects, 2.19
compound subjects, 2.19
compound terms, 2.45
    See also compound adjectives,
        hyphenation for
concise writing, paraphrasing for, 4.5
conference titles, 2.110
conjunctions
    coordinating, 2.7, 2.25, 2.90
    subordinating, 2.90
consistency
    for additional information in in-text
        citations, 6.15
    in bilingual quotations and their
        citations, 6.75
    in capitalization of identity references,
        3.4
    in comma usage, 2.23
    in date styling, 2.138
    in headings and subheadings, 1.5
    in lists, 1.11
    with numbers, in using spelled out vs.
        numerals, 2.138
    personal names and, 2.72
    in spelling, 2.1
    in styling of titles of works, 2.110
    in translation, 2.125
    in transliteration, 2.98, 6.76